International Development: Socio-Economic Perspectives

International Development: Socio-Economic Perspectives

Edited by Elizabeth Swinton

Clanrye International
www.clanryeinternational.com

Clanrye International,
750 Third Avenue, 9th Floor,
New York, NY 10017, USA

ISBN: 978-1-63240-856-3

Cataloging-in-Publication Data

International development : socio-economic perspectives / edited by Elizabeth Swinton.
p. cm.
Includes bibliographical references and index.
ISBN 978-1-63240-856-3
1. Economic development. 2. Social change. 3. Human capital. 4. Globalization.
I. Swinton, Elizabeth.
HD82 .I58 2019
338.9--dc23

For information on all Clanrye International publications
visit our website at www.clanryeinternational.com

CLANRYE INTERNATIONAL

Printed in China.

Contents

Preface

I am honored to present to you this unique book which encompasses the most up-to-date data in the field. I was extremely pleased to get this opportunity of editing the work of experts from across the globe. I have also written papers in this field and researched the various aspects revolving around the progress of the discipline. I have tried to unify my knowledge along with that of stalwarts from every corner of the world, to produce a text which not only benefits the readers but also facilitates the growth of the field.

International development is a concept concerned with the level of development on an international scale. The countries are divided into developed, developing and least developed on the basis of this parameter. International development is used in a multidisciplinary context in the fields of human development, quality of life, competitiveness, etc. The major theories that fall under this discipline are modernization theory, dependency theory and world systems theory. Some of the focus areas under international development include education, human rights, quality healthcare, sanitation and shelter among many others. The topics included in this book on international development are of utmost significance and bound to provide incredible insights to readers. It picks up individual branches and explains their need and contribution in the context of a growing economy. As this field is emerging at a rapid pace, the contents of this book will help the readers understand the modern concepts and applications of the subject.

Finally, I would like to thank all the contributing authors for their valuable time and contributions. This book would not have been possible without their efforts. I would also like to thank my friends and family for their constant support.

Editor

1

Economic Development of the Black Sea Riparian Countries during 2004-2012

Romeo Bosneagu[1], **Florin Sorescu**[2], **Rodica Elena Faida**[3]

Abstract: The Black Sea is politically divided between the European Union, countries aspiring to join the EU and the Russian Federation. From an economic perspective, the area has a huge potential for development and is "claimed" by the same political actors. In 1992, BSEC (Black Sea Economic Cooperation) was formed and it includes, along with the six riparian countries, eight countries in order to meet their economic power in order to achieve regional development. In the period 2004-2012 the economy Black Sea countries experienced strongly fluctuated, which was strongly connected to the global economy, the inflow of capital in the region and the influence of the global economic crisis.

Keywords: crisis; riparian countries; population

1. Economic Power of the Black Sea Countries

For the Black Sea riparian countries, the past decade has meant a special period politically, socially, and economically difficult, characterized by a prolonged transition needed to adapt to the new standards imposed by the Euro-Atlantic integration of Romania and Bulgaria – NATO states since 2004, and European Union members since 2007), and Turkey (NATO member with European integration aspirations), Ukraine and Georgia who were going through a long process of development and modernization to ensure conditions for the entry into NATO and the EU. Also, the Russian Federation was going through a lengthy process of development and adapt to the market economy laws. The economic power of the countries bordering the Black Sea states, in summary, as follows[4]:

a) population (Table 1 and graph.1);
b) GDP (Table 1 and graph.2);
c) GNI per capita- Atlas Method (Table 1 and graph. 3);

[1] Associate Professor, PhD, Naval Academy" Mircea cel Batrân", Romania, Address: Strada Fulgerului 1, Constanța 900218. Corresponding author: romeobosneagu@yahoo.com.
[2] Senior Lecturer, PhD, Tomis University, Constanta, Romania, Address: 100 Vulcan Petru Str., Constanta, 900628, Romania, E-mail: flosorescu@yahoo.com.
[3] Master Student, Spiru Haret University, Bucharest, Romania. Address: 13, Doamnei Str., Bucharest, Romania, E-mail: rodica.faida.if@mfinante.ro.
[4] www.data.worldbank.org.

Table 1. Population, GDP and GNI for the Black Sea riparian countries in 2012

Country	Population (mil.)	GDP (current mil. USD)	GNI per capita – Atlas Method (current USD)
Romania	21,3	192,70	8820
Russia	143,5	2015,00	12700
Bulgaria	7,3	50,97	6840
Turkey	74,0	789,20	10830
Ukraine	46,0	176,30	3500
Georgia	4,5	15,75	3270
Total/average	*224,6*	*3249,92*	*7650*

- compared to the European Union, which has a GDP of about 17 800 million USD for a population of about 507 million[1], Black Sea riparian countries have a GDP of only 18.4%, a population that represents 44% of the EU population, which shows a difference concerning the need of considerable economic development for the Black Sea;

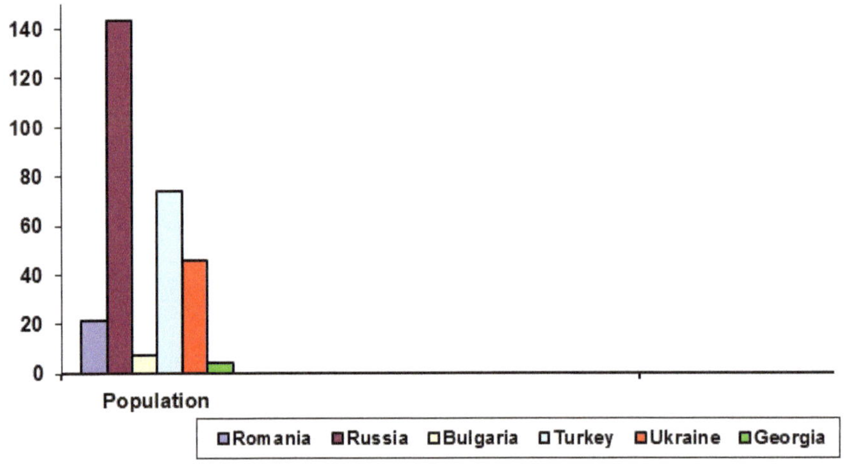

Graph 1. Black Sea countries population in 2012 (million inhabitants)

- Black Sea riparian countries are divided into: large countries (Russia), medium countries (Ukraine and Romania) and small countries (Bulgaria and Georgia);

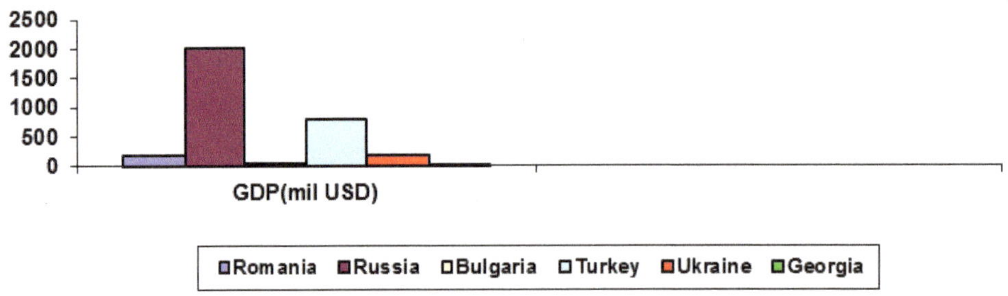

Graph 2. GDP Black Sea riparian countries in 2012 (million USD)

- GDP ranges from minimum (Georgia, 15,75 billion USD) to the maximum (Russia, 2,015 billion USD), with a total of 3,249.92 billion USD;

---

[1] www.europa.eu

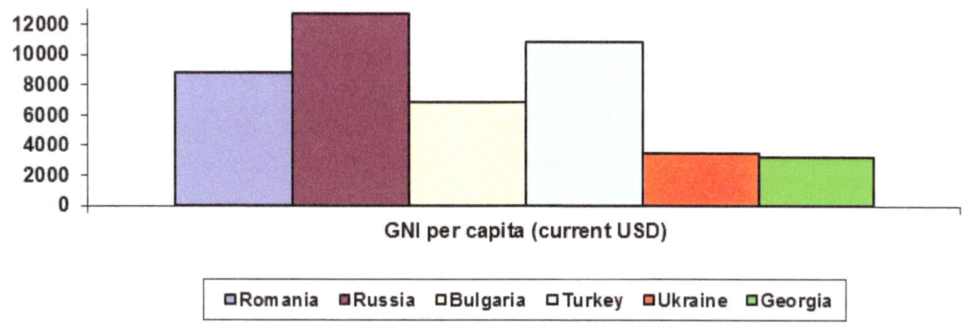

Graph 3. GNI Black Sea riparian countries in 2012 (Atlas Method – million USD)

- GNI per capita ranges from minimum (Georgia 3270 USD per capita), to the maximum (Russia 12700 USD per capita).

2. Economic Development of the Black Sea Riparian Countries during 2004-2012

Black Sea GDP of the riparian countries was generally dictated by the evolving of the global economy[1] before and during the current global crisis (Table 2 and graph.4); it can be observed the decrease in the value of GDP from 2009 to 2010:

Table 2. GDP of the Black Sea riparian countries in the period 2004-2012 (U.S.$ million)

Country Year	Romania	Russia	Bulgaria	Turkey	Ukraine	Georgia
2004	75,5	1439	25,3	392,1	64,9	5,1
2005	98,9	1431	28,9	482,9	86,1	6,4
2006	122,6	1425	33,2	530,9	107.7	7,7
2007	169,3	1421	42,1	647,2	142,7	10,1
2008	204,3	1419	51,8	730,4	179,9	12,7
2009	164,3	1419	48,6	614,5	117,3	10,7
2010	164,4	1424	47,7	731,1	136,4	11,6
2011	189,7	1429	53,5	774,7	163,4	14,4
2012	192,7	1435	50,9	789,3	176,3	15,7

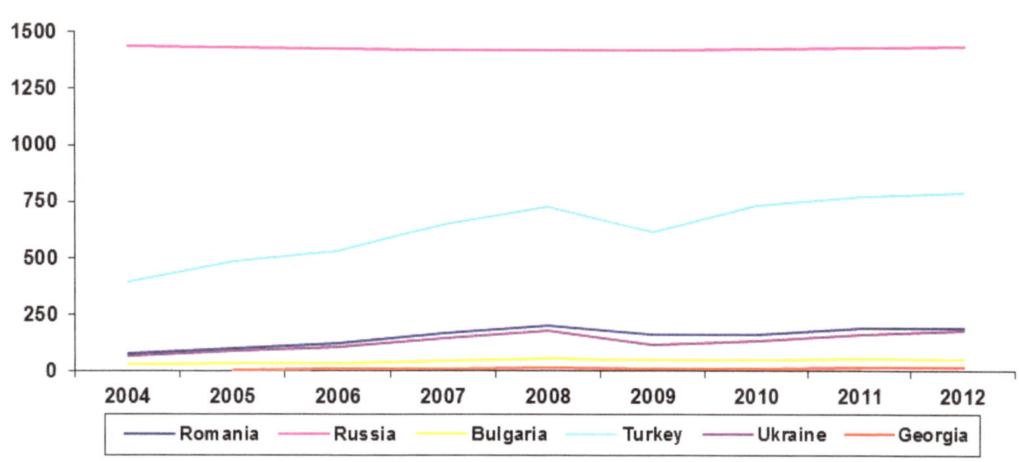

Graph 4. GDP Black Sea riparian countries during 2004-2012 (U.S.$ mil.)

[1] www.worldbank.org

Statistical analysis of the evolution of the Black Sea economies listed below (Table 3 and graph.5) has some issues, as follows[1]:

Table 3. GDP of the Black Sea riparian countries during 2004-2012 [in percent]

Country Year	Romania	Russia	Bulgaria	Turkey	Ukraine	Georgia
2004	8	7	7	9	12	6
2005	4	6	6	8	3	10
2006	8	8	6	7	7	9
2007	6	9	6	5	8	12
2008	8	5	6	1	2	2
2009	-7	-8	-5	-5	-15	-4
2010	-2	5	0	9	4	6
2011	3	4	2	9	5	7
2012	3	3	1	2	0	6

- the best economically years were 2004, 2006, 2007;
- the worst economically years were 2009 and 2010;
- the year 2012 was weaker than the previous year;
- the development trend of GDP is declining in the past two years that have been analyzed.

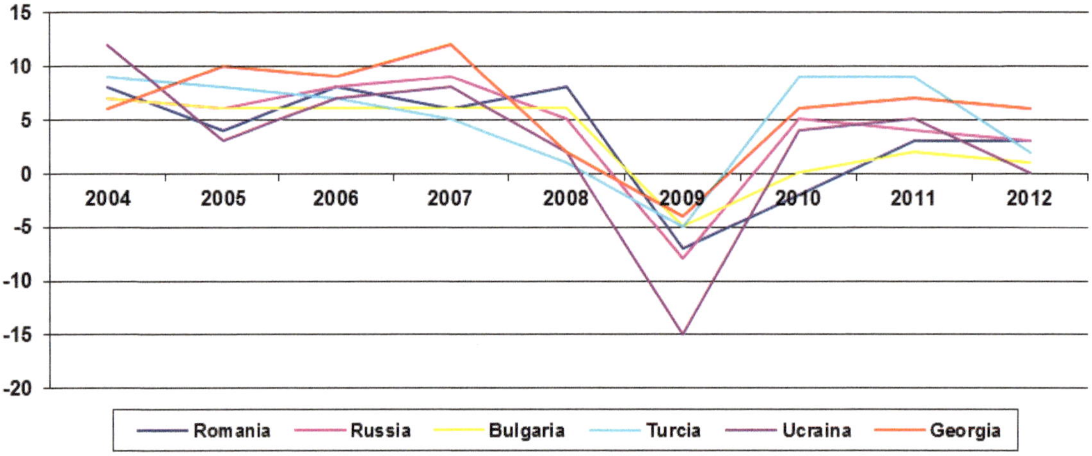

Graph 5. GDP evolution of the Black Sea riparian countries during 2004-2012

3. GNI per capita in the Black Sea Riparian Countries

GNI per capita, PPP (Purchasing Power Parities - the current international USD) shows a steady increase in the analyzed period for the Black Sea riparian countries, with a decreasing period, between 2009-2010, as a result of the global economic crisis (Table 4 and graph.6).

Table 4. GNI per capita in the Black Sea riparian countries during 2004-2012

Country Year	Romania	Russia	Bulgaria	Turkey	Ukraine	Georgia
2004	8540	10030	8970	10150	5160	3270
2005	9280	11560	9840	11390	5520	3650
2006	10890	14500	10800	12860	6120	4120
2007	12640	16350	11390	13880	6820	4680
2008	14550	19850	13230	15000	7200	4830
2009	14580	18600	13270	14340	6130	4660
2010	15260	20110	13700	15810	6540	4910
2011	16660	21700	14790	17070	6970	5260
2012	16860	22720	15450	18190	7180	6770

[1] *Ibidem.*

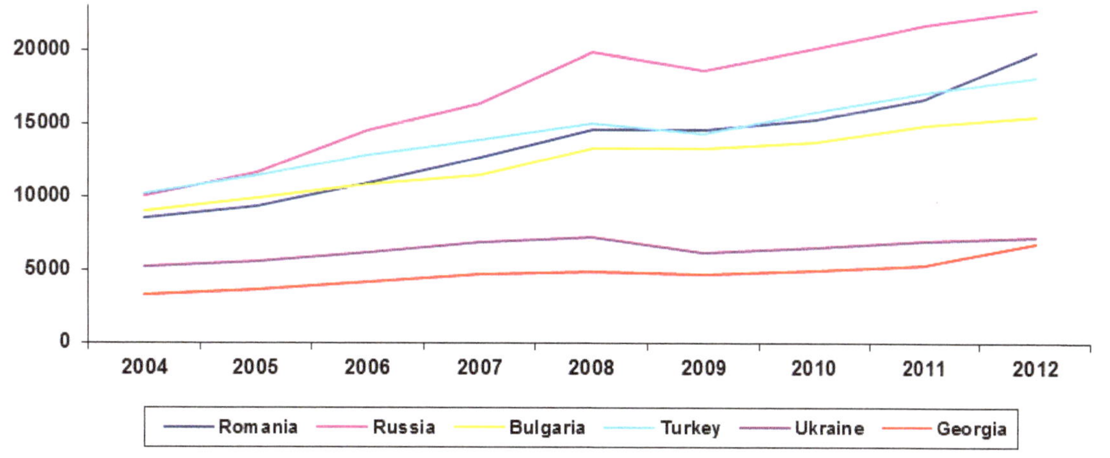

Graph 6. GNI per capita evolution in the Black Sea riparian countries during 2004-2012

4. Foreign Investment in the Black Sea Area

Since the domestic capital needed for investment and development is insufficient, the economic development of the Black Sea riparian countries is closely linked to the level of foreign investment. The UNCTAD statistics show the evolution of the capital who fluctuated in and out (table 5 and graph.7), from 36,562 million USD (2004) to 83,881 million USD (2012), dictated by the current global economic crisis.

Table 4. Foreign investments in adjacent areas of the Black Sea (U.S.$ million) during 2004-2012

Area	BSEC (Black Sea Economic Cooperation) [US$ mil.]
2004	36562
2005	47200
2006	89533
2007	112256
2008	141410
2009	66142
2010	68502
2011	91447
2012	83881

Thus, it is obvious that the level of FDI in the economy of the Black Sea adjacent and riparian countries, BSEC states, followed the global economy after strong growth in 2004-2008, nearly four times (from 36,462 million USD in 2004, to141,420 million USD, in 2008), the collapse in 2009 (66,142 million USD) and then a slow growth, and a decline in 2012 (83,881 mill, compared to 91,447 million USD in 2011).

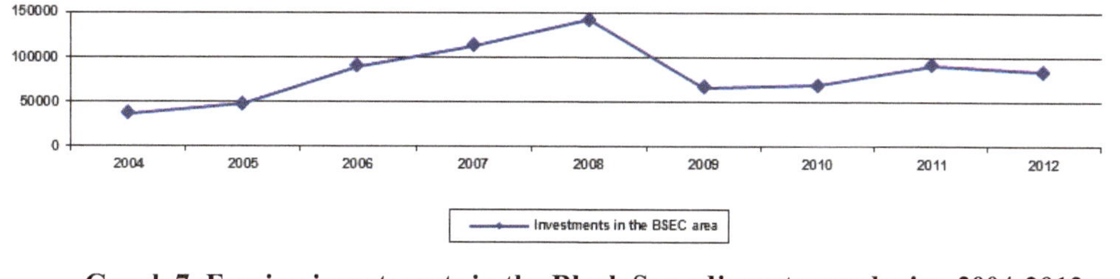

Graph 7. Foreign investments in the Black Sea adjacent area during 2004-2012

5. Conclusions

The Black Sea is a region between Europe and Asia whose geopolitical and economic importance is strongly emphasized by the recent political, military and economic actions in the area.

The Black Sea basin has six riparian states, which share the influence of political, economic and military power according to their economic and political affiliation to the strong political and military organization (EU, NATO, CIS), and other Black Sea "adjacent" countries, that wish to make their presence and influence visible here.

In the period 2004-2012, GDP of the Black Sea riparian countries grew, as it follows: GDP of Romania and Bulgaria increased approximately 2.3 times, GDP of Russia has remained almost constant, Turkey has doubled its GDP and Georgia tripled, with a total regional of about 3,950 billion in 2012, though the growth trend (percentage), GDP in the region has been declining in 2011-2012.

GNI per capita in the Black Sea riparian countries was increased overall during the period 2004-2012, however, the reductions imposed by the global economic crisis in 2009-2010, so in Romania, Russia and Georgia doubled, in Bulgaria and Turkey almost doubled, while in Ukraine it increased 1.4 times.

Although the population of the Black Sea countries, representing 44% of the EU population, compared to the amount of their GDP, is only 18.4 % of EU GDP, which demonstrates the need for many future strong investment programs, and the great opportunities for development that this area has (during 2011-2012, the trend of foreign investment in the region is declining).

6. References

Boşneagu, R. (2004). *Geographic Conditions Influence on the Maritime Trade Routes in the Black Sea Basin (West Basin).* Bucharest: University Book Publishing House.

*** www.imf.org.

*** www.unctad.org.

***www.worldbank.org.

*** www. europa.eu.

*** www. eurostat.ec.europa.eu.

2

Analysis on the Taxation in the EU Member States

Ana Alexandru[1]

Abstract: The purpose of this paper is to perform an analysis on the tax revenue collected by the Member States. The analysis takes into account the period 2000-2013 and highlights the main reasons reforms Member States' tax systems

Keywords: taxation; fiscal revenues; tax rate

1 Introduction

In 2012, the level of taxation in EU-28 was 39.4% of GDP. The level of taxation in the EU is high compared to countries like Russia 35.6%, and New Zealand, 31.8%. Countries which are less developed usually have a relatively low weight. High tax rate in the EU is not new; it makes its presence felt since the last third of the 20 century. In that time, the role of the public sector was expanded, this led to a large increase in tax rate 1970, and to a lesser extent, in the 1980s and early 1990. Member states have adopted several packages of measures for fiscal consolidation after the first Treaty of Maastricht and the Stability and Growth Pact. In many Member States, it is possible to widen the tax base to increase revenue collection potential, opportunity to reduce the tax rate or simplify the taxation. Many standard taxation systems have various exemptions, allowances, reduced tariffs and other tax systems known as "tax expenditures" This cannot always be justified, may not be the most effective tools for social goals. Member States have a more effective strategy in terms of raising legal tax rates. In some states, the process of consolidation was mainly based on the restriction or reorganization of primary public expenditure and in others the focus was on tax increasing.

2 Tax Rate in EU-28

2.1 General Overview

Tax rate in GDP surpassed the crisis in 2012 and will continue to increase in 2013. The tax rate in GDP began with a decrease in tax 2000 and increased by 2007 in the euro area and the EU-28. Income tax decreased in 2010 in both the euro area and the EU-28.

[1]Student, Faculty of Economic Sciences, "Danubius" University of Galati, Romania, Address: 3 Galati Boulevard, 800654 Galati, Romania, Corresponding author: anamariaalexandru1994@yahoo.com.

There are many reasons why government tax revenue varies from one year to another. Main reasons are changes in economic activities (affecting the level of employment, the sale of goods, services, etc.) and tax legislation (affecting tax rates, tax based) and changes in GDP.

Table 1. Total Taxes % of GDP

	2000	2001	2002	2003	2004	2005	2006	2007	2008	2009	2010	2011
Belgium	45,1	45,1	45,2	44,7	44,8	44,8	44,4	43,9	44,2	43,4	43,8	44,2
Bulgaria	31,5	30,8	28,5	31,0	32,5	31,3	30,7	33,3	32,3	29,0	27,5	27,3
Czech Republic	33,8	33,7	34,6	35,4	35,9	35,7	35,3	35,9	34,4	33,4	33,6	34,6
Denmark	49,4	48,5	47,9	48,0	49,0	50,8	49,6	48,9	47,8	47,8	47,5	47,7
Germany	41,3	39,4	38,9	39,1	38,3	38,3	38,6	38,7	38,9	39,4	38,0	38,5
Estonia	31,0	30,2	31,0	30,8	30,6	30,6	30,7	31,4	31,9	35,3	34,0	32,3
Ireland	31,5	29,7	28,3	28,8	30,1	30,6	32,1	31,5	29,5	28,1	28,0	28,2
Greece	34,6	33,2	33,7	32,1	31,3	32,2	31,7	32,5	32,1	30,5	31,7	32,4
Spain	34,1	33,7	34,1	33,9	34,8	35,9	36,8	37,1	32,9	30,7	32,2	31,8
France	44,2	43,8	43,3	43,1	43,3	43,8	44,1	43,4	43,2	42,1	42,5	43,7
Croatia	:	:	37,9	37,5	36,7	36,6	37,1	37,4	37,1	36,5	36,4	35,3
Italy	41,5	41,1	40,5	41,0	40,4	40,1	41,7	42,7	42,7	42,9	42,5	42,4
Cyprus	30,0	30,7	30,9	32,2	33,0	35,0	35,8	40,1	38,6	35,3	35,6	35,3
Latvia	29,7	28,9	28,6	28,6	28,6	29,2	30,6	30,6	29,2	26,6	27,2	27,6
Lithuania	30,9	29,4	29,1	28,8	28,9	29,1	30,0	30,2	30,7	30,4	28,5	27,4
Luxembourg	39,2	39,8	39,3	38,1	37,3	37,6	35,9	35,6	37,5	39,8	38,1	38,2
Hungary	39,8	38,7	38,0	38,0	37,7	37,4	37,3	40,4	40,3	40,1	38,1	37,3
Malta	27,3	28,9	30,0	30,4	31,3	32,9	33,0	33,9	33,0	33,4	32,2	33,0
Netherlands	39,9	38,3	37,7	37,4	37,5	37,6	39,0	38,7	39,2	38,2	38,9	38,6
Austria	43,0	44,9	43,6	43,4	43,0	42,1	41,5	41,7	42,7	42,4	42,1	42,2
Poland	32,6	32,2	32,7	32,2	31,5	32,8	33,8	34,8	34,3	31,8	31,8	32,3
Portugal	31,1	30,8	31,4	31,6	30,5	31,4	32,1	32,8	32,8	31,0	31,5	33,2
Romania	30,2	28,6	28,1	27,7	27,2	27,8	28,5	29,0	28,0	26,9	26,8	28,4
Slovenia	37,3	37,5	37,8	38,0	38,1	38,6	38,3	37,7	37,3	37,2	37,7	37,2
Slovakia	34,1	33,1	33,0	32,9	31,5	31,3	29,3	29,3	29,1	28,7	28,1	28,6
Finland	47,2	44,8	44,7	44,1	43,5	43,9	43,8	43,0	42,9	42,8	42,5	43,7
Sweden	51,5	49,4	47,5	47,8	48,0	48,9	48,3	47,3	46,4	46,5	45,4	44,4
United Kingdom	36,3	36,1	34,8	34,4	34,9	35,4	36,1	35,7	37,1	34,3	35,0	35,8

Source: Taxation trends in the European Union, Statistical books, 2014 edition, European Union, 2014

The crisis, along with fiscal policy measures has a strong impact on tax revenues in 2009 and the first effects became visible in 2008. In 2012, tax revenues in terms of GDP, substantially increased and reached its highest level since 2001, as we can see in table above.

2.2 Incentives for Research and Innovation

Experiencing concerns about decreasing competitiveness, many countries have introduced tax changes which had hoped to limit crises effects. These measures targeted to help small businesses and stimulate private investment in the Member States.

The vast majority of Member States apply tax incentives to stimulate private investment and innovation. This has become increasingly attractive in the start of the crises. In this period, about half of Member States have introduced or announced changes in terms of taxation that are offered support for research and development. Latvia introduced a new form of tax incentives for certain costs related to research and development.

Several Member States have introduced or expanded tax measures designed to stimulate entrepreneurial activity, investments in certain sectors. Some Member States have introduced tax incentives underlying goal of stimulating reinvestment of profits, for small enterprises (Spain, France). Sweden launched a new tax incentive for business in December 2013 in which individuals acquire the shares of small and medium enterprises can deduct half of the amount of acquisition. United Kingdom has introduced a new measure of tax relief for investments.

2.3. Direct Taxation

The direct tax rate in GDP has exceeded pre-crisis levels. Proactive fiscal measures taken by Member States in the last year was correcting their deficit economic recovery.

Direct taxes have decreased since 2008 (13.7% of GDP to 12.7 % of GDP in 2009). After a continuous decrease, direct taxes have increased. Starting from 2009-2010 direct taxes in the EU -28 increased from 12.8 % to 13.2 % of GDP. This could be due to an increase in income taxes of companies. Main components of direct taxes are income tax of individuals and corporate. We cans see this image in the table above.

Table 2. Direct Taxes as % of GDP

	2000	2001	2002	2003	2004	2005	2006	2007	2008	2009	2010	2011	2012
Belgium	17,5	17,8	17,6	17,2	17,5	17,6	17,3	17,0	17,2	15,9	16,4	16,8	17,4
Bulgaria	6,9	7,5	6,4	6,2	6,0	4,9	5,2	8,2	6,7	5,9	5,4	5,2	5,3
Czech Republic	7,9	8,3	8,8	9,2	9,2	8,9	8,9	9,0	8,0	7,2	6,9	7,2	7,2
Denmark	30,5	29,5	29,3	29,6	30,4	31,9	30,7	30,1	29,7	30,0	29,9	29,9	30,6
Germany	13,0	11,4	11,0	11,0	10,8	11,1	11,9	12,2	12,4	11,8	11,2	11,7	12,1
Estonia	7,7	7,2	7,5	8,0	7,9	7,0	7,1	7,4	7,9	7,5	6,8	6,5	6,8
Ireland	13,6	12,7	11,6	11,9	12,4	12,3	13,2	12,9	11,7	10,9	10,6	12,3	13,1
Greece	10,0	8,8	8,8	8,0	8,2	8,8	8,3	8,3	8,3	8,5	8,0	8,8	10,2
Spain	10,6	10,5	11,0	10,4	10,8	11,5	12,3	13,5	11,1	10,0	10,0	10,0	10,6
France	12,5	12,6	11,8	11,4	11,7	11,9	12,2	12,0	12,0	10,3	11,0	11,7	12,4
Croatia	:	:	6,1	6,0	6,0	6,2	6,9	7,4	7,2	7,2	6,5	6,2	6,1
Italy	14,4	14,7	14,0	14,7	13,9	13,3	14,3	15,0	15,2	15,4	14,8	14,8	15,2
Cyprus	11,2	11,3	11,3	9,7	8,8	10,2	10,8	13,8	12,9	11,2	11,1	11,7	11,1
Latvia	7,3	7,6	7,9	7,6	7,9	7,9	8,5	9,2	9,8	7,2	7,4	7,4	7,7
Lithuania	8,4	7,8	7,4	7,9	8,7	9,0	9,5	9,2	9,3	6,0	4,7	4,4	4,9
Luxembourg	15,0	15,3	15,4	14,8	13,1	13,7	13,2	13,2	14,2	15,0	14,7	14,5	14,8
Hungary	9,9	10,2	10,2	9,6	9,1	9,1	9,5	10,4	10,6	10,0	8,6	7,0	7,5
Malta	9,0	9,7	11,0	11,5	11,0	11,7	12,0	13,3	12,7	13,6	12,9	13,0	13,9

Netherlands	12,0	11,7	11,8	11,0	10,7	11,7	11,9	12,2	12,0	12,1	12,2	11,7	11,2
Austria	13,2	15,0	13,8	13,7	13,5	12,8	12,9	13,4	14,0	12,8	12,8	13,0	13,4
Poland	7,2	6,7	6,9	6,6	6,4	7,0	7,5	8,6	8,6	7,5	7,0	7,0	7,2
Portugal	9,6	9,1	9,1	8,5	8,3	8,3	8,6	9,5	9,7	9,0	8,9	9,9	9,4
Romania	7,0	6,4	5,8	6,0	6,4	5,3	6,0	6,7	6,7	6,5	6,1	6,2	6,1
Slovenia	7,4	7,6	7,8	8,0	8,2	8,7	9,1	9,2	8,9	8,3	8,2	8,0	7,8
Slovakia	7,4	7,5	7,1	7,1	6,1	6,0	6,1	6,2	6,5	5,5	5,4	5,5	5,6
Finland	21,4	19,3	19,1	18,1	17,8	17,8	17,6	17,8	17,8	16,4	16,2	16,6	16,3
Sweden	22,6	20,8	19,6	20,2	20,9	22,0	22,2	21,2	19,8	19,6	19,2	18,5	18,3
United Kingdom	16,5	16,7	15,6	15,0	15,2	16,0	16,8	16,5	18,2	15,8	15,5	15,6	15,1

Source: Taxation trends in the European Union, Statistical books, 2014 edition, European Union, 2014

3 The Distribution of the Tax Burden according to the Type of Taxation

Considerable variation between Member States showing the distribution of total tax revenue by type of taxation base (labor, capital and consumption). The largest source of income comes from income tax in the work, and half of all revenues are coming consumption tax, followed by capital. Tax structure is different between Member State.

3.1 Consumption Tax

In 2012, the revenue collected from taxation of consumption remained at the same level as the previous year. The level of consumption was climbed back in 2007. The evolution from 2000 to 2012 is described in the figure below.

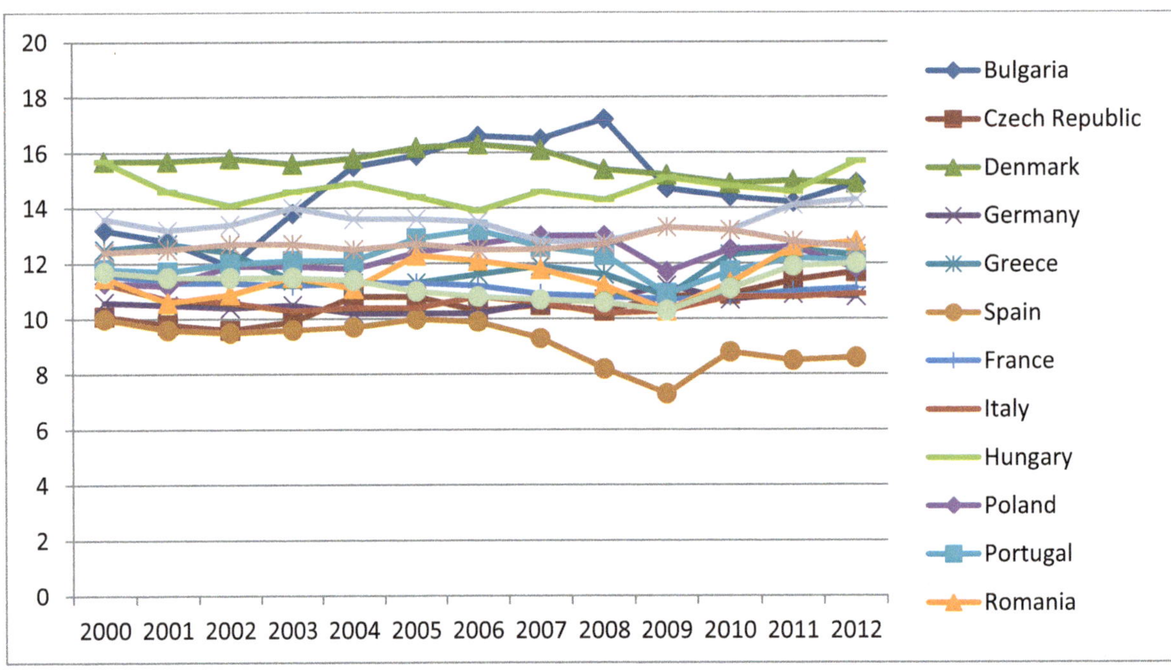

Figure 1. Taxes on Consumption as % of GDP

Source: Taxation trends in the European Union, Statistical books, 2014 edition, European Union, 2014

3.2 Labor Taxation

In 2012 the increasing of the tax burden on labor have place. Starting from the economic crisis won the arguments in favor of reducing the tax burden on labor, but the achievement of this goal remains difficult.

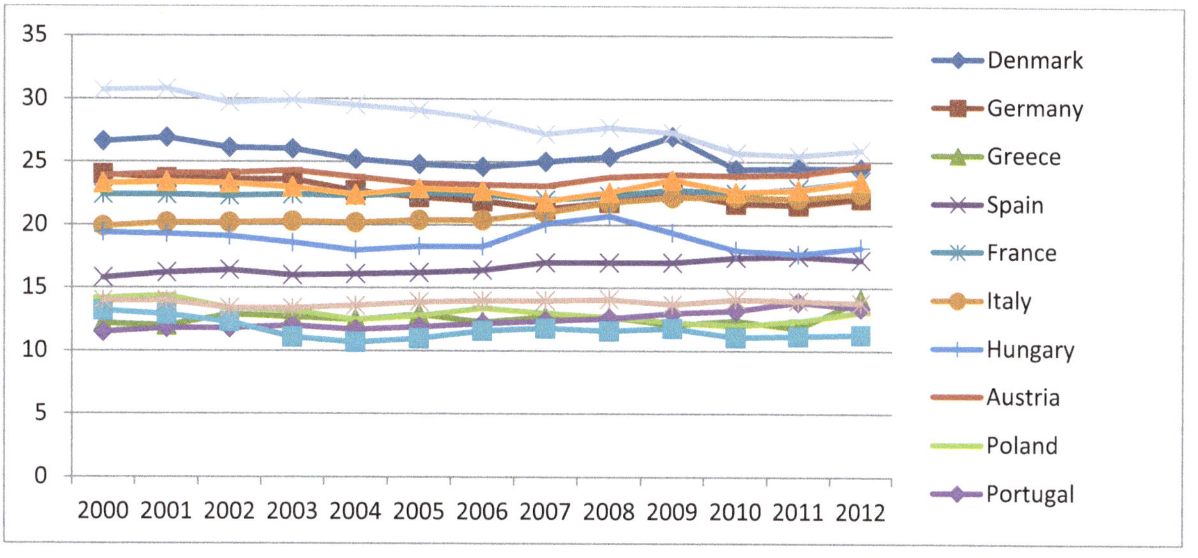

Figure 2. Taxes on Labor as % of GDP

Source: Taxation trends in the European Union, Statistical books, 2014 edition, European Union, 2014

The 28 Member States recorded an increase in employment in 2012, the highest growth being recorded in Greece, followed by Poland and Cyprus, each with two percents. The tax burden on labor varies between Member States. The higher direct taxes on labor are registered in Belgium with a share of 42.8% in 2012, Italy (42%) and Austria (41.5%) and the small direct taxes are recorded in Malta (23.3%), Bulgaria (24.5%) and the UK (25.2%). In the context of the economic crisis, given the high level of unemployment, high taxes on labor the effect was harmful in terms of work incentives for individuals and firms. Labor tax increases were relatively rare in this time and especially took the form of restrictions tax credits or tax exemptions for people with higher incomes.

4 Conclusions

Reforms that were introduced in the Member States in 2013 and 2014 shows that many Member States have taken measures to increase indirect tax. Taxes on consumption and environmental taxes was being considered less harmful, although most of the Member States have taken steps to improve the tax structure, and some states have taken steps to adopt new reduced rates. In the field of labor taxation (personal income tax and social security contributions) many countries only increase the fiscal burden.

6 References

European Comission, Tax reforms in EU Member States, Tax policy challenges for economic growth and fiscal Sustainability, 2014 Report.

Consiliul fiscal, Raport anual, 2013/ Fiscal Council, Annual Report 2013.

Taxation trends in the European Union, Statistical books, 2014 edition, European Union, 2014.

3

Analyses on the Possible Brexit through the Lisbon Treaty

Ana-Maria Teodora Andronic[1], Andy Pușcă[2], Anișoara Popa[3]

Abstract: Europe is facing a social crisis like never before, and this comes just after an economical one. The huge flow of migrants that started crossing into Europe at the end of 2015 was just the straw that broke the camel for Great Britain, because the Brits were threatening to leave the EU for some time. Prime Minister David Cameron has warned his European counterparts that his country might leave if his demands are not met. He clearly affirmed that he wants to stay in the EU, but under different rules. He negotiated a package of reforms, demanding concessions from a frightened Brussels, that has seen almost inevitable the change in some EU treaty terms. The PM used the 2011 European Union Act at the negotiations, document which requires any EU treaty that passes new powers to Brussels to be put to an internal British referendum. On June 23rd there is set a referendum on the country's membership to the EU. But this amount of uncertainty led to the fall of the pound (reaching its lowest level since 2009), to fear for the investors and furious debates between the political parties. We shall further analyze the Lisbon Treaty, in order to better understand the legislation behind this European-wide tension, and to explain the implications of such an event.

Keywords: Brexit; European Union; referendum; Lisbon Treaty; United Kingdom; employees' rights; migration

1. Introduction

Voluntary Withdrawal from EU of a Member State- Before the Lisbon Treaty

It is necessary to state that never before since the creation of the Economic Community of Coal and Steel in 1951 until today, none of the member states left the EU, in neither of the versions in which it has presented itself. The possibility of voluntary withdrawal was not mentioned in the Constitutive Treaties, before adopting the Lisbon Treaty in 2009 (signed in 2007). But neither the Accession Treaties of every member state don't have such a clause, although in theory, this right is recognized. Procedural forms to support such an initiative were not established, and this is due to an accumulation of reasons.

According to the European doctrine, the lack of regulation in the EU is due to the absolute confidence that the countries' leaders have had in the stability and durability of the construction of Europe. And the presence of such regulations would have put to doubt the arrangement between the nations, allied to achieve common objectives, assumed by the founding Treaties. It would have boosted the risk of

[1]Assistant at the International Cooperation Center and Master Student at Danubius University of Galati, Romania, Address: 3 Galati Blvd., Galati 800654, Romania, Corresponding author: aanateodora@yahoo.com.
[2]Associate Professor, PhD, Rector of Danubius University of Galati, Romania, Address: 3 Galati Blvd., Galati 800654, Romania, Corresponding author: andypusca@univ-danubius.ro.
[3]Professor, PhD, Department of Comunications International and Relation, Danubius University of Galati, Romania, Address: 3 Galati Blvd., Galati 800654, Romania, Corresponding author: apopa@univ-danubius.ro.

such an event, because the regulation should have been accompanied by a procedure and an overview of the possible consequences.[1]

Two separate interpretations were generated due to lack of express clauses from the constitutive treaties. The first stipulates that unilateral right of withdrawal exists even in the absence of clear provisions under the right of any sovereign state to withdraw as a signatory to the treaties concluded. A second interpretation is that there exists a supreme commitment between the member states in order to accomplish the mission and the vision of the Union, evidence of the irreversible nature of unification, and so contrary to exit clause. Proof of the constant effort to maintain the integrity and unity of the European structure is the fact that exactly the concluding of the treaties is done indefinitely. Besides this there are restrictions on the right to renegotiate the treaties of accession[2] the acquis communautaire acceptance by all Member States the principle of solidarity and others.

Public international law and the Vienna Convention on the Law of Treaties (1969) are sources for a possible interpretation of this dispute. The *Pacta sunt servanda*[3] principle is enshrined by the Vienna Convention, acknowledging the right to terminate a treaty. Situations where this might happen is either if that right is expressly provided[4] or may be deduced from the content / nature of a Treaty[5], or if applicable the *rebus sic stantibus* clause, meaning where there is a fundamental change of circumstances which has occurred with regard to those existing at the time of concluding a treaty which was not foreseen by the parties, if: the existence of those circumstances constituted an essential basis of consent to be bound by the treaty and this change had the effect of transforming the radical nature of the obligations remaining to be performed under the treaty.[6]

Of these three possibilities under the Vienna Convention only the last (rebus sic stantibus) may apply in case of withdrawal of an EU Member State given the "absence of a clause to that effect in the constituent treaties and the impossibility of deducting a right of withdrawal, or even approved, from the content or nature of the treaties"[7]. Also, extremely limited is the application of the doctrine that provides change of circumstances in exceptional situations, and a more permissive interpretation could endanger the very stability and inviolability of treaties.

---

[1]Miheş, Andreea, Voluntary withdrawal and exclusion from the EU and Economic and Monetary Union, 2012, Juridice.ro http://www.juridice.ro/201796/retragerea-voluntara-si-excluderea-din-uniunea-europeana-si-din-uniunea-economica-si-monetara.html

[2]The renegotiation took place in favor of the UK in January 2016.

[3]The principle of binding force regarding treaties on legal pact.

[4]*Article 54 of the Vienna Convention*: "Termination of or Withdrawal From A Treaty Under Its Provisions Or By Consent Of The Parties. The termination of a treaty or the withdrawal of a party may take place: (a) In conformity with the provisions of the treaty; or (b) At any time by consent of all the parties after consultation with the other contracting States."

[5]*Article 56*: "Denunciation of or Withdrawal from a Treaty Containing No Provision Regarding Termination, Denunciation Or Withdrawal **1**. A treaty which contains no provision regarding its termination and which does not provide for denunciation or withdrawal is not subject to denunciation or withdrawal unless: (a) It is established that the parties intended to admit the possibility of denunciation or withdrawal; or (b) A right of denunciation or withdrawal may be implied by the nature of the treaty. **2**. A party shall give not less than twelve months' notice of its intention to denounce or withdraw from a treaty under paragraph 1."

[6]*Article 69:* "Consequences Of The Invalidity Of A Treaty **1**. A treaty the invalidity of which is established under the present Convention is void. The provisions of a void treaty have no legal force. **2.** If acts have nevertheless been performed in reliance on such a treaty: (a) Each party may require any other party to establish as far as possible in their mutual relations the position that would have existed if the acts had not been performed; (b) Acts performed in good faith before the invalidity was invoked are not rendered unlawful by reason only of the invalidity of the treaty. **3.** In cases falling under articles 49, 50, 51 or 52, paragraph 2 does not apply with respect to the party to which the fraud, the act of corruption or the coercion is imputable. **4.** In the case of the invalidity of a particular State's consent to be bound by a multilateral treaty, the foregoing rules apply in the relations between that State and the parties to the treaty."

[7]Miheş, Andreea, Voluntary withdrawal and exclusion from the EU and Economic and Monetary Union, 2012, Juridice.ro.

Sovereignty although cited in the existence of a right of withdrawal of states does not fully guarantee action. Miheş (2012) discusses the example of Costa / E.n.e.l.[1] in whose verdict rendered by the European Court of Justice noted the limitations of the principle of sovereignty by joining the EU and by signing the founding Treaties. Thus, the transfer to the European system from the law of the Member States of rights and obligations bring a permanent limitation of their sovereign rights. One element that distinguishes the constitutive treaties of other international treaties is the transfer of sovereignty of the first set Member States have limited their sovereign rights by creating a community of unlimited duration of operation, possessing its own institutions which subsequently acquired legal personality and to which powers have been transferred from its members.

In conclusion, we believe that states can invoke the sovereignty principle with great difficulty to denounce previously concluded treaties. Prior to adoption of the Lisbon Treaty (2009) there was only one theoretical possibility you could withdraw from the EU, based on negotiation, all of it embodied in an agreement ratified by all Member States.

The Lisbon Treaty

The Lisbon Treaty has brought enshrining the right to voluntarily and unilaterally withdraw by several provisions designed to shed light on this delicate issue. Art 59[2] "Voluntary withdrawal from the Union" enshrines explicitly the right of withdrawal of any EU Member State, in accordance with its own constitutional procedure. Thus, as a direct consequence, European law becomes inapplicable to the State which decides to withdraw, from the withdrawal date set in the agreement or up to 2 years from the date of notification of withdrawal, according to the Constitutional Treaty. The state which has undergone the procedure can change his mind later, wanting to be again a member state of the Union, but then it will be required to follow a new procedure for accession, like any new candidate (art. 49-The general procedure for accession).

Article 50, paragraph (1) of the TEU stipulates that "any Member State may, in accordance with its constitutional rules, withdraw from the Union" with procedural formalities set out in the following articles. Thus, the state shall notify the European Council regarding its intention to withdraw, and the Union shall negotiate and conclude an agreement with the state (agreement negotiated in accordance with art. 218 paragraph (3) TFEU). In it are inscribed the conditions for the withdrawal procedure, taking account of the nature of its future relationship with the Union. It shall be concluded by the EU Council, with the approval of Parliament, with a qualified majority. The state representative cannot attend for reasons of procedural matters at the debates in the European Council and the Council. Also, Article 50 sets out the conditions for termination of the application of EU law into national law, namely from the entry date into force of the withdrawal agreement or two years from notification of intention to withdraw. There is an exception though, if there is a unanimous decision to extend (the default delay) from the European Council, in agreement with the Member State that submitted procedure.

[1]CJCE, decision from 15th July 1964, *Costa/E.N.E.L*, 6/64, (Mihes, 2012).

[2]1. Any Member State may decide to withdraw from the EU in accordance with its own constitutional requirements. 2.A Member State which decides to withdraw shall notify the Council of its intention; the European Council shall examine that notification. In the light of the guidelines provided by the European Council, the Union shall negotiate and conclude an agreement with the State, setting out the arrangements for its withdrawal, taking account of the framework for its future relationship with the Union. That agreement shall be concluded on behalf of the Union by the Council of Ministers, acting by a qualified majority, after obtaining the consent of the European Parliament. The representative of the withdrawing Member State shall not participate in Council of Ministers or European Council discussions or decisions concerning it. 3.This Constitution shall cease to apply to the State in question from the date of entry into force of the withdrawal agreement or, failing that, two years after the ratification referred to in paragraph 2, unless the European Council, in agreement with the Member State concerned, decides to extend this period. "

Article 50 of the T.E.U.

The wording of Article 50 TEU is very permissive, in that the State in question may either carry a negotiation followed by an agreement for the withdrawal to operate, or may be about a unilateral withdrawal. The state concerned is not required to sign an agreement that would draw new relations with the EU, negotiations could fail and still the notification of its intention shall take effect. In the absence of an agreement, the state will no longer be subject to union rules, even after the expiry of two years' time from the date of notice of its wish to withdraw. Each state has full freedom of decision and can act in accordance with their own constitutional rules, and the withdrawal decision cannot be censored at EU level.

Aside from the questions of the nature of the process, there is another aspect of the recall, which is highly debated in the current situation in the Union. After the announcement from the Great Britain of its intention to leave the Union, the EU could face a massive withdrawal of Member States who wish to negotiate separate agreements with numerous advantages, to determine their stay in the EU. The European Council was forced to negotiate special clauses in order to change Britain's intention to leave, and also to act with great care, in order to prevent a dissolution of the Union.

2. Brexit- General Discussion

Britain has a long history as a signatory of international treaties and as a reliable partner of various international alliances. FCO or Foreign Affairs Office of the British Government (Foreign and the Commonwealth Office) made a census of treaties, from 1834 to the present. The result was no less than 13,200 documents of bilateral treaties, agreements, pacts and acts establishing the UN and NATO.

The word that generates many disputes between the parties involved in the delicate situation with the possible Brexit is sovereignty. This supreme illustration of power, this quality to exercise unrestrained political power both internally and in relation to external forces cannot be taken away from what it is *de facto*. Parliament's sovereignty is and will remain intact even if the authority is delegated. The members of the Parliament can always abrogate treaties in force, whether we are talking here about the EU, NATO or the UN. Philip Stephens, Financial Times[1] editor, said about EU membership that it represents "the most extensive and complex exercise of delegation of authority to a supranational organization."

Britain, as a sovereign state, has global interests, which lead, in consequence, to extensive vulnerabilities. Economic and strategic interests weigh heavily in the balance, in trying to make a decision on leaving the EU. And the decision will take into account, of course, the implications of Brexit on the security and prosperity of the nation.

Implications of a Possible Brexit

Exiting from the European Union would have broad implications over the United Kingdom, especially adverse implications on a large number of fields. The main impact would be on the economy (remember that in late February 2016, the pound recorded a historic low, from its lowest level in 2009, and continued to fall). Secondly, national security would be at great risk, taking into account terrorist

[1]Financial Times, http://www.ft.com/intl/cms/s/2/26b6a12c-daf2-11e5-a72f 1e7744c66818.html?ftcamp=social/free_to_read/brexit_sovereignty_comment/awareness/editorial&segid=0100320#axzz41DSGPEp4.

threats and negative signals from some countries (Russia Korea Iran, etc.). Many analysts believe that Britain could better negotiate personal advantages remaining in the EU than outside it.

Countries outside the European Union who stand and watch this unwanted situation should realize the danger. Brexit would mean a severe blow, both "physical" and psychological, on a Europe already weakened. It would mean breaking the fifth largest economy of its market outlets, and the fifth largest arms buyer among its allies[1]. Brexit campaigners believe that Britain is held in place by the European Union when it comes to progress; in theory, UK could continue external trade in the event of leaving the Eurozone. But in reality, the European Union would allow access to a restricted common market under special conditions. If we were to look at Norway or Switzerland, we would see that the UK should still accept free movement of people, along with a substantial payment to the EU budget, before having unrestricted access to the common market. In terms of the years 2000-2016, the EU has come to absorb about half of the total export mass of goods/products from the United Kingdom, while imports from the Union do not exceed 10%. British trade deficit is linked mainly to Germany and Spain, and not necessarily to the rest of the 25 Member states[2].

For some skeptics all these difficulties and restrictions which may be imposed in the event of a Brexit do not represent a major impediment, since the Kingdom would recover its sovereignty. This means regaining complete freedom of decision against the will of the EU which interferes in every sector of citizens' lives, from the bonuses received by bankers and limits to weekly working hours. Specialists wonder to what extent this statement is an illusion. For a completely globalized world, power is being used as the most powerful weapon. The British state gave up part of their sovereignty to be members of NATO, the IMF, the EU and so on. Alliances are a double-edged weapon: the act of signing treaties involves obedience to the collective rules, in exchange for compensatory gains.

The immigration issue is extremely sensitive in the current refugee crisis, and an integral part of the early 2016 Brexit negotiations. The year 2015 brought to Europe the largest flow of migration seen in modern times, coming from the Eastern part of the continent and from the Orient. Half of the migrants that are being accepted in the UK on a daily basis come from the EU, and there are no actual measures that the British Government can take in order to restrict them. Only in the case of a British exit-Brexit, this could be done, but restraining immigrants from coming to the UK has some cons, and the damage is yet difficult to estimate. We mean, of course, losing the access to the common market, plus Britain would lose the young workforce, most of them qualified, and the services sector would suffer a huge decline, since it is based on the Italian doctors, French bankers, Romanian IT specialists or Bulgarian builders.

Another area of activity that will suffer if a Brexit happens is science and research. Although Britain is a generous contributor to the EU fund, it attracts every year more research money than their pay. Between 2007 and 2013, the UK has contributed with over 5.4 billion Euro in the R&D (Research and Development) Fund of the Union, but attracted an enormous amount of 8.8 billion euro, cited Steve Connor, editor for The Independent. [3]

[1]The Economist, http://www.economist.com/news/leaders/21693584-leaving-eu-would-hurt-britainand-would-also-deal-terrible-blow-west-real-danger.

[2] The Economist, http://www.economist.com/news/leaders/21693584-leaving-eu-would-hurt-britainand-would-also-deal-terrible-blow-west-real-danger.

[3] The Independent, http://www.independent.co.uk/news/uk/politics/eu-referendum-british-science-would-suffer-badly-in-event-of-a-brexit-scientists-warn-a6898376.html.

Brexit- Effects on Workers' Rights

Frances O'Grady, general secretary of the largest union for workers in the Kingdom, warns that workers' rights are in danger in the possibility of a Brexit. Separating Britain from the European Union would adversely impact on the right to work, on maternity leave for women, on payroll and payments policy field between men and women, on redundancies and so on.

Kathleen Morrison, attorney for the law firm Brodies LLP, has offered for The Independent newspaper 11 examples of workers' rights from British law which came from European legislation.[1]

3. Working Time

Employees' working programme was not highly regulated before the introduction into UK law of the 1998 act called UK Working Time Regulations (WTR). The regulations have met the implementation of the European Directive of Work (European Working Time Directive), and include 48 hours-working week, the right to have daily and weekly breaks, and working time limitations for workers on night period.

1. Vacations

The European Directive for the Work Program has prompted all Member States to give employees holidays of four weeks every year, period when they could exercise their right to leave (but leaving is up to workers). Since its adoption, however, Great Britain has brought changes to the UK legislation, meaning that now, the four weeks holiday was extended to five weeks of vacation annually.

2. Protection of Workers in Case of Business Transfer

Employees are protected by their rights when a business is changes ownership, and so they are transferred to the new owner; they are kept under the same terms and conditions as when they were employed. They are protected from dismissal due to a possible transfer, and in the case of major decisions regarding employees, they are informed and consulted.

3. Employees with Temporary Status

Also called agency workers, they are entitled to the same basic working conditions (right to be remunerated for their work and leave entitlements), as have the employees with a permanent status, but only if they had worked in a place for at least 12 weeks (3 months).

4. Collective Redundancies

If an employer wishes to start a series of collective redundancies of over 20 employees within 90 days, he is obliged by law to engage into collective consultations with the employees' representatives. Starting date of a round of negotiations must be established with a sufficient period of time ("in good time") before the actual redundancies.

5. Discrimination

Discrimination is not moral nor legally accepted in the UK, when it comes to gender maternity, race, religion, beliefs disability, age, sexual orientation or gender reassignment. There are also attempts to lessen the gap between the salaries received by male and female employees.

---

1 The Independent, http://www.independent.co.uk/news/business/news/eu-referendum-tucs-frances-o-grady-warns-that-workers-rights-are-being-forgotten-in-brexit-debate-a6897801.html.

6. Fixed-Term Employees

EU laws prohibit less favorable treatment for fixed-term employees, compared with permanent workers.

7. Part-time Employees

Workers employed part-time are protected against less favorable treatment compared to permanent employees by the European law.

8. Maternity and Pregnancy

Some rights regarding pregnancy and child care period came from the European Union legislation, although British regulations go beyond what provides as a basis in the European legislation. Thus, the United Kingdom provides for a period of 52 weeks maternity leave for its female employees, unlike the European minimum of 14 weeks.

9. Parental leave

Employees who are eligible for parental leave are entitled to up to 18 weeks of unpaid leave for each child, a period that can be used until the child's eighteenth birthday.

10. Privacy

Data Protection Act in the United Kingdom (UK Data Protection Act) was specifically designed to implement the data protection system in the European Union and for its citizens. Workers' rights are being threatened by negotiations on the Brexit case, and principles such as paid holidays and the right to employment of part-time workers are on the list of cuts. European law mandates each Member State to comply with its agreements on workers' rights. For example, the principle of equal pay for equal work has existed since the formation of the Treaties.[1]

On the other hand, there are opinions that wages will rise in the UK because of a limited access to employment of foreigners in the case of Brexit The number of migrants will suffer a decline and existing workforce will have to be paid in addition to the current payroll. Lord Stuart Rose, former chief executive of Marks and Spencer, told The Telegraph[2] that Britain staying in the EU will mean "one way street" for immigrants. Labour migration to developed countries is constantly growing as, shown in recent statistics. Thus, in Great Britain, more than 257 000 citizens from the EU member states came to the UK in 2015, and more than 630 000 EU citizens were registered to receive a social insured number (National Insurance Number)

3. Conclusions

Permanent development of the European Union by increasing the number of new members with a high level of political and economic integration has changed the face of Europe, as it is known to us today. The European Union was established as a comprehensive cooperation project, with a distinct role in maintaining economic and social stability, peace and to ensure a "lifeline" for Member States which are in difficulty. All agreements signed so far have established a legislative framework of the

[1]The Independent, http://www.independent.co.uk/news/uk/politics/eu-referendum-workers-rights-paid-holiday-brexit-labour-angela-eagle-a6901146.html

[2]The Telegraph, http://www.telegraph.co.uk/news/newstopics/eureferendum/12181385/Wages-for-British-workers-will-rise-in-the-event-of-a-Brexit-head-of-in-campaign-says.html

European construction, leaving room for an increased level of integration of its members, and also ignoring an essential criterion: that of withdrawal of a state.

At the beginning, the economic crisis came from the United States (2008), and continued with a massive economic recession, political differences and extremist parties gaining ground in the last election, aging of population in the EU, exchange rate fluctuations, crisis and wars, migrants flow, and all this, however, confront us with problems whose solutions are proving to be extremely difficult. This raises the increasingly problematic question that an exit from a member country would pose to the European Union.

Close ties between states have prompted a considerable transfer of attributes that are nothing but enshrined the national sovereignty of each state. European institutions, empowered by the transfer of sovereignty, have attracted in recent years discontent from some states. Increasingly obvious politicization of EU directives and regulations which must be integrated into national legislation, contributions in cash for the survival of poor countries are reasons of dissatisfaction in strong democracies.

And given the current context, in which uncertainty leaves room for speculation and concern for the stability of the Union, and given the fact that no further than 2013 Greece was in a position to be saved with a huge financial aid to prevent its withdrawal, now the year 2015 brings a clear attempt of the UK to leave the Union, we consider justified treating this theme. Whether we are talking about the revanchist politics of Russia, or the terrorist threats and the expanding sphere of influence of ISIS (ISIL DAESH), nuclear proliferation, environmental degradation, huge debts from the states and diminishing resources, we understand how important the negotiation on a possible Brexit is.

4. Bibliography

Miheş, Andreea (2012). *Voluntary withdrawal and exclusion from the EU and Economic and Monetary Union.* Juridice.ro http://www.juridice.ro/201796/retragerea-voluntara-si-excluderea-din-uniunea-europeana-si-din-uniunea-economica-si-monetara.html.

The Vienna Convention.

A consolidated version of the Treaty on European Union, the Treaty on the Functioning of the European Union and the Charter of Fundamental Rights of the European Union.

4

Perspectives of the Press Council in Romania

Daniela Aurelia Popa[1]

Abstract: A review of self-regulatory operational systems at international level can offer a practical vision on media responsibility tools such as press council, which represents the main focus of this study. The Press Council is a flexible structure (Zlatev, 2011, p. 18) whose complexity depends on the political, cultural, historic and cultural context of a country and the professional culture of the journalists. There are many models of press councils, so we can conclude that there is no universal model, better or less good. This study aims at providing the current prospects for the functioning of such an instrument of professional responsibility of journalists in Romania and it is based on a qualitative research based on in-depth interview.[2]

Keywords: self-regulation; moral court; prestige; sanction

1. Introduction

As a tool for self-regulation media, the Press Council is an *independent agency whose responsibility is of monitoring the daily performance of mass-media* (Dominick, 2009, p. 454) or a more complex definition: that apolitical and non-governmental structure whose purpose is to ensure the smooth and sane development of the life of information environment, particularly through monitoring the good journalism practice and by judging cases of malpractice (Runcan, 2002, p. 324). The Press Council has the following characteristics (Ristow, 2009, p. 5) it may cover *written press and audiovisual media* - consisting of members such as journalists, representatives of public community, covering a wide geographical area; it can be established by *a statute* - by: companies, professional media organizations or independent groups.

Most northern European countries benefit from the existence of Press Councils, News Councils or Mass-media Councils, which have expanded their activities and they are now responsible for journalistic publications. Solving complaints against the mass-media remain a vital task of the Press

---

[1] Assistant Professor, PhD, Danubius University of Galati, Faculty of Comunication and International Relations, Romania, Address: 3 Galati Blvd, Galati, Romania, Corresponding author: daniela.popa@univ-danubius.ro.

[2] For conducting interviews, the researcher has had a number of questions that have served as a guide for the interview and which were addressed not in a strict order, but according to the conversational flow and the reactions interviewees. By conducting interviews, the researcher was able to obtain the perceptions of journalists on the objectives of the study. The interpretation of the collected data was achieved by calling the content analysis based on categories grid. Some text units were coded according to the main and secondary themes and text passages containing similar information were placed in a grid of categories. For accurate rendering of relevant information were used both citations and paraphrases but only to support the basic text. The interviews were conducted face to face, during February-April 2013 on a non-probability sampling consisting of 15 people (journalists and media activists).

Council, but the Western countries have several roles, being complemented by academic activities, training institutions and supervisory groups (watchdog), such as: training of journalists, publishing guides of public records, helping to write and publish codes of ethics, ensuring institutional voices against government interventions, supporting a free and responsible press (Risow 2009, p. 8).

For such a council to be established, Deaver (2004, pp. 183-184) suggests the existence of certain requirements such as: a *free mass-media system*, of certain means of *private mass-media* and an *ethics for social responsibility*. Also, in addition to these conditions it must be taken into account that this board cannot be *funded* by the state or the mass-media, as the censorship would interfere, official coercion, undermining the credibility, and it may not have as members, government officials or politicians. Where these councils function, they are the first legally recognized as being entitled and obliged to judge the quality of journalistic practice (such as Medical Colleges, Councils Bars) as protection institutions, but also as media accountability. As for the members of a Press Council Miruna Runcan (2002, p. 324) considers that it should journalists union representatives, representatives of employers and representatives of the public.

2. The Favorable Framework: the Democratic Corporatist Countries

At the moment there are about 50 such press councils in the world, but it is almost impossible to determine accurately the total number of press councils around the world, especially since not all are members of an organization such as the Alliance of Independent Press Councils of Europe (AIPCE)[1] and the World Association of Press Commissions (WAPC).[2]

The corporate-democratic countries tend to have relatively strong systems formalized by the media self-regulation. The first example of international press council was provided by Sweden in 1916. With durability until today, the **Swedish Press Council** receives approximately 400 complaints annually, of which 10-15% consists of official criticism (Ristow, 2009 p. 8) and it has a high level of legitimacy among Swedish journalists and editors. According to researchers Hallin and Mancini (2004, p. 172), there are several elements that make the well-known Swedish Press Council particularly powerful: it has the power to fine newspapers and ask them to publish its decisions; it is headed by a judge, and the representatives of the media industry represent a minority of its members; it is supplemented by the Press Ombudsman who helps investigating complaints.

In **Britain**, where journalists have exceeded for a while the bounds of professional decency early and mid '90s, the parliamentary committees have called for the establishment of a statutory regulation, but the UK press has avoided this by establishing a system of self-regulation (Tambini, 2009, p. 66). The Press Complaints Commission in the UK (PCC) is an organization established in January 1991 by the mass-media to enable injured parties to challenge the way in which the events were presented (Bland, Theaker, & Wragg, 2004, p. 17). In the UK, the board is made up of people with expertise in media (academics, former lawyers and representatives of the public) and it is designed to deal with complaints from the public regarding inaccurate or deficient media reports (Dominick, 2009, p. 454). The Code of Good Practice, under which the Commission operates, is updated regularly and it operates alongside the Code of Ethics developed by the National Union of Journalists, and possible

---

[1] http://www.aipce.net/members.html accessed on 14.03.2015.

[2] According to a study (Ristow, 2009, p. 17) in 2009 the following countries press councils were members of an association: Armenia, Azerbaijan, Bangladesh, Belgium, Bostwana, Bulgaria, Cyprus, Denmark, Estonia, Finland, France, Germany Hungary, India, Ireland, Israel, Italy, Kenya, Kosovo, Luxembourg, Malawi, Malta, Nepal, Netherlands, Norway, Peru, Russia, Spain, Sri Lanka, Swaziland, Sweden, Switzerland, Tanzania, Thailand, Turkey, Uganda, UK, Ukraine, Zambia, Zimbabwe.

violations of the Code are the responsibility of the Press Complaints Commission, dealing with complaints and it imposes the necessary sanctions. The English self-regulation patters consider that the Press Complaints Commission plays the role of the last resort. The Press Complaints Commission is financed by the Finance Council for Press Standards (PressBoF), a body established in 1990 specifically to coordinate the actions from the media industry.[1]

Jared Obuya makes a description in his study (2012, p. 40) on the composition of functional press councils in Western Europe. To get a view, we detail as follows: **Netherlands** - a president, three vice-presidents (lawyers), at least ten members who are not journalists and at least ten journalists (some nominated by the Dutch Union of Journalists, others by the Chief Editors Society in Netherlands); **Sweden** - a president, three vice-presidents (legal powers), 14 members (four publicists, two from the journalistic associations, two from the press club, six members of the public) and 14 substitutes, identically distributed; Denmark - a president (member of the Supreme Court), a vice-president (lawyer), six members (two journalists, two editorial managers, two members of the public), six substitutes identically distributed; **UK** - 17 members (of which ten are members of the public including the President and seven Chief editors); Germany - 28 members (14 advertisers and 14 of the journalists associations).

The CIMA study shows that the independence of the press councils is maintained by keeping away the state's institutions from the activity of appointing or approval of the members of the press council (Ristow, 2009, p. 9). The financial aspect is another sensitive issue as press councils funding can come from different sources such as grants, international NGOs, multilateral organizations such as UNESCO, the average annual fee charged to the members of the institutions, subsidies from governments in the West, or even specific projects[2] or even from the state (such as the Press Council of Turkey), which is to be avoided.

3. The Unfavorable Framework: How about a Romanian Media Council?

The conducted study (Popa, 2014), the assessments of respondents in terms of *authority* with responsibilities in the *accountability Romanian journalists* had a common path: that of highlighting ***the need*** for it. This occurred within the context of several failed initiatives of the media organizations in Romania to create a functional press council. From the respondents' answers have created the following *categories grid*, in supporting the results:

Necessity: *can be a type of self-regulation structure (...) or it can be a coordinated and controlled institution as CNA (S1); it should be implemented by the press itself, through self-regulation (S4); something to arbitrate things (S12); it may be set as an association with a purpose, with budget and all (S14); it may be formed even by journalists (S15).*

Even if *the name of the forum is less important in the land of forms without substance* (S4), we note that respondents attributed this structure some names and after the analysis of the frequency terms, the

---

[1] http://www.publications.parliament.uk/pa/cm200607/cmselect/cmcumeds/375/375.pdf accessed on 14.03.2015. *Self-regulation of the press*, Seventh Report of Session 2006-07, by authority of the House of Commons, Culture, Media and Sport Committee, published on 11 July 2007, London, p. 6. Initially, the British commission should have been financed by the contributions from industry press, organized by the Council of financing Press standards (Wilson, 2004, p. 36).

[2] For example, the Press Council of Bosnia and Herzegovina in 2009 organized an international conference gathering 40 representatives of press councils in the region and in Europe, in order to develop a common strategy self-regulation media, the conference being funded by the German Embassy in Sarajevo and Konrad Adenauer Foundation (Ristow, 2009, p. 20).

predominant use of the term is ***council*** (of honor, ethics, media)[1] followed by the term ***forum*** and then ***court***. Next we use the media council term.

Out of the desire to follow a functional model, such as Swedish Press Council, created by an honorary court of justice established by the Publicist Club (Hallin & Mancini, 2004, p. 172), the Romanian respondents imagined creating this media council by the guild itself[2], hoping to trigger a "mass accountability".

The only such authority should be implemented by the press itself, through self-regulation. The organization is as follows: there are professional associations, unions; it should also be a single forum of the Romanian press, which would deal specifically with this stuff: self-regulation, involving also the press accountability. (S4)

I could see it coming only from our guild and not from the political realm. That would be ideal for journalists to manage to organize a professional association or more which would have as purpose, as I said, not a police case for those who violate these rules, but simply to encourage their compliance as there are codes of ethics, deontological norms. (S8)

This media council is the mechanism for implementing the deontological code unique. It is a traditional mechanism, which operates very well across the European countries and it represents the authority that may make the difference between the quality of journalistic activities and the others. For this reason, the court must have the task of establishing the professional rules, the arbitration slippages and application of *sanctions*.

During the interviews, there were brought into discussion also issues that might impede or facilitate the creation of such moral authority to oversee and monitor the deviations of the Romanian journalists. Firstly, this moral authority must be made up of a group of journalists that *are respected by the guild and with indisputable reputation*, to rise in defending the profession and rescue the deterioration of the media landscape in Romania, so that full authority would be recognized by the journalists. The interviewees considered that these journalists exist, but they are not united so as to form a critical mass. Those polled exemplified other accountability systems that exist, such as the RAC[3] (Romanian Advertising Council)[4] and that of MediaSind.

(...) It is indicated how the RAC, where there are also advertisers and there are virtually all players in the industry. From what we see, even though often enough their solutions were not satisfactory, at least there are there, I have been to a meeting, they are discussing, I do not know if the decisions were made in advance, there are all kinds of agreements or even if they vote for real, but you can make a complaint, you can go there, you are interrogated, even if it is only formally, but it is there. It is a start ... I cannot make trial of intent as I do not have sufficient evidence. They have agreed with us several times. (S14)

---

[1] Titles: *commission, board of honor, college, comitia (S1); honor council (S2); moral instance, non-coercive court (S3); authority, unique forum of the Romanian press (S4); a board (S7); an informal forum (S8); entity (S11); a body also for the press (S12); press ethics council, media council (S14); moral court, a forum (S15).*

[2] *Created by the guild: it should be implemented by the press itself (S4) it is coming from the guild (S8) structure of self-regulation type (S1) institutional authority but not bound by the state (S14)*

[3] RAC is the only Romanian self-regulatory body recognized by the National Audiovisual Council. Since 2003, NAC and RAC interact based upon a protocol of cooperation. According to it, the RAC and NAC became partners in solving complaints regarding advertising. The decisions in these cases are adopted under the Code of Advertising Practice developed by its members. Available at http://www.rac.ro/autoreglementarea-in-romania, accessed on 14/03/2015.

[4] The Self-Regulation of the advertising industry is considered the most effective tool to stop the excesses and illegalities (Middleton, Trager, & Chamberlin, 2002, p. 158).

All collective agreements, including the one in mass-media, constituted a Joint Commission, whose decisions are required by law, they are compulsory for the parties, for all the institutions of mass-media and for all journalists. Those who make a mistake are required to make public in their institutions the decision of this committee, and from the moment, me as a journalist or as patron have such a judgment, I immediately go to court, and based on it, the court judges. (S5)

3.1. The Structure of Media Council in Romania

Respondents' assessments regarding the structure of Media Council showed the journalists as key members of this forum, as we can see in the next ***categories grid***:

Journalists: *guild representatives (S1); employee's representatives (S5); only journalists (S6); only journalists (S14); people from media and I do not mean the central one but also the local one (S10); pressmen (S8); we have journalists and but also editorial management (S13); five people, written press two (S2) journalists with at least 20 years of experience (S4) personalities from this guild that are beyond any suspicion (S11); a forum made up of five respectable people (S15); some more experienced journalists (S7).*

Some respondents considered that journalists need to compose the main forum, that they should be senior journalists in newsrooms. A more important aspect is that respondents felt that ***the reputation and prestige of those journalists***[1] is essential. They must be able *to stand up for defending the profession* (S3). From this point of view, some respondents believe that these journalists exist; others believe that they are there too few to form a critical mass and they are always challenged. At the same time, it would be recommended that these journalists stop working in other newspapers, to avoid conflict of interests.

I think it is needed of some more experienced journalists with a solid undoubtedly professional profile (S7)

I think if we could succeed in gathering credible people, not only among the journalists but also among the public opinion, in time it could work. On one condition, however that the people who formed an authority do not work in a media institution, so as not to suspect them of favoring their own institution. (S3)

It is conclusive, as we noted above, the fact that the majority of the respondents considered that journalists are the ones who should not miss in this court with responsibilities in journalists' accountability. In addition it should also be taken into consideration ***the members of the public***[2] (or media consumer associations, as their criticism is always constructive) and representatives of various ***organizations***. On the other hand, other respondents did not agree with representatives of the public as it would be difficult their selection and their number might not be representative for the entire population. Regarding the professional organizations, unions and employers, the subjects considered important for the employers' associations to be part of this council, as the decisions made by the council must be accepted and implemented at the guild and employers' level. Respondents also mentioned for the structure of moral court the representatives from academia, jurists, lawyers, judges, journalists from abroad, independent experts from academic and NGOs environment, to be consulted

[1] Prestige: with a professional spotless prestige, as much as possible (S4); with a solid undoubtedly professional profile (S7); credible people (S3); to be above suspicion, representative people (S11); respectable people (S15).

[2] Members of the public: *the public is part of this phenomenon (S1); I would give a seat to the civil society representatives (S5); Always listening to their critics (S6); Absolute (S7); it is very important to communicate with the public (S14); members of the public could take people to represent them, the opinion leaders (S15).*

when there are more delicate cases; and that etic council needs independent opinion or from the exterior. Regarding state institutions, respondents felt that they should not be part of that court.

3.2. The Ways of Sanctioning Slippages

According to the MediAct study (Popa, 2014, p. 199) from 2012 at the level of journalists in Romania, they found in a percentage of 63% that self-regulation should include a form of sanctioning. Asking respondents to indicate the most effective types of sanctions, they considered that the media council should monitor, supervise slippages and that it should enforce only moral sanctions, and subjecting to the public opprobrium - *name it and shame it* as some interviewees called the process. Respondents considered that it is needed some time to accommodate, where the self-regulatory system would not sanction, precisely as *"the guild must be cleaned of impostors and cheaters*" (S4). At the same time, the moral authority should find solutions for the economic and employers pressures to which the journalists are submitted, and that is because the sanctions will be imposed on the individual journalist and not to the media institution.

After the analysis of responses, most of the respondents agreed with the sanction of public reporting of slippage (public opprobrium)[1], as shown in the following ***categories grid***:

Public opprobrium: *subjecting them to public opprobrium (S1); if he would release information that it would take an act of reprehensible press (S3); there is a circular kind, where all media are informed that this journalist has committed a slippage (S6); indicating with arguments the journalist who violated the code of ethics (S8); to make it public (S11); a public shame, name it and shame it (S14); that is all you can do "Name it and shame it". You name him or you can put a limit between him and you. (S15).*

In this way, the obedience of the journalist to the ***public opprobrium***, the employing media institution would be directly affected and monitored by the public interested in knowing how to solve the slippage. This would bring a plus or a minus to the credibility of the regarded media institutions, depending on the attention that they will give to the journalists' accountability. The arrangements for public reporting of these *reprehensible press acts* proposed by respondents were those through press or circular releases, clearly showing who is to blame and what happened.

I still believe in common sense and I think delimitation and a reasoned indication of the journalist that violates the Code of Ethics should be enough. I do not think the license withdrawal would be something too dramatic, I do not believe in such solutions, I think that a rather public delimitation of such a character is more important. (S8)

Respondents considered appropriate for the disciplinary sanctions to be applied to journalist by the media institution where he works. Media Council will retain *only the attributions of moral instance*, to report and make public, and based on the decision of the council, that media institution will have to apply other sanctions. In this way, the accountability of the media institutions, from owners to editorial managers will be implicitly achieved.

The Labour Code in Romania provides to media institution, the disciplinary prerogative by which the employee may apply to the journalist, disciplinary sanctions whenever deemed to have committed a disciplinary offense. Misbehavior can be triggered whenever he does not met his obligations, under the

---

[1] The essence of accountability is to appoint, to shame and to apologize (naming, shaming and claiming) (Obuya, 2012, p. 17).

individual employment contract, the collective contract at mass-media sectoral level or he violates at fault the ethical standards set by the codes of professional conduct, such as the one annexed to the collective contract, in the case where the media institution has not joined to other media code of ethics. Respondents supported[1] this way of internal sanctioning of journalists.

We do not discover the wheel when we already are journalist and you already have the responsibility of writing, which would be a very serious matter, there are two types of sanction: the internal sanction applied by the editorial and the sanction that the prejudiced person demands in court. (...) (S9)

A final way of punishing, but also the most often mentioned by respondents, is the suspension and / or removal of the profession. This type of punishment is the extreme solution that can be reached and it seems that we have to resort to it, when self-exclusion no longer works. After analyzing the responses of respondents, there was a majority of their tendency to apply the sanction of public opprobrium conducted by the Media Council and the sanction of suspension or exclusion from the profession, as shown in the following categories grid:

Suspension or expulsion from the profession: *it relates to the access to the profession (S1); the sanction of exclusion from the profession (S2); reaching the point of temporary or permanent exclusion (S4); withdraw the press pass (S4); it should suspend the journalist (S6); should no longer find a vacancy (S7); suspension for a certain period of time (S7); you do not belong in this business (S9); press card withdrawal and the right to profess for a period of time (S10) to the exclusion (S11) the interdiction from further practice (S12); cannot work any longer (S13).*

The sanction ***definitive exclusion from the profession*** was one of the respondents' options, which can be applied, but after committing a serious disciplinary offense. Definitive exclusion from the profession is not a disciplinary sanction expressly provided for in the Romanian Labor Code, so it is necessary a specific regulation as for a lawyer or public notary professions there are specific rules setting the conditions for exclusion from the profession. Disciplinary sanctions provided for by the Labor Code stops only for the termination of the individual employment contract, i.e. dismissal.

The definitive exclusion from the profession is a more serious sanction, which requires withdrawal of press card (if the journalist has it) and prohibition of activity implementation and writing press materials. The definitive exclusion from the profession of journalist is difficult to achieve, on the one hand because some respondents say that it violates the right to freedom of expression, on the other hand this cannot be controlled as anyone can write anonymously on the Internet.

3.3. Funding Sources of the Moral Court

Such a council is in charged with the supervision and monitoring breaches of professional journalists norms and in order to analyze and sanction these slippages it is necessary to have a budget from which members can be paid. For this budget there is a need for certain funding sources that respondents found them to be the journalists' *contributions*[2] to the professional associations or unions and from

[1] **Internal Sanctioning:** *sanctioned disciplinary by the entity where they work (S14); there are disciplinary sanctions provided for in the Labor Code (S5); the internal sanction applied by the editorial (S9); sanctioning the reporter (S11); to sanction as a warning (S7); It would be the warning (S2); warnings (S10) the sanction that works best is the financial one (S12, perhaps a stoppage of pay (S13), for the second violation, the journalist would be dismissed (S6) contract termination. (S7)*

[2] Contributions of journalists: *by the actants sustaining that they are involved, the contribution of journalist members (S2); the journalists' contributions to association (S14); the associations of journalists, are paid by journalists based on subscription. (S8); A single annual fee, paid directly and immediately by each of journalists (S4); the contribution would be achieved (S7); by each of the journalists (S4).*

media institutions contributions[1] offered by employers' organizations. These professional organizations, trade unions and employers in turn must provide a fee (monthly or yearly) to this media council. In the case of journalists not affiliated to any association, they will have to pay that fee directly to the council. This is an advantage for increasing the associativity of journalists and implicitly the solidarity in the guild.

In relation to other stakeholders, such as companies, advertisers, respondents felt that their contribution is not suitable as conflicts of interest may arise. At the same time, however, it was noted the public interest that characterizes the media services provided by the council "*the product of this body is a public asset; you produce ethics, professional morals*" (S1). This could lead to state levies, collected from the taxes the population pays or from specific funds.

3.4. The Jurisdiction Area of the Moral Court

Respondents expressed largely the support for a media council that would carry out activities and expand their duties in the online and audiovisual media sector, as in terms of profession, the principles are the same regardless of the sector. Slippages are the same, with prevailing visibility in the television area and online press.

Total Competence: *it should cover the whole guild (S4); there is a moral court to judge all these products, whether it's print, online, TV, radio (S6); you must respect the same rules (S8); it is same thing (S10); the very serious slippages are in audiovisual media sector (S15).*

Respondents see no need for such an institution unless it is working properly, being dissatisfied with the operation of the CNA's (The National Council of Audiovisual). Considering transfer of the mass-media to online, the self-regulation system should function especially for the online area.

Regarding online self-regulation mechanisms, the Code of Good Practice, which is in force now in the UK has expanded the journalists' accountability also in the online versions of publications. In the preamble it specifies that editors and publishers must ensure that the Code's provision will be strictly respected by all editorial staff and external collaborators, including non-journalists, both for hard copies and online publications. The code provisions extend therefore more than it would seem at first glance, as it covers freelancers, photographs and reporters. Many of press councils cover both written press and audiovisual media, as it is the case of Finland and Denmark councils; others have competence only in the written press, as in the case of Sweden and the UK (Zlatev, 2011, p. 20). Thus, this alternative of self-regulation media, extended to the audiovisual and online media, has gained ground since it responds to many pressures that the media is facing, by the flexibility and the ability to meet the challenges of a changing industry.

Most respondents considered that the media council should focus only on issues within the guild, without having other roles in the Romanian society. However, there were respondents who considered that this moral court such as the media council, may have other duties related to the accountability of the press *such as training for young journalists"* to arm themselves with some correct tools and benchmarks in the early career." (S3)

[1] Contributions of media institutions: *a share from employers (S14); There are also employers' associations that can also contribute (S2); each media organization should contribute to this body (S10); media institutions concerned to clean the landscape. (S3); media trusts (S13); the press (S11).*

4. Conclusions

Some experts[1] consider that the press councils operate effectively in countries where there are other independent institutions, regardless of the field. Another view[2] is that the efficiency of such boards can be seen in civil society where the rule of law is respected and the mass-media manifests high standards. In an oppressive environment, such as the countries with tough laws and governing offenses against human dignity, the Press Council cannot be recognized and people resort to the courts. In Indonesia the press law approved in 1999 the creation of an independent press council needed to solve the press disputes release. In this country, the ambiguities left by the law still allow an appeal to the courts (Ristow, 2009, p. 23).

According to a 2002 study, *The Right to Tell* (*apud* Ristow, 2009, p.24), there are five factors that can determine the success of press councils and that we add to the prospect of a press council in Romania:

1. The intention to create a council must be a desire coming from inside the press. Government and NGOs can encourage its creation, but the impulse must come from the media;
2. The Council shall have the support of the media institutions obliged to respect them;
3. There must be a conduct and a genuine desire to improve the media profession;
4. There should be a Press code or something. Designing the ethical guidelines which balances the freedom of the press and it activates highly the accountability;
5. The standards should be applied consistently.

5. Bibliography

Bland, M., Theaker, A., & Wragg, D. (2004). *Effective Media Relations.* London: Kogan Page.

Deaver, F. (2004). *Etica în mass media/Ethics in the mass-media.* Bucharest: Silex.

Dominick, J. (2009). *Ipostazele comunicării de masă, Media în era digitală/The aspects of mass communication, The media in the digital age.* Bucharest: comunicare.ro.

Hallini, D. C., & Mancini, P. (2004). *Comparing Media Sistems. Three Models of Media Politics.* New York: Cambridge University Press.

Obuya, J. (2012). *Self-regulation as a tool for media accountability. The report card on Kenya.* Lexigton: Lambert.

Popa, D. A. (2014). *Autoreglementare și responsabilizare profesională în media/Self-regulation and professional accountability in the media.* Bucharest: Editura Universității din București.

Ristow, B. (2009). *Sword and Shield: Self-Regulation and International Media.* Center for International Media Assistance (CIMA).

Runcan, M. (2002). *A patra putere-legislație și etică pentru jurnaliști/The fourth power - law and ethics for journalists.* Cluj-Napoca: Dacia.

Tambini, D. (2009). Transformation of the Public Sphere: Law, Policy and the Boundaries of Publicness. In J. Harrison, & B. Wessels, *Mediating Europe. New Media, Mass Communication and the European Public Sphere* (pp. 47-72). New York, Oxford: Berghahn Books.

Wilson, J. (2004). *Să înțelegem jurnalismul/Understanding journalism.* Iasi: Institutul European.

Zlatev, O. (2011). Media Accountability Systems and their applications in South East Europe and Turkey. In Unesco, *Professional Journalism and Self-Regulation* (pp. 17-39). Paris: Unesco.

---

[1] Joel Simon (Executive Director of the Committee to Protect Journalists), interview, taken from the study *Sword and Shield: Self-Regulation and International Media*, a report of the Centre for International Media Assistance (CIMA), author Bill Ristow, May 5, 2009.

[2] Drew Sullivan (Director of the Center for Investigative Reporting Center, Sarajevo, Bosnia-Herzegovina), interview, taken from the study *Sword and Shield: Self-Regulation and International Media*, a report of the Centre for International Media Assistance (CIMA), author Bill Ristow, May 5, 2009.

5

European Conservatism as a Present Political Ideology

Ionuţ Ştefan[1], Sergiu Pîrju[2]

Abstract: The historical beginnings of conservative ideology were felt during the Revolution in France and the next decades that followed this event reference of modernity. The conservative thinking has evolved in the nineteenth century and in the early part of the twentieth century, it has experienced major changes in civilization and has known phenomena of crisis, identity and solutions, crisis that has exceeded it during the second of the last century, when it was restructured as neo-conservatism. Without having a single and concrete definition, conservatism has always represented all those who declare themselves political partisans to any social system, is concerned to ensure the continuity of social and political order, historically legitimated and strive to reject revolutions that would, inevitably, change it. The conservatism peculiarity was highlighted by rejecting the ideological organization of any systematization form of its ideas, because society can be organized by appealing to programs and theories. Conservatism is the political and social doctrine which renders the system a conservative spirit, focused on the ideal of social order and stability. Modern conservatism, located at the right of liberalism, was and shall remain the doctrinal and ideological opponent of all systems of ideas that are situated on the scale policy guidelines on its left. While tradition is indispensable for the existence of conservatism, it was forced to adapt to modern requirements and to modernize itself over time, maintaining however the main features that characterizes it.

Keywords: conservatism; political doctrine; European construction; tradition

1. The Definition of Conservatism

The term "conservatism" is part of the semantic field of the verb "conserve" which means to keep, to preserve, to save; "conservator of a museum", the usual significance in the nineteenth-century French vocabulary and then in the Romanian one, known because penetrates in Romanian through the French branch.[3] The conservatism is considered both a political vision as well as a way of being, an ideology that focuses on "the historical identity of the people, the spiritual realities and unlike the leftist vision, is not intended as denial, but the affirmation of values, their conservation"[4] .Thus the conservatism is one of three significant political ideologies in the last two centuries Occident, along with liberalism and socialism. The etymology of the term ideology comes from the Greek word "eidos" = image and "logos" = science, meaning learning about ideas (Nisbet, 1998, p. 19). The ideology is a wealth of

---

[1] Senior Lecturer, PhD, "Danubius" University of Galati, Faculty of Communication and International Relations, Address: Galati, 3 Galati Boulevard, 800654 Galati, Romania, E-mail: ionut.stefan@univ-danubius.ro.

[2] Senior Lecturer, PhD, "Danubius" University of Galati, Faculty of Communication and International Relations, Address: Galati, 3 Galati Boulevard, 800654 Galati, Romania, Corresponding author: pirjusergiu@univ-danubius.ro.

[3] http://filosofiepolitica.wordpress.com/elemente-de-doctrina/partidul-conservator/istoria-partidului-conservator/.
[4] http://facultate.regielive.ro/cursuri/stiinte-politice/conservatorismul-istorie-universala-1952.html.

coherent and explanatory ideas which evaluate social conditions, helping people to understand the place they occupy in society, aiming to tradition survival, the people themselves.

But the conservative idea does not imply a full and uncensored attachment towards any tradition; this doesn't assume the old, decrepit and Manichean equation "traditional = good, new = bad". The conservative attitude should not be confused with any reactionary attitude and is not based on inversed utopia of past iteration. The conservatism axis is not an absolute rule and sacrosanct character of traditions, but only the ancestry and necessity of traditions; they constitute the essential framework of functioning of any "rational" social arrangements. Conservatism is a special kind of traditionalism. The "rational" principle losses any value when tradition hasn't created consensus on its meaning and applicability. And when it can be applied successfully, it is not because of the principle itself, its universal validity, but the public consensus supporting its functioning. Specifically, traditions legitimize any form of social order.

Those who are followers of this ideology are called conservatives. The term "conservative" simply means "preserver, who refuse to change, loyal to the currently existing ordinances" (Nemoianu, 2000, p. 75). This represents a first sense of the term. A second sense of it partially overlaps with "traditionalism", so Karl Mannheim defined conservatism as a "traditionalism becoming aware". Therefore, the conservative thinking falls within the ascendency and need of traditions. There is a third meaning of the word "conservative" which exemplifies the effort to synthesize freedom and tradition. The latter sense appeared due to the impact of modernization that was felt at all levels (economic, social, moral, political etc.). The Great writers and thinkers of the eighteenth and nineteenth centuries were concerned about how people will perceive these changes and will best respond to the evolution of society. According to John Gray, conservatives admit that before anything else, even before freedom, people need a home, a group of institutions and a way of life that they feel theirs. (Gray, 1998, p. 142).

Regarding the conservative relations with the other two political ideologies, liberalism and socialism, the first one reproaches them that they advocate for community life settlement on the basis of deliberate "rational" arrangements as institutions, organizational structure, legal, political or moral regulations which are deducted from intellectual abstractions: principles, ideals, theories. (Mungiu-Pippidi, 1998, p. 76).

Hence the conservative ideology doesn't have clear principles and it can't adapt to the policy based on it. The difference between conservatives and liberals can be shown by the fact that the latter believe in the rationality of certain principles such as the principle of maximum individual equal freedom and the principle of reducing freedom to equality, and require achieving peace and society consensus upon themselves; while conservatives believe that rational principles doesn't control nor determine public consensus, but their value and validity is determined by it.

Therefore, conservatism is guided by the belief that there are no "for granted" prefabricated solutions, to human community problems, or universal principles to solve them, because they have limited and local validity and nobody and nothing guarantees their future success to solve problems Therefore, conservatism is guided by the belief that there are no "for granted" prefabricated issues of human communities or universal principles to solve them, because they have limited validity local and nobody and nothing guarantees their success in future to solve the problems of the kind they have solved previously. (Mungiu-Pippidi, 1998, p. 76).

The conservative solutions are adaptive because they seek practical effectiveness, possible only by analyzing the problem and adapting the solutions to the existing reality at a given time. Hence the adaptive dimension of conservatism. The conservatism is focusing its effort not on building ideal models of social "rational" arrangement the conception of norms, rules, principles, ideals that govern social existence, but on the pragmatic objective of material and spiritual life forms development and optimization. The own political conservatism does not consist in nothing more than the usual "daily" practice, of problem solving of a human community being a "policy of imperfection" and compromise. Conservatism is not but a political pragmatism. The conservative pragmatism involves a huge skepticism regarding the economical mechanisms samples, algorithm-solutions that only needs to be applied correctly, as typical models, policy prescriptions. In the absence of universal principles and formulas, the question arises: how can conservatism aspire to an active political involvement overcoming obstacles facing the community? On one hand, by rethinking each problem-situation based on its particular, specific features. The result of this rethinking is, of course, a proposal for solving; but not one taken from a previous tank-type solutions, but one focused on a pragmatic ad hoc arrangement, based on data specific to the situation; conservative solutions are nothing more than pragmatic adaptive arrangements. The social assistance system helping disadvantaged members of the community came into being as such adaptive arrangements (they are due not to socialists, but British Conservatives who have started it in the second half of the nineteenth century). The conservative solutions are adaptive not for pursuing to perpetuate the existing situation, but pursuing the practical effectiveness, impossible to achieve without adapting to local peculiarities. The conservatism is, under this aspect, a political realism. In addition to adaptive size, conservatism has a critical dimension. It requires social barriers, not by inventing panaceas, but by criticizing any panaceas. The fabrication of panacea and universal recipes is a permanent inclination of thinking, and this inclination is manifested more intensely when both the problems and human suffering are more acute.

Conservatism cannot rely on anything other than experience. Realistic, critical thinking of a pragmatic type has no other source of inspiration than experience. David Hume, one of the founding fathers of the conservative vision says that the experience has the merit of warning us of its own reliability. The conservative pragmatism as well as the tendency to critically react to any universal recipe or canonical principles determine another very significant feature: contextualism. A well-known example in this respect is offered by the attitude of the UK Conservative Party to exercise state control of the economy; in the context of 1830, his attitude was favorable to maintain this control, so that in the context of 1890, to became negative. The conservative policies have in common the idea of moderation and gradual growth, not the one with radical and sudden change.

Conservatism is of course a gradualism; but not because it had horror of the sudden change in itself, but out of a sense of reality: for he does not believe that anything important (i.e., rooted in a form of a human life) can be changed abruptly.

So, to be conservative means having a supportive attitude of the old political, economic and cultural forms. This political doctrine defends traditional order, having political beliefs supporting the gradual development at the expense of sudden changes.

2. Conservatism as a Current Ideology of the EU Area

We considered necessary to explain the term ideology in general to show how conservatism is viewed as a current ideology of the EU area. The original meaning of ideology, in the eighteenth century, when the term appeared, was represented by the scientific study of ideas. The word "ideology" is the invention of a French scholar Antoine Destutt de Tracy (1754-1836), who attempted in the 1790s and early 1800s to found the systematic study of the ideas origins. (Ball, Dagger, 2000, p. 19)

The term "political ideology" represents all systematic and structured the ideas that, generic and functional are representative for the interests, aspirations and political expectations of a group or social class and who reflect the socio-political reality, to report people to this social-historical reality based on experience of the said group and from which results rules of political behavior and political action guidelines. (Tanãsescu, 2004, p. 66)

Karl Marx (1818- 1883), a German philosopher, economist and publicist who deal with the same theme as Tracy, spoke about the concept of ideology as a set or system of ideas whose function was to justify and legitimize the company management by the ruling class. The latter differs from one society to another, but there will always be the class which controls the material forces. The ideology masks the management of this class by presenting existing social relations as being normal, natural, necessary and eternal.

According to Mannheim, the knowledge sociology requires us to make a distinction between the concepts of "total" and "particular" ideology. In his opinion, the term "particular conception" is used when we say that the ideas and positions of a group of people whom we oppose, such as political parties or interest groups are "ideological". "The overall concept" on ideology, by contrast, refers to characteristic ways of thinking of a whole class or society or historical periods such as medieval society or the modern age.

Extending the concept therefore, Mannheim made it more difficult to define ideology, the term becoming too vague to be useful, this being the prospect of some social analysts of the twentieth century. Therefore, for many people, the term "ideology" remains a pejorative one. In their concept, ideologies are not good because it always simplifies and distorts the problem. Even worse, ideologists encourages its supporters to believe that their ideology has monopoly over the truth. Those who disagree are enemies that stand in the way of truth, justice and progress - an enemy who either must be convinced or defeated. (Ball & Dagger, 2000, p. 22)

One of the most important components of community for conservatism is tradition, because is trying to continuously improve the human condition through it. Although tradition is indispensable for the existence of conservatism, it was forced to adapt to the modern requirements and to modernize it over time. For this reason, appeared a new type of conservatism. The instruments used by it are freedom of the press and autonomous associations in all areas, the aim being to create a conservative spirit from the good ones, a spirit against innovation and "hasty" improvisation on the intellectual and social field. In order to implement a new conservatism, an attempt was made to remove the destructive tendencies of mass democratic society by expanding civil society sector, preserving certain values determined to save the intellectual and moral integrity of each and every one. In other words, it was meant to save the individual from the tyranny of the majority and gain autonomy of civil society in the detriment of the bureaucratic apparatus oppressor generated by the mass democratic society.

3.1. The Conservative Doctrine in the European Union

The European Union is currently the political and legal environment in which takes place the European integration process as well as the form under which is constituted and stands political--legal, economic, social and cultural construction - the essential kernel, engine of the European unity, around which a number of increasingly large countries of the world, of primary importance in international life. (Anghel, 2007, p. 4)

The European Union is an international entity officially published on the international scene in 1993 with the entry into force of a treaty signed a few months earlier in the Netherlands by several western states. This treaty recorded the participating States willingness to strengthen economic, social and political links between them to achieve a union of growing ties between the European people. (Ghica, 2007, p. 25)

In terms of conservatism within the European Union, at first, it fell under the clear influence of Romanticism, seaming that this is the doctrine ideological destiny. Its political dimension was not profoundly different from that of its ancestors, only radicalizing its position regarding state liberalism, which was supposedly highly inappropriate in the manifestation of social freedom (meaning that the default social hierarchy was not accepted anymore, minimizing the nobility role in the society construction, especially after the emergence of popular parliaments). Also, the religious position became, both in the UK and Germany, highly percussive, perceiving modernity as a permanent spiritual revolution, but not necessarily beneficial. Through romanticism, conservatism becomes imagine of a strong current, permeated by ideological direction of the ruling classes, idea not altogether true, but apparently highly pertinent. Through romanticism, conservatism makes the condoning of country life, the peasant family, traditionally medieval, capable of simple happiness of continuity compared with the proletarian and petty bourgeoisie class, which is in a permanent cultural or national identity crisis and manages to take over the nationalist dimension of liberalism.

Conservatism assumes the national dimension of the party that opposes the liberal state attempt to broaden the nation's citizen base since 1830, the official birth year of the Conservative Party in the UK. For conservatives, the return to the national community was paramount, no longer assuming the risk posed by the contrast between rich and poor, which could lead to the destruction of the English nation, which could barely be formed at all.

A great reformer of conservatism, Disraeli, claimed the nationalism with strong social focus. Its proposed reform strongly influenced the British and European society in the middle of the nineteenth century. He established government bodies or state guarantees to ensure workers' pensions, social assistance for children and disadvantaged people, compulsory schools etc. In addition, he obtained British unemployment reduction, so that the British workers would lead a better life both materially and politically. The applied conservatism by the Conservative Party in Britain after Disraeli, has developed a policy with strong paternalistic overtones which allowed the posting of the Liberal Party and also the entrance in competition with the Labor Party.

Of course not in all countries conservatism had exactly the same behavior. In Central and East European countries, the conservative parties played an important role in the cleavage of land owners versus agricultural workers. Their role was less modernized than Western conservatives, being considered rather reactionaries than modernizers, issue that persists today in the perspective of the generally conservatism.

Starting with the twentieth century, the main ideological opponent of conservatism becomes the socialism. In the first instance, conservatism is in a rather difficult situation in relation to socialism which at that time was the bearer of an ideology extremely attractive and seemingly fair. Then, the organization of the Party was completely new and stable (mass party model) having an electoral body dedicated to the Party, led by unions and, finally, a stable ideology proposing radical transformation of the state. To these realities, the conservatives could not answer it only with the old political and moral principles of the nineteenth century. Secondly, the Socialists gave the appearance of a trans-European political union, while conservatives from each country refer only to their political society, without statutory links between the various parties, and after World War I a large part of the conservative parties on the continent disappeared. The conservative idea however did not disappear, but attempted once more to adapt to the new society. In the interbellum period, conservatism had an extremely difficult situation especially in relation with fascism, that he ideologically intensified it, and tried in some cases even to assume it, particularly in cases form countries within Central Europe - Poland, Slovakia and Hungary.

This ideological distortion marked the era after World War II, when it became very heavy the destruction of conservative connotations. However, in this era, the conservatism, either in opposition (most often) or in power begins to build a new identity and economic policy that will become effective in the 50s, identity that will mark forever its image.

The conservatives have placed their resistance to collectivist and scheduler socialism, calling upon the indissoluble link between economic and political freedom. They believed that despite ideological prejudices, capitalism is the only form of economy that leads to happiness, for it is the only fair and free economic form. The socialism, in his desire to equalize the whole society, led to injustice and poverty due to economic planning and excessive bureaucratization of society. Those who promoted this type of current political and economic theory were not necessarily members of a conservative party, but their theory was quickly embraced by conservatives who build a new political dimension based on these ideas, which, in short time have been implemented by the governments of conservative families.

The Romanian conservatism resembles European conservatism in general. But, unlike liberalism, it is claimed also from a Romanian reality of its own in its own traditions. Even partially, it inherits the ruling class ideology of the Romanian Principalities.

The connection to the modern era of Romanians and their Northand West neighbors has no special significance. When Romanians entering modernity and seeks close contact with Western civilization, they set it directly with the British, French, Germans, Austrians, without intermediaries. The European Union has designated its own motto in 2000: “Unity in Diversity”. For its elections, a contest was held in the European Union schools, with the participation of 80,000 young people aged between 10 and 20 years. Finally, were selected six proposals and the European Parliament decided which one will be adopted. The winning creators’ nationality remained secret so far. (Neguţ, 2007, p. 14)

The term conservatism has undergone a denigration in the last centuries of European history and civilization. A denigration promoted by both the winning liberalism and democracy, and also by the left and the extreme left ideologies. The term conservatism has served as antithesis to progress and became more or less an insult. It's also true that there have been successful conservative analysis in a constructive way. The most important come from British and German culture.

All conservatives share the desire to preserve something, usually the traditions and customs of their society. However, as a distinct political position, conservatism is more than a simple desire to oppose change. For example, the classic conservatives defended the traditional social hierarchy, insisting on a government strong enough to direct people's passions and they were skeptical of the attempts to promote individual freedom and equal opportunities in a competitive society. Regarding the Conservatives at the end of the twentieth century, they are individualists, pleading for reducing the government size and aims, to let individuals to freely compete for profits. This conservative current actually resembles to classical or neoclassical liberalism. The human belief of conservatives is that human beings are and will always be weak. Many call conservatism as a “political philosophy of imperfection"[1].People are not as smart as they think, and their reason is not able to anticipate all the decisions consequences. Therefore, the best intentions often end up causing the greatest harm.

In the twentieth century, conservatives were against mainstream society, not welcoming with enthusiasm, the change felt at the time. From their point of view, it first lead society to chaos, then to despotism. They believed that in any society there is a small group that is suitable to govern, through capabilities, experience and temperament, while the whole is totally inappropriate. Therefore, conservative supporters opposed leveling, the main characteristic of mass society because they were suspicious of attempts to reach a large democracy or equality. Cultural leveling is as dangerous as financial leveling. But nevertheless, although initially antidemocratic, conservatives have supported democracy in societies where it evolved and became a part of the social fabric, of the traditional and customary way of life.

3.2. The Conservatism in France

In this country, the first political parties appear with the 1879 Revolution, but they will exist only for a short period of time, because most of these "parties" were extremely divided and there is no actors' consensus regarding the constitutional framework. In a rather odd way, the French parties are born much later, even though is assumed that democratic and partisan expression is born and function together. Thus, since the 20s, in France appear "five political families' constant on the political scene: communist, socialist, radical, on the center-right - Christian-democratic and on the right - conservative. In the eighteenth century, conservative groups represented the nobility and Church image. They were formed to fight against the principles of the French Revolution and to defend the old regime, representing the historical right. Conservatisms were inclined to a kind of aristocratic populism, founded on the idea of traditional forces and undivided loyalty of the people opposing the bourgeoisie (the Liberals), in its turn detested by the Jacobins. But in the nineteenth century with the advent of labor movements, they were directed toward liberalism, although they opposed it, arguing the nobility. Conservative Party appears as a party of competence, intelligence and reason: a party of teachers, like Guizot, and publishers, like Thiers.

Conservatives had great respect for the Church, this being, according to them the order, hierarchy and discipline and having a role of social cohesion, which could maintain peace among all citizens.

In most of the nineteenth century and the early twentieth century, France was ruled by "moderates". There is some ambiguity between the terms "conservative" and "moderate" but these terms cannot be avoided. They belong to the same political spectrum and are easier to practically place than to define from a theoretical point of view. However, when dealing with this problem, not from a philosophical standpoint, but from a political one, conservatism (moderate attitude) defines itself, not in theoretical terms, but in terms of the problems it faces. From all this, it is clear the radicals' tendencies to declare themselves conservatives, i.e. those revolutionaries who have achieved their purpose to defend the new order. But while people and parties attitudes changes with their policy, the doctrines evolves slower.

This gives us the apparent paradox of liberal conservatives, radical conservatives, of social-democrats conservatives, even of the communists' conservatives, especially when the groups' representatives obtain satisfaction and power. After 1920, took place the Communist Party founding, which would

[1]http://www.sferapoliticii.ro/sfera/153/art05-Gherasim.html.

both complicate and simplify the political situation, he Conservatives in power, no longer being able to react over their own extremists as strongly as against the left ones.

Over time, it was formed several right-wing parties which were based on a fundamental conservatism and the cult for discipline, on a parade violence expressed by noise, offices and meetings of the political opponents attack, plenty demagoguery and only a few leaders. But in 2002, these parties have joined and founded the Union for a Popular Movement. This new right political movement has more ideological influences, such as: conservatism, Christian Democracy and liberalism; unfortunately it retains its tradition in Gaullism, republicanism, populism and radicalism. The first president of the Union for a Popular Movement party was Alain Juppe, but he was forced to resign on 15 July 2004 after allegations of corruption, and on 29 November 2004, Nicolas Sarkozy, finance minister at that time, takes over the party presidency.

Thus, through this movement is tried to reduce unemployment, economic freedom, solidarity and equality from the state. Starting with May 2002, it was felt the development of the extreme right, but the French political system exceeded the enlargement policy period, returning to bipolarity. That formula of coexistence between the presidential and parliamentary majority, removed "the opposition" from the French political life, and in 2007, we witness to domination from the right over the important institutions (at central and local level).

Currently, France's conservative attitude is manifested by rejection of modern ideas and a very libertine behavior. Disagreeing with the management judgments, the French conservative struggle for justice and their welfare using street demonstrations. The problems facing France today are of economic and social type. For example, most of today's French people recognize that raising the retirement age is necessary to ensure the survival of pension system but nevertheless, according to all public opinion polls, almost 70% of the French support the demonstrators who had come out in the street to block small reforms introduced by the government of President Nicolas Sarkozy.

The French attitude is a product of combining the unique political and intellectual history and a rejection attitude of elites who are currently in power, the French people demonstrating their extremely conservative inclinations. Their resistance to changes reflects their denial of reality to some extent. Nowadays the French passion for equality is far greater than the passion for freedom and thus threaten the country's prosperity. French have not decided whether to continue to defend the old world or to face the challenges of a globalized world. Their hesitation is a source of confusion for most and a source of admiration for some. The fact is that it seems easier to explain than to understand their behavior.

3.3. The Conservatism in the UK

In this state, conservatism has rejected the ideological organization and any form of systematization of its ideas because society cannot be organized by resorting to programs and theories. However, with the introduction of universal suffrage the electoral pressure pressing on all political parties led the Conservatives to answer the moment call by providing clear principles and initiatives. Thus, the ideological outline of conservatism went on throughout the twentieth century.

The British Conservatives remain mistrustful of any positivist who in the form of some law recommends systematic actions which should be taken to achieve social welfare. Instead, the conservative thinking is particularly receptive to the benefits that tradition brings.

Conservatives do not believe there are formulations applied to achieve good governance.

The Government is a social, indigenous product and therefore must respect the history, customs and prejudices of the people. Thus, as there can't be no social welfare laws, there can't be no ideology that would provide it. Therefore, conservatism was against any ideology, refusing to form a political program, showing preference for passeisme and lessons of past history. The most important of conservative reactionaries, Count Joseph de Maistre, went so far as to reject the idea that people are able to plan and establish a proper constitution of their society. A written constitution is downright dangerous, says de Maistre because expose the Government weaknesses: "The more is wrote, the institutions becomes weaker, the reasons being obvious. The laws are only declarations of rights, and rights are declared only when they are attacked, thus, the multiplicity of written constitutional laws only shows the multitude of conflicts and danger of destruction." (Ţăranu, 2005, p. 43).

Maistre's words remain emblematic of what was British conservatism until the early twentieth century. The fear of any form of systematization led the British conservatives declare that their party has no ideological basis. They realized that the lack of political deals and critique brought to the mass society could no longer provide, under the system of universal suffrage, the party maintenance in power.

The early twentieth-century finds in the first instance the British conservatism in a rather difficult situation in relation to socialism, which at that time was the bearer of an ideology extremely attractive and seemingly fair. In front of the mass parties, conservatism, with the old political and moral principles could no longer respond to a reality that does not comply with the old models of political organization of society. Under the pressure of universal suffrage, conservatives are forced to respond to the needs of doctrinal clarity required by the electorate.

But eventually, they returned to the principles that define them and especially to liberal values from the early nineteenth century, adapting and reevaluating them for the British society after War World II. The conservative tradition has become an ideological commitment giving doctrinal clarity of which the party needed to compete in the election of the twentieth century. The head of the Conservative Party today is William Hague, elected in 1997. He introduced the principle of party leadership election by members, trying to rejuvenate the party, to make it more attractive to young voters and to increase the number of its members. The current Conservative Party members are former students of private schools, working in private firms. Over 90% of them are owners of housing and a quarter have consistent income. For example, in 1994, they earned more than £ 30,000 per year.

Many members of the Conservative Party in the UK have expressed Euroscepticism over time, being slightly more reluctant to everything that the EU means. For example, from the perspective of Conservatives, the UK will never adopt the euro, even more, it definitely should leave the European Union.

Thus the danger for Britain to leave the EU is not imminent, but a positive vote would show how little faith was left in the island for the European project, given that Europe is facing the biggest crisis since the establishment of the common market. Regarding this issue, in 2010, the Conservatives have declared their willingness to vote for the referendum, but the motion was rejected by Parliament.

But recently, the Conservative Party in Britain confirmed that it will leave the European People's Party - European Democrats, the largest group in the European Parliament. Although the British Conservative Party stands to remain in the European Union, more and more British Conservative parliamentarians keep their skepticism. Until now there has been speculation that after this event, the British Conservatives may join the Union for a Europe of Nations (UEN), second-minded conservative political group in the European Parliament. The change magnitude in mindset and policies that were generated by the Conservative Party is remarkable. This is due to the extremely difficult legacies left by the Labor Party and the fact that it failed to form a majority government, recurring, to create a coalition with the Liberal Democrats, which was not seen with good eyes by the more right-sided members within the Party. Moreover that this coalition has required certain concessions from conservatives, the most significant being electoral reform on proportional representation, although it is not known which will be the political price paid by the Liberal Democrats for cohabitation with the Conservative Party. Defending the coalition in the eyes of its own party and the conservative electorate was the first cornerstone of the Conference slogan “Together for the national interest”. The second one, not less important, is the need to support a broad policy for extraordinary austerity measures that are needed to reduce the budget deficit and reform institutions.

Social benefits will be reduced substantially, even at the beginning of the Conference, starting with allowances for children in families where one parent earns more than 43,875 pounds. Primarily the Conservatives intend to cut public spending by 83 billion pounds by 2014 and drastically reduce social benefits, although this aim cannot be achieved without freezing wages, a bigger contribution of the workers on the pension fund etc. The extremely unpopular measures are presented as the only solution for the people revival and the country’s revival. This coalition is designed as a fact in the country’s interest fighting for public exposure of the indecent high wages, salary cuts of Ministers, reducing taxes, imposing restrictions on banks so that they relieve the benefits of managerial staff and to convenient credit the small enterprises, etc. Consequently, in the UK, conservatism had the best conditions of manifestation, it being against the deep integration in the European Union. The British conservatism fits into an established regime, that defends its aristocratic character, people in the UK saying the following: “We are members of the European Union not by necessity, but by our act of will”.[1]

3.4. The Conservatism in Finland

Finland (Suomi Finnish, Swedish Finland) or the Republic of Finland (Suomentasavalta, Republiken Finland) is a country in Northern Europe, an EU member since 1995, the United Nations and the Eurozone[2].The Finnish Civil War was a conflict between the forces of "red" (Social Democrats allied with Finnish communists) and the "whites" (under the command of conservative Senate, who in the previous autumn succeeded to form a national unity government, which had the goal of maintaining the status quo (to maintain independence and constitutional monarchy).

Civil war and war are still two of the most controversial and emotionally charged events in the modern history of Finland. These two conflicts are seen as two turning points of Finnish destiny, having a huge impact on both domestic and foreign policy. The causes that led to the Civil War can be considered to be primarily the political polarization caused by major conflict between the Russian Empire and the Grand Duchy of Finland, an autonomous entity of the Tsarist Empire, which began in 1889 with the launch of pan-Slav policy and has intensified in 1899 with the first attempts of Russification of Finland. One of the first consequences of this policy was the abolition of the Grand Duchy of Finland army.

Until that moment, Senate of Finland managed to successfully lead a conservative loyalist policy towards Russia, aimed at defending the national interests of the country through main autonomy granted by the Tsarist power. It was appreciated at that time that "the people" should be removed from

[1]http://revistacultura.ro/nou/2012/02/ghici-cine-are-dreptate/.
[2]http://ro.wikipedia.org/wiki/Finlanda.

radical political approaches, which would lead to the Imperial Court irritation in St. Petersburg. As this policy in the end proved to be wrong, both the activity of the left and the right have been radicalized.

True is a political party of a populist guidance in Finland, founded in 1995 after the dissolution of the Finnish Rural Party. In the late 2000s, the True Finns have changed the balance between Finnish centrist parties increasing in popularity due to their Eurosceptic policy. Its leader is Timo Soini. In the 2011 elections, the True Finns have become a serious threat to traditional parties in the Parliament of Finland, achieving similar scores like the National Coalition Party, Centre Party and the Social Democratic Party of Finland in polls. The party combines economic policies of the extreme left, with some powerful conservative social values. Today, after a period of 30 years, Finland has a new conservative president. Sauli Niinistö, the National Coalition candidate (conservative) is the new president of Finland. His opponent Pekka Haavisto admitted its defeat. Either of the two would have won, the result would have been historical for Finland, which was managed in the last 30 years by social democratic presidents. Niinistöwill most likely have a peaceful coexistence with the Social Democrats. In April, his party won the most votes in legislative elections and his Conservatives lead a broad coalition government, which also includes the Social Democrats.[1]Finland's parliamentary elections marked a sharp increase in electorate preferences of nationalists, who stood by against the anti-European and immigration program.[2]Liberal Conservatives in Finland obtained 20% of the voters voting options in the legislative elections that took place on 05.02.2012. They were followed by the Social Democrats, with 19.1% and the True Finns Party nationalists, with 19%.On the fourth place is situated Centre Party, with 15.8% of the voting options. Out of the 200 seats for the Parliament, the Election Commission has granted 44 to Conservatives, 42 to Social Democrats and 39 to True Finnish Party (right nationalist).On the other hand, also in 2012the Conservatives remains the largest ideological group in the US. Following a research it has been reached a result whereby 40% of Americans continue to describe their perspective as conservative, 5% describe themselves as moderate and 21% liberal. This is the third year in which the number of conservatives surpassed that of the moderates, after a decade in which statistics indicated a close competition between the two groups.

4. Conclusions

The Romanian conservatism resembles the European one, by claiming it, thou, through its own reality and traditions. Unfortunately, prominent representatives of the current managed only partially to set social policy formulations. Speaking purely doctrinaire, they have excelled and there isn't, with few exceptions, works with ideological content, programs, platforms etc. In the past, it was put great emphasis on elocution (let's not forget that most politicians of that time lacked training in the legal field). Therefore, we discover rather an ideological orientation, clearly articulated, and less a doctrine itself, as a coherent system of principles, completed with key programmatic documents. In order to make quality policy, it is vital that it is done in accordance with a moral policy. The latter implies efficiency, the ability to fulfill the promises the power understood as a means, not as an end. For the true politician, holding power is the chance in fulfillment of national interest of electoral commitments and not an exercise in itself or, worse, a display of its own pride. The countries where we find traditional conservative parties are Denmark, Finland, Norway, and Sweden. They are characterized by a moderate opposition to state intervention in social and economic life, having a consensual approach to policymaking. The political parties of a conservative type are more important than the

[1]http://www.adevarul.ro/international/finlanda-presedinte-homosexual_0_640736348.html#.
[2]http://www.romania-actualitati.ro/conservatorii_finlandezi_castigatorii_alegerilor_legislative-28046.

Christian Democratic parties in many cases them being equivalent to Christian Democracy in electoral options. Both the Christian Democrats and conservative parties represent alternatives to governance and social-democratic ideologies. The development of two political families within the same political system is rather an exception. Where there is strong conservatism, Christian democratic family is often implicit as an ideology or does not exist.UK, Scandinavia, Greece, Spain are examples of situations in which, if the family is strong conservative, cancels the Christian Democratic family. Austria, Belgium, Italy, the Netherlands are examples of the opposite situation: where the Christian Democracy is strong, the conservative family is weak or not at all represented. In conclusion, conservatism is an important trend that manifests itself in many countries within the European Union, ensuring in this way a harmonious combination of tradition with modernity, supporting democracy in societies where it is installed.

5. References

Anastasie, Iordache (1999). *The origins and formation of the Conservative Party in Romania*. Bucharest: Paideira.

Ball, Terence & Dagger, Richard (2000). *Political Ideologies and the democratic ideal*. Iaşi: Polirom.

Bréchon, Pierre (2004). *Political Parties*. Cluj-Napoca: EIKON.

Căpreanu, Ioan (2009).*Romanian history of political parties (From 1859-2002)*. Iasi: Tipo Moldova.

Coman-Kund, Liviu, (2008). *European Community law*. Course. Galati.

Iorgulescu, Adrian (2000). *RIGHT. Principles and Perspectives*. Cluj-Napoca: Dacia.

Iliescu, Adrian, Paul (1994). *Anglo-Saxon conservatism*. Bucharest: All.

Ghica, Lucian (2007). *Encyclopedia of the European Union*. Bucharest: Meronia.

Gray, John (1998). *Beyond conservatism and liberalism*. Bucharest: All.

Gusti, Dimitri (1924). *The doctrines of political parties. 19 public lectures organized by the Romanian Social Institute*. Bucharest: Cultura Naţională.

Mungiu-Pippidi, Alina (1998). *Political Doctrines. Universal concepts and Romanian realities*. Iasi: Polirom.

Matei, Horia; Neguţ, Silviu & Ion, N. (2007). The *European Union States*. Bucharest: Meronia.

Nemoianu, Virgil (2000). *Romania and its liberalisms. Attractions and opposition*. Bucharest: Fundaţiei cultural române.

Nisbet, Robert (1998). *Conservatism*. Bucharest: Du Style Publishing House.

Patapievici, H.R. (1995). *The sky seen through lens*. Bucharest: Nemira.

Petre, Dan (1995). *The doctrines of political parties*. Bucharest: Garamond.

Stănciulescu, Ştefan (1998). *Violence, myth and revolution*. Bucharest: All Educational.

Stanomir, Ioan (2004). *The conservative conscience*. Bucharest: Nemira.

Tănăsescu, Florin (2004). *Doctrines and Political Institutions*. Bucharest: Fundaţiei România de mâine Publishing House.

Ţăranu, Andrei (2005). *Modern and Contemporary Political Doctrines*. Bucharest: Fundaţiei Pro Publishing House.

http://filosofiepolitica.wordpress.com/elemente-de-doctrina/partidul-conservator/istoria-partidului-conservator/.

http://facultate.regielive.ro/cursuri/stiinte-politice/conservatorismul-istorie-universala-1952.html.

http://filosofiepolitica.files.wordpress.com/2008/03/lect-andrei-taranu-doctrine-politice.pdf.

http://www.cadranpolitic.ro/?p=3444.

http://revistacultura.ro/nou/2012/02/ghici-cine-are-dreptate/.

http://www.sferapoliticii.ro/sfera/153/art05-Gherasim.html.

http://www.ziare.com/social/romani/romanii-sunt-printre-cei-mai-conservatori-cetateni-din-ue-studiu-1125126.

http://www.adevarul.ro/international/finlanda-presedinte-homosexual_0_640736348.html#.

http://www.romania-actualitati.ro/conservatorii_finlandezi_castigatorii_alegerilor_legislative-28046.

http://ro.wikipedia.org/.

6

Geopolitical Evolutions in the Eastern Space in Romania's Proximity

Florin Iftode[1]

Abstract: We will debate some aspects related to the geopolitical equation of space in Romania's proximity where we have bigger actors (Russia), smaller actors (Republic of Moldova), as well as actors without international legitimacy (Transnistrian Republic). The geopolitical issue includes the analysis of the intersections between the Russian border and the Euro-Atlantic area, on the border line represented by the Republic of Moldova. The effect of the geopolitical tensions on the internal dynamics of R. of Moldova's policy, exclusively the dependence on the Nistru crisis and the geopolitical and security blockage, is represented by the "frozen conflict" in Transnistria. We will show with arguments why the states in the Black Sea - Caucasus - Central Asia region have a double hypostasis: seen from Brussels, they are part of the eastern neighborhood of the EU, but seen from the Kremlin, they are part of the "close neighborhood" of Russia. Therefore, each of these states resembles the pieces on the chessboard waiting to be moved. In conclusion, the problems that the area raises are countless - interethnic conflicts, a mosaic of religions, frozen conflicts, instability, the presence of non-democratic institutions, collapse of states, economic backwardness, authoritarian regimes. Of the above list, no feature has positive features, which is an alarm signal.

Keywords: geopolitics; the proximity of Romania; Transnistrian Republic; frozen conflict

1. Introduction

The lack of natural boundaries has fueled a national obsession in Russia about the need to control territories as a cover against invasions. Historian G. Patrick March said that the vulnerability of the Russian territory gave rise to a "higher tolerance for tyranny" (March, 1996, p. 73). We believe that this finding could help to understand some of President Putin's tough political decisions.

The western media loves to hate him, because he does not fit the templates - a sort of liberal leader who receives cheering in chic conferences. What the media should see in Putin is not really the totalitarian authoritarian, but only a Russian, ordinary semi-dictator whose cynical neo-imperialism is the result of deep, very deep geographic insecurity.

Putin wants a dominant influence in the Baltic states. He wants state buffers in Eastern Europe. He does not accept the collapse of the Warsaw Treaty. He knows he cannot reconstruct that treaty, he knows he

[1] Associate Professor, PhD, Danubius University of Galati, Faculty of Communication and International Relations, Romania. Address: 3 Galati Blvd, Galati, Romania, Corresponding author: floriniftode@univ-danubius.ro.

cannot take back the Baltic states because they are NATO members. But he will try. He will continue to press in various ways, through gas pipelines, organized crime, cyber attacks etc.

The same situation explains his need for buffer states in Belarus and Ukraine. For the same reasons, he invaded Georgia in 2008; he exerts a significant influence in Central Asia, even if he does not have the military capacity to reconstruct the Russian empire there. Putin thinks as a traditional Russian leader, because Russia is open to invasions almost on all sides. Russia is a great land-based power without natural barriers, and terrestrial powers are particularly vulnerable and insecure. They lack the security of ocean-protected marine powers.

It is very likely that Russia will not succeed in overcoming all the "holes" in its frontier protection system. It will have to consider priorities to preserve its right to state life. And the first is Ukraine. Ukraine occupies the most productive part of the Russian cereal area - the southernmost area, where it rains regularly. As the Russian capital and labor shortages accumulate, maintaining control over high productivity and low-spending land will gain increasing importance. Together with the Republic of Moldova, Ukraine controls the Bessarabian pass (low area between the Black Sea and the Carpathians). By controlling this passage, Russia will limit Turkey's ability to threaten the Russian central territories.

Ukraine holds the largest population of ethnic Russians outside the Russian Federation. Their numerical inclusion in the Russian system would improve and postpone the demographic twilight for a few years. The industrial base of Eastern Ukraine is located in the immediate vicinity of Russia. Combining them would help all parts of the Russian economy take some time. Ukrainian infrastructure transports almost half of Russian oil and gas to Europe, so Ukraine is a special economic value. The only truly navigable river in the former Soviet Union is the Dnieper, flows to the south, and allows Ukraine to integrate economically with the Black Sea, the Marmara Sea and the rest of the world. Crimean Peninsula controls the mouths of the Dnieper and is the seat of the only Russian naval base that do not freeze - Sevastopol. As long as Crimea and Sevastopol are in the hands of Russia, Ukraine cannot reach a real economic development, and foreign naval powers - the most important, Turkey - cannot dominate the Black Sea. Russia's efforts to re-anchorage began in the Crimea in 2014. But they will not stop there. Under any circumstances, a completely independent Ukraine would be a challenge for Russia.[1]

2. Frozen Conflict in Transnistria

The cold war covered the planet more completely than the other wars of the XXth century. The specifics of the period 1945 and 1990 were given by tensions between two superpowers recognized as protagonists of the Cold War: the US and the Soviet Union. The end of the Cold War "*is marked by the collapse of the Berlin Wall (1991). Although for the historians marks the end of a short XXth century begun in 1914, the end of the Cold War does not also mean the disappearance of the privileged relations between the US and the USSR, then Russia: the fallout situation and the nuclear arsenal of Russia and Ukraine make them a partner to be spared. American diplomacy, on the other hand, sees itself widowed by its Cold War ideology. Some, like Senator Paul Tsongas, even state, in the context of the economic crisis and the debate about the American decline that "the Cold War ended with the victory of Japan". This strange end, unique in history, has the gift of provoking debates; and if the Cold War is over, for historians it is just beginning, with the gradual opening of archives in the East.*"[2]

[1] Constantin Crânganu, *Russia - The Closeness of Twilight (geopolitical),* According to - http://www.contributors.ro/global-europa/rusia-apropierea-amurgului-geopolitic/.

[2] International Relations Dictionary - XX Century, Volume coordinated by (Vaïsse, 2008, p. 291).

From a geopolitical point of view, the present Republic of Moldova appears as a Romanian outpost in the Slavic world, a Romanian-speaking territory whose language was "moldavized" and transcribed in Cyrillic letters according to the needs of the Soviet power, until 1989. As a testimony to its very tumultuous history during the XIX-XX centuries, the society of the Republic of Moldova could have a special charm through its borderline character between Latin and Slavism. The demographic data converge to the same idea: in 1989, at the time of its re-emergence, the Republic of Moldova was the common home of a population of 4,335,360 inhabitants, of which 2.8 million Romanians/Moldovans, 600,000 Ukrainians, 525,000 Russians, 150,000 Gagauz, 70,000 Bulgarians and 65,000 Jews. Known more as a garden of the former USSR, an appreciated provider of vegetables, fruits, tobacco and wine, the Republic of Moldova has not excelled in industrialization during the Soviet power; even so, most of its industrial potential lies in the Transnistrian region - a strip of about 5 000 km^2 located on the left bank of the Dniester, at the border between the Republic of Moldova and Ukraine, with a population (in the same reference year 1989) of about 800 000 inhabitants, out of which over two thirds of Russian speakers (mainly Russians and Ukrainians). To keep in mind a historical detail about Transnistria: it was, in a way, the core of the future entity since 1924 when Stalin, for purely political reasons and without any historical basis, created here the Moldavian Autonomous Socialist Soviet Republic (as part of the Ukrainian RSFS) - for the simple reason that it could claim that the Moldavia itself (meaning Historical Bessarabia), located in Romania's borders after the Great War, would be under the "yoke of the occupation" of Romania (between 1918 and 1940, and then in conditions of "Romanian occupation" between 1941 and 1944).

After the creation of the Moldavian RSFS and after years of intense repression of the Russian-speaking elite - it remains unforgettable the deportation of 11239 families of Romanians, comprising 30050 people to Siberia, on the night of 5 to 6 July 1949, and totally subject to a monopolized political leadership by the Russian-speaking natives, over the nearly 50 years of Soviet history (Igor, 1991), The RSFS of Moldavia seemed to be a relatively easily manageable republic. It is probably not a coincidence that passed through here, in their first part of their political career Leonid Brejnev (first secretary of the PC Moldovans in 1950-1952) and one of his protectors at that time and later his successor, Konstantin Cernenko (secretary of agitation and propaganda in the Moldavian RSFS in 1948-1956). These totally parallel legends about the recent Romanian past of the Republic of Moldova were still to persist and still recoverable today. Probably, as an author says (Cioroianu, 2009, p. 252): "*if the Romanian state had more time, it is very possible to have succeeded in transforming the Basarabians into Romanians", but "in the short period between the two world wars, (...) homogenization efforts of the Romanian state failed to convert the pre-modern, regional identity of basarabians in a modern, national one. That is why the Soviet project to build the Moldovan nation found favorable conditions in Bessarabia*", with the mandatory mention that, according to the same interpretations, "*to the success of this project, but also contributed substantially the frustrating experience of Basarabians during the period when they were part of the Great Romania*"[1]. Area with vineyard, fruit-growing, horticultural, apicultural area a.s. enviable potential, the Moldavian RSFS remained until recently a profoundly rural one. In 1944 and 1959, it had the lowest level of urbanization in the USSR (18 and 22 percent of the population lived in cities); in 1989 only, the percentage of the urban population will reach 47 percent.

As in other republics of the Soviet Union - and in any case, as in those in which independence was obtained by fighting or at the cost of frozen conflicts - also in the Republic of Moldova it became very clear that it is impossible to find that (state) identity to please all citizens, as historian Adrian Cioroianu

[1] Cristina Petrescu, Construction of National Identity in Bessarabia, în (Heintz, 2007, p. 143).

states[1]. Not so the Russian-speaking population in the area, as Russia (through this population) reacted immediately to the possibility (rather theoretical, at that time) that the Republic of Moldova would go to Romania; and a scenario that was to be repeated throughout the former Soviet Union was put into practice.

In an article entitled *Transnistrian Conflict: Geopolitics and Geostrategy*, Oleg Serebrian, speaking of Transnistria, says that „*Moldovans had a permanent presence in the country? The colonization of the Dniester's left began especially since the XVIIth century, although migratory waves existed in the XVIIIth century. XV, but especially in the XVIth century. However, due to the fact that the Russians and the Ukrainians have not made their massive presence in the region until after 1792, it cannot be said that Moldovans would have fewer rights on the given land than the Ukrainians.*"[2] Usually, Russian and Ukrainian historiography refers to the Slavic presence in the Bugo-Nistrian interfluvial space during IX-XII centuries. *"The possibility of this presence cannot in any way be denied or the slave migration campaigns of the previous centuries, as well as the limits of the maximum extension of Kyiv Russia. But there is no evidence that the Transnistrian territory was thoroughly controlled by the Slavs and, moreover, there are no significant vestiges of the Slavic material culture of the period"*.[3] The same article shows that Transnistria was not a Moldovan political territory. Transnistrian Moldovans are the natives who, after 1792, had a regime of occupation and national pressure from the Russian Empire. The same author shows that the Romanianness of Transnistria was challenged even in Romania. "*When Marshal Antonescu ordered the passage of Romanian troops across the Dniester there were several voices reserved for this gesture. This was also the case in Chisinau in 1992, when a murmur of dissatisfaction about the losses suffered sneaked in order to maintain in the Republic of Moldova a foreign territory to the country's body*".[4] In order to be as correct as possible in expressing Oleg Serebrian's point of view, we will continue to reproduce the extract from the article quoted below, which shows that, "*in fact, those who recognized the Moldovan (Romanian) character of the Transnistrian region were indeed the Soviets when they created the Moldovan Autonomous Republic in 1924. Even if the purpose was a territorial rebellion in Bessarabia and beyond the Prut, the constitution of the Moldavian autonomy in the left bank of the Dniester set the beginning of Moldovan political-geographic presence in Transnistria. In August 1940, with the transformation of the Moldovan Autonomous Republic into the union republic, five of the eleven Moldovan Transdniestrian districts were attached to Ukraine- Kodima, Balta, Kotovsk, Red Salt Mines and Ananiev. Din pacate, foarte adesea uitam ca Basarabia a pierdut în august 1940 nu doar patru raioane la nord şi 9 raioane la sud, ci şi aceasta parte a Transnistriei, în care mai locuiesc zeci de mii de moldoveni transnistreni.*"[5]

With a population of about 550,000 people and a territory of 4,163 km2, the Transnistrian region has evolved since the proclamation of "independence" in 1991 and to date in a de facto state entity not controlled by the Moldovan central authorities[6]. The attempts of political settlement of the conflict in Transnistria have achieved poor results. The political negotiations involving Transnistrian and Moldovan parties, as well as representatives from the OSCE, Ukraine and Russia failed to identify a solution regarding the status of the region. This is why the Moldovan authorities have attempted to

[1]Adrian Cioroianu – is a PhD in History at the University of Laval (Quebec-Canada) and the University of Bucharest. He is specialized in the contemporary history of Romania, and in October 2008 inaugurated at the Faculty of History of the University of Bucharest a Masters course dedicated to the history of post-Soviet Russia.
[2] http://transnistria.md/ro/articles/0/542/.
[3] http://transnistria.md/ro/articles/0/542/.
[4] http://transnistria.md/ro/articles/0/542/.
[5] http://transnistria.md/ro/articles/0/542/.
[6] *EU Action Plan - Republic of Moldova*, ADEPT Guide, Gunivas Publishing House, Chisinau, 2006, p. 61.

internationalize regulatory efforts by involving, since 2005, the US and the EU in the negotiating mechanism as observers.

Why is Russia interested in keeping control of this enclave and why many Russian parliamentarians and officials see Transnistria[1] as a "*region of privileged interest*" for Russia? The answer is an elementary strategic consideration. Transnistria (located in the "coast" of Romania, the Republic of Moldova and Ukraine) alongside Kaliningrad[2] (the Russian enclave that no longer has a border with Russia, but it is also on the "*coast*" of Poland and Lithuania) and the Crimean peninsula pulled from the territory of Ukraine in 2014[3], are all three parts of a security cord useful to Russia from a geopolitical point of view, especially since NATO has penetrated significantly in the East of the European continent. The alibi of the rebellion of the Russian-speakers in Transnistria was originally a linguistic one: the declaration by the Parliament of the Republic of Moldova in 1990 of the Romanian language as an official language was rejected to the left of the Dniester in the most concrete way possible. Transnistria is the first to become a target in the war against terrorism, being a paradise for illegal smuggling of arms and smuggled goods and a pre-designed place of rest for mafia and terrorist groups. The business here is feeding the accounts of terrorists from all over the world.[4]

Referring to the origin of the Transnistrian conflict, Oleg Serebrian shows that "*if we remember the problems of 1988-89, when the conflict arose, we would notice a little nuance - we then opted not for ethnic, but linguistic identity, not for national independence, but for the revival of national culture. Ideas regarding the union with Romania, independence from the USSR, or anticommunist slogans were not very noticeable. Hence, neither ethnic nor political factors could have been the source of the conflict. The Transnistrian problem has originated more an intercultural conflict, which, after November 1989, became more and more pronounced from geopolitical point of view.*"[5]

The Transnistrian conflict represents „*only a geopolitical conflict, and the ideology or political regime in the present case has no importance. Besides, even Western observers do not hurry with such ratings. Speaking of the geopolitical and geostrategic value of the conflict, some political analysts in Chisinau attribute an exaggerated dimension to it, even if Transnistria is said to be a "Russian knife stuck in the back of Ukraine", and when it is said that Transnistria would be a base of Russia for the Balkan "direction". If we are talking about the Balkans and its "gates", let us not forget that the old and metaphorical qualifier of Bessarabia as the "gate of the Balkans" was valid for Russia in its geographic configuration at that time.*"[6]

According to Oleg Serebrian "*the geopolitical value of Transnistria is one that states not the control of the Balkans nor the threat of Ukraine, but only the control of the Republic of Moldova. Paradoxically, the Republic of Moldova largely owes its existence to the Transnistrian problem, and this is not only that legally contemporary Moldovan statehood has its origin in Transnistria of 1924, but also because if this conflict did not exist, then the story of the independence of the Republic of Moldova, with its*

---

[1] Transnistria - surface about 5 000 km², population of about 800 000 inhabitants, mostly Russian-speakers. Enclave, which is part of the Russian Federation, is - geopolitically speaking - a point of control over the Republic of Moldova, Romania and Ukraine.

[2] Kaliningrad - the former capital (Königsberg) of Oriental Prussia, the city was a war trophy obtained by the USSR in 1945. After the collapse of the USSR, the city (about 415 000 inhabitants) and the surrounding region remained part of the Russian Federation - even if no boundaries with it. Geopolitically, Kaliningrad offers an exit to the Baltic Sea and control over the North of Poland and the West of Lithuania.

[3] The right of residence of the Russian Federation's fleet in the port of Simferopol - Sevastopol, was prolonged until 2017 (s.n.).

[4] Republic of Moldova - Anti-democratic Sinking of Galagious Government, Country Report 2003, Coordinator: Iulian Chifu, Politeea-Snspa Publishing House, 2004, p. 261.

[5] http://transnistria.md/ro/articles/0/542/.

[6] http://transnistria.md/ro/articles/0/542/.

dominance in the Chisinau political elite in December 1991, would have ended with the fall of the Soviet flag in Kremlin and by the reunification of Bessarabia with Romania."[1]

Speaking of the interest of US[2] and EU on Transnistria, in his work on the geopolitics of the Transnistrian conflict, Oleg Serebrian shows that „*Americans and Europeans rarely manifest glimpses of interest, but this is generated not by the conflict itself, but by the stockpiles of weapons and the paths that that weapon comes surprisingly through the most undesirable corners of the Earth."*[3]

3. Points of View on the Transnistrian Issue

Ion Leahu[4] analyzed the tensions between Chisinau and Tiraspol, as well as the "convenient" intervention of the Organization for Security and Co-operation in Europe (OSCE) mission. At the same time, he also mentioned the contribution that Romania should have in the conflict between the Republic of Moldova and the self-proclaimed pro-Russian republic, the Nistrian Moldavian Republic (Transnistria).

He declared that *the JCC's (Joint Control Commission) activity does not in any way affect the basic aspirations of the Transnistrian region, such as the coveted sovereignty or control regime in the security zone completely dominated by the secessionist regime. At the same time, due to an informational tradition, the Commission's activity awakens a certain interest and can be interpreted as an indication of bilateral or multilateral relations in the negotiation process*. Major changes will not occur if Moscow is not interested.

Former member of the Moldovan delegation to the Joint Control Commission, Ion Leahu, said the representatives of Austria, holding the presidency in the OSCE for 2017, announced the availability to have no less than two meetings in the format "5+2". *Berlin, when chairman of the OSCE, had the "Mezenberg process" in which it had something to propose to Moscow in exchange of boosting negotiations on the Transnistrian issue. Austria only has the protocol of June 2016 in Berlin. Tiraspol and Moscow, however, will not abandon the examination of this deeply erroneous document, a factor that may have been conditioned by the abdication of Vienna from the convening of the format "5+2".* Starting from this finding, obviously, we cannot expect dynamism in the settlement of the conflict.

Regarding Moscow's position, the Moldovan expert showa that this *is limited by the financial factor, a factor that has greatly influenced how to react to changes in the region. Previously, Moscow could afford the delivery to Tiraspol $ 100, 200 million a year to ensure its indisputable dedication to the population. Then these transactions became more and more difficult to bear for Russia, being aggravated by massive embezzlement by the former Transnistrian leader Igor Smirnov and his family. Russia cuts out of financial assistance.* Not long ago, Moscow encouraged Tiraspol to expedite the application of the Russian Federation's legislation in the Transnistrian territory. Obviously, the action is a response to Bucharest's evolutions in relation to the North Atlantic block and Chişinău with Brussels. At that time Tiraspol decided to habg the Russian tricolor at the same time as the red-green bicolor one, applied as its "own flag".

[1] http://transnistria.md/ro/articles/0/542/.

[2] *The vast country, as the entire European continent, with a large exit to the two largest oceans of the planet (Pacific and Atlantic) and with huge ground and underground resources, the United States were predestined - as some American personalities have expressed, over time - to dominate the world. The events of the last decade of the XXth century propelled the United States into a singular world position, the world's only superpower. cf.* (Negrut, 2005, p. 109).

[3] http://transnistria.md/ro/articles/0/542/.

[4] Former member of the Moldovan delegation to the Joint Control Commission, an expert in Transnistrian settlement.

According to the experience of the Moldovan expert, Leahu said that *the involvement of the OSCE in the settlement of the Transnistrian conflict is not one that corresponds to the mandate of the mission and the capabilities of this international structure.* The OSCE mission practices a tactic, both comfy and inefficient, which could be exposed in the following way: "*The OSCE will support all the agreements reached by the parties involved in the conflict*". Because of this passive position, the parties commit serious deviations, which condition the absence of positive effects. *The nonessential reaction of the OSCE to the serious deviations from the provisions of the basic acts, which regulates the peacekeeping operation in the Transnistrian region of the Republic of Moldova and the regulatory process supported by the Russian Federation and Transnistria, contributes to the complete depletion of these norms.*

As a result, the peacekeeping mission in the Republic of Moldova no longer has mechanisms to influence the situation, to ensure peace and stability. Annually, about 10 extremely serious situations (conflicts, altercations, murders (Vadim Pisari's case of January 1, 2011), involvement of force structures) are committed. They are caused by the inability of the OSCE Mission to demand unconditionally compliance with the prescribed rules. Basically, there has been no assessment of the crisis situations. I believe that the OSCE Mission has the obl to require permanent monitoring of compliance with legal rules for the implementation of the peace process, the settlement of the dispute and the adoption of decisions.

On Romania's contribution to solving the Transnistrian conflict, Ion Leahu said that *Romania in its current quality as an EU member state and North Atlantic block obviously is limited in actions. It promotes the policies developed and proposed by the designated bodies.*

As for the contribution made by civil society, the media, the possibilities are enormous in this respect. The problem, however, is the position of Chisinau. It is necessary for the Republic of Moldova to prepare a well-argued strategy of collaboration with the Romanian partners, to use the capacities of the state and the Romanian society in support of Moldova. The involvement of the Republic of Moldova in international structures, of which Romania is also part, would be a very positive support. It would be useful to explain the nature and content of economic relations between Romania and the Transnistrian region. Tiraspol exports a lot to Romania. From there, it procures raw materials and technologies. To explain, what reasons condition this collaboration, at first glance, untested in the aspect of Russian anti-Romanian propaganda. *Romania has a rich experience in the issue of interethnic relations, especially the "Lipovans". There is no doubt what would be the positive effect of establishing some contacts, relations between the Danube Delta inhabitants and those from Moldova and Transnistria.*[1]

"*The notion of special status is an instrument of reexpansing Russia in the former Soviet republics, especially in Ukraine and the Republic of Moldova. Russia has had federalization projects for both Ukraine and the Republic of Moldova. The word federalization is rightly provoking such fears that the new denomination of federalization is a special status*"[2], says Vladimir Socor[3], in an interview with HotNews.ro. Socor argues that Russia's interest in the Republic of Moldova is limited to the opening of a precedent in Transnistria, but the Kremlin is not able to support Chisinau. In his opinion, Romania is more influential in Moldova than Russia at the moment. Socor Vladimir supports some important ideas about the Russia-Moldova relationship, such as:

---

[1] https://www.dcnews.ro/conflictul-din-transnistria-expert-de-la-chi-inau-pozi-ia-formatului-5-2-comoda-contribu-ia-romaniei_535667.html

[2] Vladimir Socor, analyst at Jamestown Foundation

- The Republic of Moldova is not a priority of Russia's foreign policy. Russia has its hands full in the area with Ukraine and in another area with Syria, and now at the official level it suddenly manifests a deep disappointment to Donald Trump. Russia's leadership had great hopes in Trump;

- In the Kremlin's vision, Putin's gesture with that map was a sarcasm or a malicious gesture free of charge. Free from a political point of view. Neither Dodon nor Putin have the intention of creating a large Moldavia in the Carpathians;

- Russia is unable to support the Republic of Moldova. If Dodon's party by absurd came in the Republic of Moldova, economic support would fall into Russia's taks. Russia is not capable of supporting not even Transnistria, certainly not the Republic of Moldova. Russia has a limited interest in Moldova that Moldova should pursue a policy of balance between the West and Russia and consult Russia on major economic and foreign policy decisions;

- Russia wants to establish some precedents in the Republic of Moldova for use in other situations. For example, the precedent to renegotiate the EU-Moldova Association Agreement, to subject it to a three re-examination with the participation of Russia. An approach that Russia would like to impose on Ukraine. Success in Moldova would be a precedent;

- Granting a special status to Transnistria. The official goal of the 5 + 2 negotiations is to finally reach a special status. It has become the official, declared purpose, and that's why I think it would be a very dangerous thing. The notion of special status is an instrument of reexpansion of Russia in the former Soviet republics, especially in Ukraine and the Republic of Moldova;

- Russia has had federalization projects for both Ukraine and the Republic of Moldova. The word federalization rightly provoks such fears that the new denomination of federalization is a special status. This status would integrate the secessionist territory and its representatives formally into the recognized state political system, but the territory would continue to be under Russian control and that territory would delegate its representatives to the political system of the reunified state with blocking powers. Decisional blocking for foreign policy decisions etc.

- In Transnistria there was a change for the worse after the election of Krasnoselski (the new president, replacing Sevciuc from December 2016). Transnistria opened a representative office in Moscow. It is called the representation of the Transnistria' president in the Russian Federation, which is a sort of first step towards the establishment of diplomatic missions;

- If Transnistria receives a so-called special status in which Transnistria would be part of the Republic of Moldova to a sufficient extent to be represented in institutions, but to an extent insufficient to be controlled by the Chisinau government, so it would remain under Russian de facto control, if Moldova accepts such a thing, we will wake up with a cascade of claims for special statutes. The Gagauzia administration has already announced that if Transnistria receives a special status, Gagauzia will ask to raise its status at the same level as Transnistria. The city of Balti will surely require a special status, it is populated by 70% of Russian speakers. So we will witness a cascade of claims of special statutes, with the danger of dismantling the Republic of Moldova;

- The question to which Western diplomats cannot answer is: if a special status for Transnistria is reached, what will happen to the Russian troops? No Western diplomat has been able to give me assurances that the Russian troops will withdraw. All political negotiations took place with the presence of Russian troops on the ground. The connection that had existed between granting special status and withdrawal of Russian troops disappeared. I think it is completely wrong for any Western diplomat to

press the Republic of Moldova to consent to a special status as long as the Russian troops are on the ground and as long as no one can guarantee that the Russian troops would withdraw;

- At the present stage, the Republic of Moldova is incapable of absorbing Transnistria. The state in the Republic of Moldova is practically a collapsed state. Transnistria is a kind of proto-state supported by Russia, but otherwise Transdniestria is in some ways more viable than the Republic of Moldova. It has an internal propaganda that instills to population the feeling of belonging to a state and a specific type of identity, a post-national identity linked to the Russian world. The Republic of Moldova is not appealing for the ordinary population of Transnistria. The reintegration of Transnistria into the Republic of Moldova in this situation would lead to the complete disintegration of the Republic of Moldova. The institutions are so crashed, they will not be able to absorb Transnistria;

- Romania has instruments of influence in the Republic of Moldova with a major impact, which I sometimes feel under-appreciated. The Embassy of Romania, compared to Russia, is very influential in Chisinau. The Russian Embassy in contrast is not relevant in Chisinau, while the embassy of Romania and others are always consulted. Unfortunately, Romania has failed to complete the gas and electricity connection projects, this is a big drawback. Romania for the first time after the 90s is able to provide budget assistance to the republic of Moldova. I think Romania becomes more influential than Russia in Chisinau.[1]

4. Russia's Internal and External Actions

About what Putin has done in recent years, both externally and internally, Cosmin Popa[2] shows that the political inventiveness resources of the regime are exhausted, and force and intimidation are beginning to play an increasingly important role in promoting Russian interests. Using and abusing power, outside and within the country, Putin potentiates the availability of those whom Russia regards as opponents to use force in their turn.

Started as a new, seemingly paradoxical modernization experiment, putinism turned into a catalyst for the return to classic realism, in which the alliances succeeded with stunning repetition, and the interests changed according to the personal perspective of talented politicians or monarchs full of political vitality. The historic role of the Russian Empire, the USSR, or the Russian Federation, believe Russian leaders, is to intervene decisively in the political game or in war when the confrontational camps are weak enough to be imposed conditions.

In fact, the country that occupies the sixth part of the land, which has the largest reserves of raw materials, which gave the world geniuses of science and culture and has an impressive arsenal of weapons of mass destruction, thinks international relations at the scale of a power medium-sized, preoccupied to ensure survival between the empires.

The attraction by Russian officials of governments and corporations in Western Europe in a "miracle" business line, in order to undermine Euro-Atlantic solidarity, is only a reflection of traditional Russian "realism". *In order to stimulate the pride of a continent unable to find itself politically, since Stalin,*

---

1 http://www.hotnews.ro/stiri-esential-21631527-video-cum-juca-rusia-moldova-transnistria-vladimir-socor-notiunea-statut-special-este-instrument-reexpansiune-rusiei.htm.

2 Cosmin Popa is a scientific researcher of the Nicolae Iorga Institute of History of the Romanian Academy. He is specialized in the history of the USSR/ Russia and the history of Central and Southeast Europe, the communist and contemporary period. He studied in Bucharest and Moscow and is a member of the bilateral Commission of Historians from Romania and Russia.

Russia still complained of Europe's pitiful mercy, subjugated by American "imperialism" or reduced to neocolonial status.

Putin tried and partly managed to cheat "Old Europe", helped by the mirage of a price of oil, which was only to grow, constanly whispering to his ear that Russia healed the imperial obsession and that the profit was the new ideology of the Kremlin.

So, Germany, France, Italy, but also good defenders of rights and freedoms, such as the Netherlands or Austria, have been pretending for years that they do not see how the institutions are formed and how the laws of putinist kleptocratic authoritarianism appear, nor how Georgia, Moldova and Ukraine were held in a kind of political imponderability by local politicians, perfectly integrated into mafia networks led by people in Putin's entourage. The August 2008 Georgian and February 2014 Ukraine forced the old European democracies, not without a healthy US pressure, to agree in some respect the claimed principles, the political declarations and the concrete actions.

Cosmin Popa analyst shows, in this context, Russia mistakes went on and on. *Annexation of Crimea, an act that came out somehow from the logic of Russian traditional political action, although allowed Putin to call himself "the unificator", like Stalin, meant leaving by Russia the "Ukrainian front", at least for the near and medium future.*

The challenge and support of the pro-putinist rebellion in Southeast Ukraine is nothing more than another desperate attempt to keep a number of strategic positions in the Ukrainian state by imposing a federalism to turn it into a nonfunctional entity.

The concerted pressures of Germany and France on Ukraine to accept the absurd terms of the "armistice" in Minsk in both versions show that Berlin and Paris have rushed to close the "file", accepting Russia's illegitimate interests in Ukraine, but trying, in parallel, to maintain its external worthiness. The non-application of the Minsk I and Minsk II provisions shows that the Russian-German-French stratagem to anchor Ukraine on the Moscow trailer, under the appearance of a democratic truce, failed, and Washington it is not alien to this.

Eventually, in their chaotic effort to reconcile action and claimed principles with their historic obsessions, Berlin and Paris ended by disappointing Russian "partners" and irritating American allies.

It is no surprise that the "New Europe' saw in the Ukrainian crisis an opportunity to reset the Euro-Atlantic security system, relying on a direct agreement with the US. As the Russians say, "farther, more". The international isolation of Russia and the imposition of sanctions have stimulated the creativity of Russian political propaganda. On all channels and through all major political actors, Russia accredits the idea that, while they officially support sanctions, Western countries are able to use any pretext to cancel them.

A number of marginal politicians in Western countries, a plethora of "reputable analysts", all kinds of exotic characters are strongly promoted by Russian environments, with statements stating the "absurd" of sanctions and the idea that Ukraine was "abandoned" by the West.

Sergei Lavrov does not forget to "remember" in every interview, and the last is no exception, that all "relevant" European countries, even the Americans, whisper to his ear that if they organize a new referendum in the Crimea after all the rules that Russia would win anyway, the sanctions would be immediately lifted. "Realism" makes Russia's leaders believe that anything can be traded in a lunch break, regardless of the number and quality of international obligations assumed by "partners".

Direct involvement in Syria, a decision meant not only to secure the Russian military presence in the Eastern Mediterranean, but especially to retrain Putin as a frequent partner of the West, is also a risky bet. Besides the fact that Russia has become the object of the hatred of an important part of the population that opposes Bashar al-Assad, Putin must avoid, almost at any price, a confrontation with ISIL extremists. Once attacked, they would create Russia a series of major "nuisances" in the North Caucasus and Central Asia. As things evolve in Syria, it is hard to believe that at the end of the war, Russia will only have to agree with Bashar al-Assad to maintain its bases in Tartus and Latakia.

In the meantime, Moscow is in full political and economic war with Ankara, and if the oil that President Erdogan's close friends, as Russian officials say buy it from ISIL is so much, the Islamic fundamentalists' reaction will not delaye to appear.

Soon, Lavrov will have to mediate between Syrian Kurds and Bashar al-Assad, which is perfectly plausible in the Middle East, but that will reduce Russia's maneuvering space in Syria, forcing Putin to diversify the targets of the attacks of Russian aviation.

The alliance with China. Moreover, in search of markets for its resources and high tech suppliers for a number of strategic industry sectors, Russia claims it is about to conclude a major alliance with China. The noisy campaign around the start of the "Siberian Force"energy project, the transport system meant to link China to Russian resources, suspended for the time being because of the stubborn Chinese negotiation of the price of Russian gas, contrasts with the heavy silence surrounding the project.

Trying to prove to the West that he can resist without selling it oil and gas, Putin is about to "surrender" to China, knowing well that after Mongolia, Russia is the most exposed country to China's formidable expansion at all levels. True policymakers, the Chinese do not rush to respond to Russia's stingy signs of goodwill, expecting Moscow's bargaining margin to fall. The Great Dragon is now "only" experiencing an acute shortage of cultivated land, which Russia has in full use, being already connected to the international oil and gas supply system.

The "Russian variant" would immediately increase China's autonomy, but it would link it to a series of agreements that it should respect in the future, and it could bring better auspices than it does today. China can afford to wait. Russia?

Russia's policy towards European neighbors including Romania. Neither Russia's policy towards European neighbors does not excel in creativity, even if this does not make it less damaging. Although they kept all the force lines of imperial policy, the Bolsheviks brought a distinct note in foreign policy, where the dominant elements were violence and institutionalized lie.

The interval between the two wars can be considered the "golden age" of the subversive Russian foreign policy, with destabilizing effects.

The interposition of the "sanitary cordon" based on Romania and Poland between Soviet Russia and the Republic of Weimar strengthened Lenin's conviction that if Russia cannot control a country then it must at least be destabilized.

Propaganda, pure lying, corruption, subversive actions, the stipending of some local political forces, the instigation to rebellion and the intensification of internal and international dissensions have since become Russia's favorite tools in relations with the states of the area, which they perceive as hostile.

In his last interview, Lavrov, the one who constantly makes the parade of "retention" and "balance" of Russian diplomacy, did not hesitate to draw loosely a real "list of shame" with the states he considered "hysterical".

Romania, Poland and the Baltic states, the old pillars of the "sanitary cordon", were accused by the refined Lavrov that, instigated by Washington and assisted by the United Kingdom, "stir the myth of Russian dangers up to hysteria".

As it has been accustomed to throughout its contemporary history, when it rages with its smaller neighbors, Russian propaganda leaves aside any diplomatic inhibitions, excelling in pettinesses, more bizarre. It is expected that the Russian press will fill again, in the following period, with articles and reports about poverty and crisis in the named states, as well as a series of Russian journalists' stories, which are more fanciful.

Schematic in its external actions, unable to overcome the era of state interests, Russia persists in not understanding that the international influence of a state is directly proportional to the progress it generates. *Putin's economic and social model, based on a massive state presence in all spheres, but funded by a huge oil price, almost collapses silently.*

Sadly for her, but also for the Europeans, Putin's Russia is not ready to put anything else in its place, trying to fill the void created with the brutal force and the illusion of an imperial restoration.

The primitive way in which he acts does not make it less devastating, but it gives those who are targeting precious indices of how it can be countered.

Putin's conservatism, imposed on society as a formula for reconciliation with the past, now in a state of crisis, rekindles the war of the Russians with their own history, urging them again to approach to them not only hatred and bias, but also the acute feeling of an incomplete accomplishment.[1]

5. Putin's Battle to Maintain His Power in Russia

Vladimir Putin's authority is increasingly challenged, which worries the Kremlin leader. As a result, the President of Russia has begun to take measures to prevent instability and to stifle potential dissidence movements. Even if Putin surrenders to many Kremlin elites, he will not get away from political purges if necessary. And Putin's most dangerous opponent might turn out to be even someone close to him - the leader of the lower chamber of the State Duma, Viaceslav Volodin, according to an analysis by Stratfor.

A report by Moscow's Carnegie Center, quoted by Stratfor, shows that the battle for power in Russia will be given in the State Duma. If until now the Russian parliament was a tool used by Vladimir Putin to give him legitimacy and to strengthen his power through various legislative acts, now it is not anymore the Russian President the one giving the orders but the new president of the lower chamber of the Duma, Viaceslav Volodin.

Ever since he came to the leadership of Russia, initially as prime minister, then as president, Vladimir Putin did everything in his power to strengthen his power over the State Duma, writes Stratfor. In order to ensure that he keeps control over the Russian Parliament, Putin needed to appoint a strong and loyal leader at Duma's leadership. He chose Viaceslav Volodin, the one who helped him manage the crisis created in Russia in 2012 after the parliamentary vote was defrauded. Stratfor writes that *Volodin has long wanted to be part of the Kremlin elite, but he has never had the necessary power. Normally, his job now does not allow him to achieve this goal, but his position is much more important in the context of Putin's need for laws to pass through the Duma to receive more much power. In this context, Volodin began to take steps to strengthen his own power.*

[1] http://www.ziare.com/vladimir-putin/presedinte-rusia/realismul-rusesc-sau-diplomatia-obsesiilor-1408241.

Stratfor writes *that what happens to Volodin is not at all new, on the contrary it fits in a pattern. In recent years, several close friends of Putin preferred to pursue their own goals, even if it meant defying the Russian president.*

For example, in 2016, Rosneft chief, Igor Secin, took over a majority stake in rival company Bashneft behind Putin. He also ignored the orders of the Russian leader to sell the company's shares to buyers on an approved list and has chosen his own partners. Stratfor also writes that the president of Chechnya criticized on social networks the Ministry of Finance's initiative to cut federal subsidies for his region, suggesting that, in the absence of funds, the country already affected by the war, could become unstable. And Sergei Cemezov, the head of the Rostec defense state giant, bought various companies to make sure his company infiltrated every arm of the Russian military-industrial complex, an action Putin tried to prevent in the past.

But this is not the most worrying, says Stratfor, and even unexpected. *A surprise, however, is that politicians in the second or third echelon began to deviate from the Kremlin line, especially leaders from regional governments. Some have removed local government structures to ensure their stay in power. Putin's answer has not been expected: in the past three weeks he has dismissed six regional leaders.* Also, on February 17, it was also he the one who organized a Security Council meeting to claim that a huge sweeping purification operation would develop aimed at regional governments.

Stratfor writes that *Vladimir Putin needs loyal close friends to implement his strategy. And if at the moment Viaceslav Volodin is one of them, the situation could become disastrous for the president of Russia if the president of the lower chamber of Duma will gain more power.*

Russia is a country that is almost surrounded by land, with difficult access to the sea, and this defines its geopolitical strategy as its most, to fight to push its frontiers to the West, according to American analyst George Friedman[1], in a Forbes article. That is why, he shows, *Russia is more like Sparta, not Athens, if we look at the ancient models of development.* A nation that pulls its strength not from wealth, like the West, but from the effort to overcome the hardships and vulnerabilities it faces, is more united, and from its simple geography it can actually reveal the danger to the West, however bad would be its economy, Friedman considers.

The American shows that *the most important feature of Russia is that it is caught nearly complete between lands. The European Peninsula is surrounded by three sides of the Baltic Sea, the North Sea, the Atlantic Ocean, the Mediterranean Sea and the Black Sea. The division to Russia is seen on the map if we draw a line from St. Petersburg to Rostov on Don. The line almost coincides with the eastern border of the Baltic countries, Belarus and Ukraine.*

Moreover, *Europe controls Russia's access to the oceans*, says George Friedman. European Russia has three points to access international maritime trade: through the Black Sea and the Bosphorus Strait - a Turkey-controlled route that can easily be blocked through the Denmark waters from St. Petersburg - and this passage is easily blockable, and through the Arctic Ocean, to Murmansk, crossing Greenland, Iceland and the UK. The access of a country to the sea can greatly influence its economic and political power.

The Russian population is concentrated along its western border with Europe and at the southern border with the Caucasus (the region between the Black Sea and the Caspian Sea). Siberia is sparsely populated, and its rivers and infrastructure are heading west. The heart of Russia's agriculture is in the southwest. North Russia cannot support agriculture, which makes Russia's border with Ukraine and that of the

---

[1] George Friedman – the manager of *Stratfor Analysis Group.*

Caucasus and Central Asia vital. As in the population, the west and south are the most productive Russian agricultural areas.

The importance of these two regions - the West and the South - can also be seen from Russia's transport infrastructure. Railways remain critical in Russia, and they are oriented to the West and to the former Soviet republics. Only two routes link European Russia to the Pacific maritime region, and Siberia is almost isolated, shows the Amercian analyst.

Being a terrestrial power, Russia is vulnerable, being situated on the European Plain with few natural barriers to defend it from Western enemies. To the east of the Carpathian Mountains, the plain goes south, and the gate of Russia is open, says Friedman. To this is added that Russia has few rivers, which makes domestic transport difficult and reduces economic efficiency. That is why, *Russia's strategy is to move its frontier as far as possible. European countries fro the first Eastern line - the Baltics, Belarus, and Ukraine - provide Russia with the depth from which Russia can project its power and present economic opportunities.*

At present, the Russian border has not been so close to Moscow for a long time, losing control over both country lines from the European Peninsula. The West absorbed the Baltic countries in NATO, bringing St. Petersburg a few hundred kilometers from the North Atlantic block. To stabilize the situation, they fought the Chechens, intervened in Georgia and sent troops to Armenia.

However, after 1991, the key country for Russia was Ukraine, because the border with it was passing through the heart of Russian agriculture, the most populated areas and the transport nodes.

In the current conflict with Ukraine, Russia assumes that Europeans and Americans have a goal beyond creating a pro-Western regime in Kiev. From their perspective, this buffer zone was lost, and Ukrainian forces hostile to Russia advanced near the Russian border. The situation is precarious for Russia at this time, and this means that things will not remain like this in Ukraine, because Russia cannot assume that the West's interests in the region come from good intentions. At the same time, the West cannot assume that Russia, if occupying Ukraine, will stop here. That is why we are in the classical situation where two forces assume the worst one about the other. However, Russia is in a weaker position, shows Friedman.

Although Russia has been involved in the conflict in Syria, demonstrating its military capabilities and gaining strength against the West, this operation is peripheral to Russia's interests, for which the western border and Ukraine as well as the southern Caucasus remain the main objectives.

It is clear that Russia's economy, based on energy exports, is doing badly because of the collapse in oil prices, but Russia's economy has always been bad. That did not prevent her from winning the Second World War. The difficulties unite the Russians. Why Russia is Sparta rather than Athens. Tucidide distinguished Athens and Sparta, showing that Athens is closer to the sea and has an excellent port in Piraeus, while Sparta was not a maritime power. Athens was much richer than Sparta, because it could make international trade much easier than Sparta, surrounded by land. That is why Athens was rich, but there were two flaws here: the luxury that corrupts and the vast experience that creates moral ambiguity. On the other hand, Sparta was much poorer than Athens, not based on trade, but on hard work. It did not know the world but had a robust sense of good and evil.

This distinction could also be made between the European Peninsula and Russia, according to George Friedman. Europe pulls its power out of wealth, but it is also prone to internal struggles. Russia, though provincial, is rather united and pulls its power out of difficulties.

It is not prosperity that unites the Russians, but the idealized vision of loyalty to the Russian Mother, and from this point of view there is a deep fault between Europe and the US, on the one hand, who use prosperity as a justification for loyalty, and Russia, where loyalty derives from state power and the inherent definition of being Russian. All this gives the Russians an opportunity. No matter how bad the economy would go, the simplism of their geographical position gives them the ability to surprise their opponents and perhaps make them more dangerous, Friedman says in the conclusion of his analysis.[1]

6. Conclusions

Moldova is considered to be decisive for the redesign of the regional geopolitical configuration. Located on the southern flank and considered a NATO and Russia buffer zone, it was wickedly compressed between two powerful force fields, with little chance of finding a way out.

The Transnistrian problem is no longer an internal problem of the Republic of Moldova, it is an international one and it can be solved only with the help of the international community and only after the Russian military retreat from the region. The real democratization of the Transnistrian region could only begin after the withdrawal of the Russian troops, after the demilitarization of the region and the liquidation of the structures in the region to suppress the democratic values. The presence of Russian troops on the territory of Moldova is the main cause of the failure to democratize the country and its autonomous development, and the influence of force instruments is felt in all sectors of political life. Transnistria is maintained in the so-called "frozen conflict" but everyone is aware that Moscow can always "warm up the situation" if it sees its interests threatened.

This military outbreak is an essential factor in keeping Russia's control over the entire area. No political analysis can disregard the presence of the regional military force. Hence the discussion about the real authority of the Moldovan state. This is the brief summary of Bessarabian issues...[2]

From a geopolitical perspective, Russia has two major problems: a bad demography and difficult/ impossible to defend frontiers. At present, Russia's south and west borders stretch over 11,000 km, from the Caucasus Mountains to the Arctic Circle. Russia already does not have enough troops to defend this border, and due to negative demographic trends it will have fewer available soldiers in the future. That is why Russia needs to shorten its border to about 1,500 km, much easier to control/ defend. Russia would only need some clever moves on the geopolitical chessboard: to head west and occupy three major cities: Riga, the eastern half of Warsaw and Bucharest. Is it possible? What will NATO do?

We do not know the answer. But we saw how Russia can do it: in a way that NATO and other countries of the European Union do not appreciate at the real scale and significance of the Russian territorial advances until it is too late. We have seen relatively recently how Russia has quickly entered a country, either officially or unofficially, as in the case of Ukraine, under the pretext of protecting native Russians or Russians from the former Soviet Union. It happened in 2008, when Russia invaded Georgia, and much more recently, when Russia invaded Crimea and vast portions of eastern Ukraine. In both cases, the international response was just a noisy indignation and some occasional economic sanctions. However, NATO has never felt the need to trigger a war due to the two invasions. I think NATO will have the same reaction when Russia moves forward in Ukraine, Moldova and the Caucasus. But if a Russian invasion of the Baltic countries is to come, I think NATO will react. But the Baltic countries will be conquered very quickly, possibly in a weekend, and NATO will not be able to defend them initially.

---

[1] http://www.gandul.info/international/zece-harti-care-explica-strategia-rusiei-15089856.
[2] http://cyd.ro/tinta-geopolitica-rusiei/.

An analogy between the pre-World War II situation and what is now happening with Russia is a must. The great historical lesson of Munich should not be forgotten. Even if in Russia the geopolitical twilight is approaching.[1]

The EU's contribution to conflict resolution in the European space was mainly in the form of economic aid. European funding is an important support for conflicting communities, but it is not the most effective solution to conflict resolution. The EU has also been involved in supporting the dialogue between the parties, but has failed to remove the existing borders between the various conflicting communities.

Addressing conflicts in the immediate neighborhood is important for the EU, both because of their negative effects on neighboring countries and the security risks they pose to the EU. The problems faced by the Republic of Moldova, and here I am referring especially to the Transnistrian conflict, are major obstacles in the process of democratization and, at the same time, sources of instability for the rest of Europe.

However, the EU is not generally perceived as an important actor, but rather as a "neutral benefactor". This has its advantages, but also underlines the limited role that the EU assumes in the transformation of conflicts. The EU is not an independent actor, because its actions depend on local political conditions, nor does it have a direct impact on society.

7. Bibliography

International Relations Dictionary - XX Century, Volume coordinated by Maurice Vaïsse, (2008). Polirom.

(2006). EU Action Plan - Republic of Moldova. ADEPT Guide. Chisinau: Gunivas Publishing House.

Republic of Moldova - Anti-Democracy Sinking of Galagious Government, *Country Report 2003*, Coordinator: Iulian Chifu (2004). Politeea-Snspa Publishing House.

Igor, Caşu (1991). *National Politics in Soviet Moldova (1944-1989).* Paris: France Loisirs Publishing House.

Cioroianu, Adrian (2009). *Matrioskai's Geopolitics - Post-Soviet Russia in the New World Order*. Bucharest: Curtea Veche Publishing House.

Crânganu, Constantin *Russia the Closeness of (Geopolitical) Twilight,* According to - http://www.contributors.ro/global-europa/rusia-apropierea-amurgului-geopolitic/.

Petrescu, Cristina (2007). *Construction of National Identity in Bessarabia* In Monica Heintz (coord.), Weak State. Uncertain Citizenship. Studies about the Republic of Moldova. Bucharest: Curtea Veche Publishing House.

March, Patrick G. (1996). *Eastern Destiny: Russia in Asia and the North Pacific*. Greenwood Publishing Group.

Oleg Serebrian in *Transnistrian Conflict: Geopolitics and Geohistory* http://transnistria.md/ro/articles/0/542/.

Negrut, Silviu (2005). *Introduction to Geopolitics*. Bucharest: Meteor Press.

http://transnistria.md/ro/articles/0/542/.

http://transnistria.md/ro/articles/0/542/.

https://www.dcnews.ro/conflictul-din-transnistria-expert-de-la-chi-inau-pozi-ia-formatului-5-2-comoda-contribu-ia-romaniei_535667.html.

[1] http://www.contributors.ro/global-europa/rusia-apropierea-amurgului-geopolitic/.

http://www.hotnews.ro/stiri-esential-21631527-video-cum-juca-rusia-moldova-transnistria-vladimir-socor-notiunea-statut-special-este-instrument-reexpansiune-rusiei.htm.

http://www.ziare.com/vladimir-putin/presedinte-rusia/realismul-rusesc-sau-diplomatia-obsesiilor-1408241.

http://www.gandul.info/international/zece-harti-care-explica-strategia-rusiei-15089856.

http://cyd.ro/tinta-geopolitica-rusiei/.

http://www.contributors.ro/global-europa/rusia-apropierea-amurgului-geopolitic/.

7

Albania-EU Relationship and the Course towards the European Integration

Jeta Goxha[1]

Abstract: The collapse of the communist regime in Albania made possible the country's opening to the west, a country that had chosen the way of total isolation. Albania was the first country in the Balkans region who signed a commercial agreement in 1992 with the European Union. This article aims to study Albania's path towards European integration. The position and role played by the European Union during that critical period for our country, as the crisis of 1997. The objective of this paper is to create a clear panorama of relationships between the EU and Albania and to highlight the problems that have come across over the years. The author of this paper will also provide an overview of the political developments in Albania after the signing of the Stabilization and Association Agreement. The method of operation is qualitative. This paper was accomplished through a bibliographic research, drawing on the European Union legislation, the agreements signed between the two countries and also the strategies of the Albanian government during these years.

Keywords: The European integration; SAA; diplomatic relations; development

1. Introduction

Albania reappeared on the international scene, immediately after the fall of dictatorships and the collapse of communist regime in Tirana. It has succeeded against a dictatorship that was known for its hardness and leaving the country in total darkness, but this instantaneous variation, caused considerable civil disturbances. The communist regime in Albania was one of the longest regimes in the Western Balkans and also one of the most regressive countries of Eastern Europe, not only in the economic viewpoint but also in the social areas.

But we cannot agree that this has been the biggest challenge of the Albanian society. The biggest problem was of a political nature, where the efforts and authoritarian ways of the Albanian political class resulted in an extremely poor dialogue between the main political parties. One of the characteristics of contemporary political life in the country is the way that Albanian politicians tend to inhibit the normal development of the post-election policy, rejecting the election results, when they are on the losing side.

The first diplomatic relationships between Albania and the European Community began in 1991, immediately after the fall of the communist regime. Until that time, the forced division of Europe was

[1] Senior Lecturer, PhD Candidate, Faculty of Law and Political Sciences SHPAL Pavaresia Vlore, Albania, Address: Bulevardi Vlorë-Skele PO. Box 4358 Posta Vlorë AL-9401 Vlorë. Albania, Corresponding author: jeta.goxha@unipavaresia.edu.al.

created by the Cold War and the mutual incompatibility of ideologies and models of economic and social development. Except for the former Yugoslavia, the Economic relationships between the European Community and Albania were more or less similar to other countries of Central and Eastern Europe.

2. Albania and the European Policies in the Balkans

Since the early 90s until today, the secession of Slovenia and Croatia, the independence of Kosovo, the political developments in the Western Balkans are characterized by a explicit attitude towards the division of territories. Since 1996, the EU has tried to create a regional approach in the context of establishing relationships with the regional countries: Bosnia-Herzegovina, Croatia, the Former Yugoslav Republic of Macedonia, Albania, Montenegro, Serbia and Kosovo.

The goal of this approach is supported by the implementation of the Dayton Peace Agreement[1] and the establishment of political stability and economic prosperity, which will be based on several principles:

a) the protection of democracy and the rule of the law;

b) Respect of the human rights and minorities;

c) the recovery of the economic activity.

In 1999, the European Commission established the terms for a new approach to the territories of the former Yugoslavia, laying the foundations for the Stabilization and Association process, which is otherwise known as the EU project for Southeast Europe.

With the approval of the Thessaloniki Agenda, in 2003, there has been a qualitative step for the relationship between the EU and the Western Balkans. One of the major challenges at the basis of the EU policy in the last decade, is the integration of the Balkans in the European Union, also a powerful incentive for the modernization, stabilization and democratization of the region.

The European Commission, in recent years in the framework of the Stabilization and Association Agreement has developed numerous instruments to support and effectively promote the integration process of the Balkans into the European Union. The Stabilization and Association Agreement is the foundation of the relationships between the EU and the Western Balkans.

The three main objectives of this process include: the stabilization of countries in transition and their rapid accession into the market economy, the promotion of the regional cooperation and the eventual membership in the EU, if the conditions for membership are fulfilled[2].

The Western Balkans continue to be one of the key challenges of the European Union. The stability of the countries that are part of this region, is closely connected to the old continent, this due to their geographic and geostrategic position. Unanimously the belief of the EU as an international actor, in majority depends on its interaction in this region (Gori, 2007, p. 5). Brussels has not invested in any other area, as much as it has invested in the Balkan region, spending there millions of euros.

We can say that unlike at the beginning, when the relationship with these countries were established,

---

[1] The General Framework Agreement for Peace in Bosnia and Herzegovina, also known as the Dayton Agreement, Dayton Accords, Paris Protocol or Dayton-Paris Agreement, is the peace agreement reached at Wright-Patterson Air Force Base near Dayton, Ohio in November 1995, and formally signed in Paris on 14 December 1995. These accords put an end to the three and a half-year long Bosnian War, one of the armed conflicts in the former Socialist Federative Republic of Yugoslavia.

[2] This process helps these countries to develop the capacity for adopting and implementing the EU legislation. The relationship between Western Balkan countries and the EU are based on the following pillars: (i) concessions (ii) economic and financial assistance (CARDS since 2007 has been replaced by IPA) (iii) the Stabilization and Association Agreement

previously in one country and later elsewhere, the EU today has all the necessary instruments, experience and all strategies to assist and come to help all the countries of the region in their European journey[1]. So if we try to highlight what is needed at the present, EU must decisively continue with the initiatives taken, which should lead to the "Europeanization of the Balkans".

In March 2006, at the end of an informal meeting of the foreign European Union ministers, held in Salzburg, was issued a statement in which was argued that the enlargement process relates not only to the fulfillment of the Copenhagen criteria of the countries that want to be part of the European family[2], but also by the capacity of the European Union to "absorb" new members. This makes us think that this issue will be in constant change, in the framework of foreign policy pursued by the EU, also by the political will of the current members.

Another approach appears in 2008 within the EU, the European Commission reaffirmed the European perspective of the Western Balkan countries. From this moment, the Western Balkans countries have succeeded in various steps, and in others less, as has been observed in their progress during these years.

Brussels has invested so much in the Western Balkans, having spent billions of euro for humanitarian assistance, the material and institutional construction, supporting with commitment and the monetary cost of five ESDP missions[3].

The Balkans have represented a fundamental test for the development of the international role of the EU. Based on EU's experience in the Balkans from the moment of the communist regimes fall, we can say that the EU has demonstrated that it has received the appropriate lessons for developing peske[4] and play an essential role in the events that also led in the fall of Milosevic.

The first European policies toward the Balkan countries were set by two crisis that disturbed the Balkans, the Albanian crisis of 1997 and that of Kosovo in 1999. In 1997, the violent protests, that erupted to denounce the collapse of the pyramidal schemes, drove the country into chaos, at the limits of civil war. Its effects were more pronounced in the southern part of the country, with the city of Vlora as the epicenter.

Faced with this dramatic situation, for the first time the EU was in trial, despite the initial premises to create a new regional approach, it showed that there were no proper mechanisms in order to resolve problems of this type. In fact the function of this organization became a secondary role, in the framework of the OSCE initiative with the generous support of Italy.

Another success, that can be attributed to the European Union, is the development of a strategy enshrined in Thessaloniki in 2003, that laid the basis for the Stabilization and Association Agreement for the progression and full integration of all Balkan countries.

Twelve years ago the leaders of the European Union, under the leadership of the Greek Presidency, in the city of Thessaloniki gave vent to the idea for a big project in the Balkan region, "*The future of the Balkans is in the European Union*", deciding the year 2014 as a time limit. By that time more than a decade has past and only two Balkan countries are members with full rights (Slovenia and Croatia).

[1] We refer to the countries that are not yet part of the European Union, so are excluded, Slovenia and Croatia, which are full rights members in the EU.

[2] This happened with the 10 countries that joined the European Union in 2004. Supported by a strong political will from the support of 15 member states, their membership was conducted with quick steps once these countries managed to fulfill the Copenhagen criteria.

[3] The European Policy on security and defense.

[4] The European Security and Cooperation policies

The year in which the project was created, was a year of great European enthusiasm: the common European single currency had been circulating for more than one year. At the same time was signed the Treaty of Athens, which ended the pre-accession process of the ten countries of Central and Eastern Europe. These countries joined the great European family in 2004. The aim of this project was that the rest of the Balkan countries would be members with full rights at the 100th anniversary of the start of World War I. We see that the situation appears quite different from what was expected to be achieved, if we try to identify the progress that these countries have made from over the years. Among the priorities of the EU, the enlargement of new countries does not seem to happen, and it is essential to overcome the economic situation. The year 2014, assumed as the "year of great changes in the region", did not conclude anything but only reduced the hopes of this region citizens.

However, we can not say that the European integration of the Balkan countries has stopped, it is an ongoing process, but a slow one. Croatia is a member with full rights in the EU from July 2013, , Serbia and Albania hold a candidate status, but Macedonia and Montenegro have also begun negotiations. Bosnia and Herzegovina[1], on February the 16-th of this year filed a formal application for membership in the European Union. This action is considered an important step not only for the region itself but also for Europe, because it marks the possibility of joining the old continent. While Kosovo has signed the Stabilization and Association Agreement and is at the first step toward the European integration, during the last two years, the situation seems to have changed.

For the countries of the Western Balkans, the clear perspective of the EU membership granted by the EU member states is a key stabilizing factor. It supports progress toward the fulfillment of the necessary conditions, including those of the Stabilization and Association Progress[2].

2. The Relationships between Albania and EU in the First Decade after the Fall of Communism

Immediately after the fall of the tougher regime in communist countries, Tirana, Albania changed its political line by opening to the west. The first contacts with international institutions were with the European Community. In early 1991 the first diplomatic relationships between our country and the EC were created. From that moment on, Albania's integration in the EU appears as the most important priority on the agenda of all the political classes of Albanian.

The first date in this historical process of bilateral relationships development between the EU and Albania dates to May 11, 1992. This date marks the moment when in Brussels, was signed an agreement between the European Economic Community and the Republic of "Albania, about trade exchanges, commercial and economic cooperation[3]. It is worth pointing out that what impresses on the agreement signed for the first time between the two contracting parties, is its preamble, where specifically stated, *"taking into consideration the political developments, Albania wants to stabilize and consolidate democracy and promote the economic and social progress"*[4]. At this critical stage for a small country such as Albania, a country that had followed a tough policy, getting close to the West was important. This deal revives a thread of hope for Albanian political leaders, but in fact will simply

[1] Bosnia and Herzegovina have signed with the European Union a Stabilization and Association Agreement on 16 June 2008.
[2] European Commission, *EU Enlargement Strategy 2014-2015*, October 2014, p. 1.
[3] The deal was negotiated and signed by the then president of the EEC, also foreign minister of Portugal, João de Deus Pinheiro, Vice-President of the Commission of the European Communities, Frans Andriessen, and the representative of the Albanian Government, Minister of Finance and Economy Genc Ruli.
[4] Agreement between the Economic European Community and the Republic of Albania, on trade and commercial and economic cooperation, the official Journal of the European Communities, dated 25.11.1992 N.

remain in principle. However by this agreement, it was decided on the development of economic cooperation and expansion of trade relationships with Albania, the establishment on a contractual basis of the political orientation of Albania towards European integration into a functioning democracy and also free market economy.

The relations between our country and the European Union become solid a year later in 1993[1], the year which coincides with the establishment of the Copenhagen criteria for the accession of new countries into the EU, as a cause of major permanent changes that had occurred on Central and Eastern Europe in recent years. It was in this historical moment, happening in Tirana, the European Commission delegation, constituting a permanent diplomatic mission to represent the European Commission in external affairs.

1996 marks the first steps to a contractual agreement with the EU. This new agreement will pave the way for a classic association agreement, but the internal political problems that were highlighted by the contested parliamentary elections of May 1996, together with the deep financial and social crisis, caused by the collapse of the pyramidal schemes, caused the failure of the initiative undertaken from the EU.

In 1997, the General Affairs Council of the EU approved "the Regional Approach to countries of the region", through which the EU set the political and economic conditions for further development of bilateral relations. The agreement mentioned above, refers to all the Western Balkan countries, part of which is also our country. In Albania, were occurring numerous disturbances, that changed the attitude of many international institutions, one of which, the European Union.

The year 1997 otherwise known as the backward year because of the collapse of "the rental firms", had reduced the liquidity in the entire country, financially destroying a large number of families, making Albania financially depended to international organizations.

The collapse of pyramidal schemes was the beginning of massive revolts against the government, which was responsible in dual ways: first due to the fact that allowed the creation and operation of these fraudulent companies and second because it interrupted their activity precisely when citizens were expecting to receive higher interests (Fuga, 2008, pp. 334-337). During this period it is noted that the EU's attitude towards Albania was very distanced.

Why did the EU not activate all the special mechanisms to cope with such a situation? The answers, we think are different; facing to the deteriorating situation, EU was left to the empty promises of the Albanian government, as the initiative containing the activation of a cooperation agreement signed in 1992; but in fact, had contrary attitudes by some members of the state. Therefore, the possibility of the European Union to take a leading role in the " land of the eagles " failed.

The situation had deteriorated, but despite this extremely precarious situation, the EU chose to cooperate in the coordination framework, which was confided to the OSCE mission, therefore it did not choose the leadership role. Brussels was left to organize and initiate the "Alba" mission in the management of the Italian country and also to sustain the initiative in order to create the necessary security conditions for the international aid.

We can state that the EU became aware, when the situation in Kosovo was irreversible. After noticing the escalated situation, this time the European Union needed to take a more significant role, perhaps

[1] Membership criteria, or Copenhagen criteria, were confirmed in December 1995 by the European Council of Madrid, in which they stressed the importance for the establishment of administrative structures in the applicant countries to join the EU. The aim was to create the conditions for a gradual and harmonious integration into the EU.

this was the appropriate time to undertake a regional approach. Realizing also the importance of maintaining a decisive role not only in the European continent, but also towards international actors (Gori, 2007, pp. 36-38).

As mentioned above the EU should assume a more active role in the Balkans, based on this context it must change its strategy, demonstrating with facts and concrete proofs, its ability to extend towards some geographical state that historically belonged to the old continent. Precisely at this moment, in 1998 the relationship between Albania and the European Union was intensified through the creation of a proper legal framework and administrative capacity. While, in 1999 a year later, at the end of July, in Sarajevo a new initiative was launched, taken by the European Union for the entire Western Balkans, the Stabilization and Association Agreement.

This process in the entire Western Balkans, would be conditioned by the desire and the will of the political forces, therefore the assessment of each of these states was done individually, a fact which proves that some of them have made significant strides, while others have still a long way to go. We can say that our country is in a very important moment, it must fulfill all the necessary criteria to make the membership request.

3. The Relationships between the EU and Albania after the Signing of the Stabilization and Association Agreement

A new and important page in the relationship between the European Union and Albania, was signed on November 24, 2000 during the Zagreb Summit. During this summit, the EU offered to the Balkan countries the perspective of a future membership in the large European family, once the Copenhagen criteria was fulfilled and they agreed about the assistance programs to help achieve these objectives. In the meantime, these countries pledged to respect the conditions set by the European Union and to use the Stabilization and Association Agreement to prepare for their route to EU[1].

The negotiations for the signing of the Stabilization and Association Agreement with Albania were officially opened in 2003, but due to problems of various nature, the signing of this agreement was made possible, on June 12, 2006, and entered into force in 2009. This historical and important moment for our country, marked the transition toward a new stage, the relations between Albania and the European Union advanced further. The NATO membership, another important issue for our country, happened in 2009.

During this period, it is worth mentioning the government program for the 2005-2009 period, where it can be evidenced the intention to undertake reforms, this as a result of the commitments provided by the SAA. Among the basic goals stand out the reforms for the development and consolidation of the democratic state, the restoration of the rule of law and the eradication of the corruption system, which will be designed and implemented in order to adapt to the European models and to get European standards.The Government Programme 2005-2009 refers to the previous government (under the leadership of the Socialist Party), calling it the major slowdown in the European path. According to the government of the time, during the socialist government, have occurred fenomens which have helped turn Albania in a catastrophic politically and economically state, as "*the creation of the corruption system, the violation of free elections and the implementation of unilateral reforms have negatively impacted the Albanian citizens, making it possible to lose confidence in state institutions, which are inefficient, opaque and deeply corrupt*".

---

[1] The final decision of the Zagreb Summit.

Compared with regional counterparts, who after the 90's, in particular in the last decade have made significant progress into the European integration process, in the Albania's case, the results have been relatively minor. However, after the accession to NATO in 2009, the country is oriented towards the integration into the Euro-Atlantic area. Albania has achieved one of the two most important strategic goals with her membership in NATO in 2009. EU integration is another strategic goal of Albania.

"EU membership" is the slogan that has characterized all the political programs of the governments of our country after the fall of the dictatorial regime, it has also been the main motto of the campaigns and public debates. Despite the political and social demonstrations, the main actors in Albania are at a constant state of "war", attacking each others with rigged election results and holding back the necessary reforms for the European integration.

Once the SAA entered into force on April 1st 2009, Albania at the end of the same month officially presented the request for membership. EU officially accepted the application in November 2009, and in the next month submitted to Albania the questionnaire about its willingness for membership.

However one of the main conditions for Albania's EU integration is the implementation of the Stabilization and Association Agreement. We find the legal basis of the mutual interaction between the contracting parties in one of the provisions of the TEU, Article 217, that specifically states: "*The European Union may conclude with one or more third countries or international organizations, to establish an association agreement, which includes the mutual rights and obligations ...* After the entry into force of the SAA, Albania has tried to respect all obligations required by the EU, although often various problems have appeared inside the country, Albania has made progress in its journey toward Europe. Referred to the above mentioned, officially since 2010, Albanian citizens have the opportunity to travel without visas in the Schengen area, as a result of the completion and fulfillment of a number of criteria by the Government.

Referred to the implementation and putting into practice the legal obligations deriving from this agreement, the Government has taken the necessary legal measures, at the same time one of the key priorities of our country, respecting the remaining recommendations after receiving candidate status[1]. Recently, on June 24, 2014, Albania has received the candidate status after a series of failed attempts.

During these years, there has been progress, but these changes have been due to impositions by the EU representatives, while the Albanian political elite have hampered this process, due to a lack of political dialogue between the political forces. However the journey of our country by itself presents a number of problems that must be resolved, to upgrade to a new stage, an application for membership.

According to the Report Progress for Albania in 2015, changes have been made in all the aspects, however there are still some that have a long way to go. For this reason Albania continued to actively participate in high level dialogue meetings, as well as in the related joint working groups on the five key priorities[2]. Continuously Albania must fulfill the five key criteria for the opening of the accession negotiations, therefore our country is a big step closer to the European family, but the whole process still seems more complicated than it had been expected.

[1] Decision of the Council of Ministers no. 486, dated 25.07.2012 on the adoption of the National Plan for the Implementation of the SAA, and the definition of institutional responsibilities for aligning Albanian legislation of any act of the European Union (which is updated annually).
[2] European Commission, *Albania 2015 Report*, November 2015, pg. 4.

4. Conclusion

In 1997 the situation had deteriorated, but despite this extremely precarious situation, the EU chose to cooperate in the framework of coordination, which was confided to the OSCE mission, therefore it did not choose the leadership role.

The European Union should assume a more active role in the Balkans, it must change its strategy, demonstrating with facts and concrete proofs, its ability to extend towards some geographical states that historically belonged to the old continent.

During 1998 the relationship between Albania and the European Union was intensified through the creation of a proper legal framework and administrative building capacity. In 1999 a year later, at the end of July, in Sarajevo was launched a new initiative taken by the European Union for the entire Western Balkans, the Stabilization and Association Agreement.

A new important moment in the relationships between the European Union and Albania, was on November 24, 2000 during the Zagreb Summit. During this summit, the EU offered to Balkan countries the perspective for future membership in the large European family, with the fulfillment of the Copenhagen criteria and the agreement for assistance programs to achieve these objectives. The negotiations for the signing of the Stabilization and Association Agreement with Albania were officially opened in 2004, but entered into force on April 1st 2009. During these years, there has been progress, but these changes have been due to impositions by the EU representatives, while the Albanian political elite have hampered this process, due to a lack of political dialogue between the political forces.

Recently, on June 24, 2014, Albania has received the candidate status after a series of failed attempts. In the past years, Albania has smoothly implemented its obligations under the Stabilization and Association Agreement. Actually, our country is a big step closer to the European family, but the whole process still seems more complicated than it had been expected. Albania continued to actively participate in high level dialogue meetings, as well as the related joint working groups on the five key criteria.

5. References

Fuga, Artan (2008). *Media, politika, shoqeria (1990-2000)/Media, Politics, Society (1990-2000).* Albania: Tirane, pp. 334-337.

Bashkim, Rama (2013). *Ballkani pas rënies se murit te Berlinit. Vetëvendosja versus tërësia territoriale/Balkans after the fall of the Berlin Wall. Territorial integrity versus self-determination.* Tirane: Botimet M&B.

Luca, Gori (2007). *Europea e Balcani Occidentali. La prospettiva europea della regione (1996-2007)/Europe and the Western Balkans. The European perspective of the region (1996-2007).* Soveria Mannell: Rubettino, pp. 36-38.

Bertino, Alessandra & Ori, Antonia (2011). *Cronologia della Politika Estera Italiana/Chronology of Italian Foreign Policy*, Gennaio-Dicembre, Documenti IAI. See to pubblicazioni.iai.it/.../Cronologia/cronologia_2011.

Agreement between the Economic European Community and the Republic of Albania, on trade and commercial and economic cooperation. The *official Journal of the European Communities*, dated 25.11.1992.

Decision of the Council of Ministers of Albania no. 486, dated 25.07.2012 on the adoption of the National Plan for the Implementation of the SAA, and the definition of institutional responsibilities for aligning Albanian legislation of any act of the European Union.

European Commission, October 2013. *EU Enlargement Strategy* 2014-2015, Brussels.

European Comission, November 2015. Albania 2015 Report.

8

Political Discourse and the Theory of Speech Acts

Mirela Arsith[1]

Abstract: The hypothesis from which we start of is that of political discourse, in its quality of practical discourse in order to be analyzed through the theory of speech acts, dominated by the use theory rule of meaning, which refers to the context of communication and human behavior. The theory of *speech acts* rise the issue of significance dependence, not the mere use of language, but the acting context of utterance, that the utterance fact, the latter not being a simple statement of something. J. L. Austin makes a first distinction between *constitutive statements,* which only say something, establishing a state of things, the truth of a fact and the performative utterances which are the performance of an action. Along with the locutionary act which manifests as utterance, as formulating sentences, the perlocutionary act, produced by the fact of having to say something, followed by the effects on a locutionary, either on the speakers, existing the illocutionary act, which is to commit *something* by enunciation, revealing a certain value and "force": information, promise, demand, order, request, warning, advice, etc. By extending the characteristics of speech acts at the level of political discourse, we can say that it manifests itself as an entity resulting from the identical meaning of producing the statements that composes it, of *the illocutionary force marking the enunciation and the effects* by which it is achieved a certain performance.

Keywords: performative utterance; illocutionary act; enunciation

1. Introduction

The argumentative foundation from which we plan to start analyzing this issue is assuming communication as always being a major social and political fact, with an essential contribution in establishing the social order. The discourse is, simultaneously, a specific way of action, a way of representation, but also a linguistic approach that speakers act upon the world and especially on their peers. Political discourse, as a species of the genre, subsumes these traits. In this context, there should be approached the performative aspects of communication ,J. L. Austin, an important representative of the "Literary" School at Oxford, in *How to do Things with Words*, made an initial distinction between *constitutive utterances* that just say something, establish a state of things, the truth of a fact and the *performative utterances* which are, by themselves, the performance of an action.

[1] Associate Professor, PhD, Dean of Faculty of Communication and International Relations, "Danubius" University of Galati, Romania, Address: 3 Galati Boulevard, 800654 Galati, Romania.
Corresponding author: arsith.mirela@univ-danubius.ro.

2. When the Words Increase and Change the World

Stating a certain phrase generates simultaneously the accomplishment of three acts (Austin, 2003, pp. 23-26):

(1) *the locutionary act* that manifests as utterance, as forms of sentences, in accordance with the grammatical rules;

(2) *the illocutionary act*, which is to commit *something* through enunciation, revealing a certain value and "force": information, promise, demand, order, request, warning, advice, etc.;

(3) perlocutionary act, which is produced *by* having to say something, followed by *effects* on the *alocutionary* or on the speakers;

Language carries *a perlocutionary force*, which is manifested by the effects obtained simply *by* saying something: that of being able or not to influence through enunciation, to be warned or being misled, to determine or to prevent a decision or action, and for the limit, the performance itself of being understood by the *alocutionary*.

In the conception of J. L. Austin, words are part of the world. Words are not objects, as any other other. We use words, and what makes them useful "objects" is their complexity, the fact that they can be built in refined instruments for modeling the world. Ordinary language contains all the distinctions men have thought it useful to make and it participates in updating and creating realities, whenever it is used in speech. Using words, people talk about facts.

By extending to the level of discourse, we can say that it represents the dynamic unity between the production of statements that create the illocutionary force of the utterance by which it is achieved a certain performance and perlocutionary action, to the extent that the three aspects of the speech act are codified and regulated according to paradigms, so to the extent in which they are "identified and reidentified as having the same meaning". (Ricoeur, 1999, p. 100) Therefore, through the discourse it is manifested intentionality, the specific human act of establishing meaning and value to the "world" that it expresses.

American philosopher John Rogers Searle, resuming the classification of illocutionary acts, identifies firstly the twelve issues that determine the differentiation of illocutionary acts, which can be grouped into three categories:

(A) differences concerning the purpose of illocutionary acts: engaging the speaker, persuading the alocutionary, assessment, etc.;

(B) differences regarding the adequacy of the words in the world and the world into the words;

(C) differences caused by the psychological states of the speaker: motivation, confidence, desire.

John Rogers Searle, taking into account these differences, reached *to five basic categories* (Searle, 1972, pp. 52-56) of these types of speech acts:

(1) *representatives*, that say "how things are", engaging the speaker to achieve the adequacy of the words to reality; these speech acts can be evaluated according to the values of truth, even if they are not outright statements;

(2) *directives* that are used by the speaker to determine the interlocutor to do something; they can have the illocutionary force of a suggestion, but a pleading or order, of an advice, a recommendation; the world must comply with words; a subcategory introduced by the philosopher is that of the questions,

which he considers them as being attempts of the speaker inciting the alocutionary to respond, that is, the determine it to fulfill an act of language;

(3) promises (commissives) whose enunciation requires the speaker to a future course of action, to follow an adequacy of the world to words; by these illocutionary acts, the locutionary is committed to do things in the future;

(4) expressive, which expresses a psychological condition specified in sincerity, about the state of things revealed in the propositional content; these acts ignore an adequacy relationship between words and things, they express their attitudes and feelings; the truth of the expressed proposition is assumed;

(5) *statements* that have its specifics in achieving the correspondence between propositional content and the reality, with in extra-linguistic institutions; by such actions there are caused changes in reality, and the adequacy between both directions, from the words to the world and from the world to the words; "the declarations cause a change in the status or position of the object or objects to which the reference is achieved only on the basis that the statement was completed successfully." (Searle, 1972, p. 57); the statements assume that to the constitutive rules of the language it should be added a system of rules that belong to an extra-linguistic institution (e.g. church, the legal system), in which the speaker and the alocutionary occupy a certain position; to pursue the fulfillment of illocutionary acts in institutional situations, it is not sufficient the linguistic competence and the fact establishment, but it becomes necessary to appeal to an authority in order to decide on what are the facts; their evaluation and decision reveals a submission of the utterance to reality, a situation in which the statements coincide with assertive statements or modeling the reality, according to certain value-normative paradigms.

The values of success or failure of the illocutionary acts are the following, in terms of illocutionary logics:

(a) *the truth or falsity of assertive*, referring to their propositional content that can be true in certain worlds and false in others;

(b) respected or violated commissives; an illocutionary commissive act is respected only if the speaker turns the propositional content into the truth, assuming and fulfilling the future course of action represented by the commissive; otherwise, the committed illocutionary act is *violated*;

(c) fulfilled or unfulfilled directive; a directive illocutionary act is fulfilled if and only if the alocutionary makes the propositional content true, fulfilling the future course of action which the directive represents; otherwise is unfulfilled; There are ways that leave out the alocutionary the option to refuse and others, an option which the recipient does not have, the only choice being obedience; between fulfilling an order or keeping of promises and the truth of a statement there is a significant formal difference: a statement is true while the propositional content is managed in the direction of matching the word-world; an order is fulfilled and a promise is kept only if the agent brings success towards matching the world-word, the "order and the promise instituting as causes, but also as ways" (Searle & Vanderveken, 1985, p. 97);

(d) the success or failure of statements; since the successful performance of the declaration conditions the propositional content of truth, a successful statement has a success matching.

In the universe of statements, the illocutionary goals are met with different degrees of strength; this differentiation is possible by using performative verbs, which make possible the illocutionary forces group in three classes:

(a) the class of strong performatives: to command, to insist, the give orders, etc.;

(b) the class of intermediary performatives: to request, to ask, etc.;

(c) the class of weak performatives: suggest, advise, recommend, etc.; when the speaker wants to make a weak commitment, he does it indirectly, sometimes as a denial of a strong commissive "I intent to do it, but I cannot promise anything."

3. Political Discourse, a Language Macro-act

The political discourse aims, par excellence, an action in concrete meaning, reaching to cause behaviors of the following type: vote or abstention, membership, street demonstrations and so on. This kind of discursive intervention is, by its nature, a recruiter vocation; it is "open", seeking to maintain the adherence of the audience who already shares her choices and values, but he also seeks to conquer the "hesitant" or to cause "changings of mind", seeking to determine the adherence of a larger segment of the population.

We believe that the political discourse maintains and exploits all the features of speech acts:

(1) *contextual determination*, that reveals social, spatial - temporal conditions of enunciation, and peculiarities of the interlocutor to whom the speech is addressed;

(2) the intentionality, which concerns the proper interpretation by the interlocutor of the speaker's intention of communication;

(3) the action dimension, which emphasizes the ability of the political discourse to change the state of the world, to produce changes;

(4) conventionality, which assumes a set of "conditions for success" of discourse in attention, which are conditioned by the circumstances of utterance, the status and intentions of the speakers and alocutionary, but also the effects pursued by utterance.

4. Applications

In our opinion, political discourse can activate all components of any illocutionary forces. To argue in favor of this assertion, we propose the analysis of some reference sequences from political speeches:

(1) "That on the first day of January, in the year of our Lord one thousand eight hundred and sixty-three, all persons held as slaves within any State or designated part of a State, the people whereof shall then be in rebellion against the United States, shall be then, thenceforward, and forever free; and the Executive Government of the United States, including the military and naval authority thereof, will recognize and maintain the freedom of such persons [...] "(Urofsky, 2000, p. 166); we consider that this fragment of "Emancipation Proclamation", stated by Abraham Lincoln in the fall of 1862 has illocutionary force of a *declaration*, since it would cause a profound change in the American social-political reality; the correspondence between propositional content and this reality is achieved within the presidential institution; the state of affairs represented by the propositional content contains the US President's belief that the situation presented is in force, it is true in the universe of the statement; thus we can identify the existence of an assertive commitment in achieving the illocutionary declarative point, with a double adequacy direction: to change the world and to represent the world as changed;

(2) "The nation has startled with pride when it heard what its soldiers have achieved at Bir - Hakeim. The brave and pure children of France have just written, with their blood, one of the most beautiful pages of glory!" (De Gaulle, 1970, p. 73); this fragment reveals an *expressive* illocutionary force, that expresses a psychological satisfaction/pride; the propositional truth content is assumed and there is no adequacy direction; we are able to highlight a strong psychological commitment that requires the political speaker to move from the psychological state of joy to the psychological state of indebtedness;

(3) "*Therefore, instead of making pacts of this kind with your political opponents, pacts which were not even always loyal, you must gain the prestige necessary for free elections, which allowed the country to be true to express its wishes in this Parliament as well.*" (Iorga, 1981, p. 299);

In this speech sequence uttered by Nicolae Iorga it is revealed illocutionary force of the *directive*; the degree of strength of illocutionary goal is expressed through a weak performative, "recommending"; the position of the speaker, a parliament member addressing his peers, does not allow the call to a stronger, prescriptive, performative, as we can see in the following passage: "All Americans should enjoy the privileges of citizenship, regardless of race. And they will receive those privileges of citizenship, regardless of race" (Urofsky, 2000, p. 251); the US President Lyndon B. Johnson, using the moral authority of the presidential institution, performs simultaneously a directive and commissive commitment: the speaker asks an adequacy of the world to the words, assuming also the involvement in fulfilling the future course of action;

(4) "*In our sphere of our attributions we work with all means to unify as soon as possible as possible all the institutions and laws of the United Principalities. We will consider the most scrupulous for that to this major reform we work closely together in understanding with the ministry in Bucharest, as such, increasingly more, the union would become an achieved factor*". (Kogalniceanu, 1967 p. 228)

Mihail Kogălniceanu formulates with the illocutionary force specific to commissive, the commitment of achieving a fundamental political program, involving the commission of future actions; thus committing himself, the political speaker cannot be honest without believing that would keep the agreement; the achievement of the commissive illocutionary point, by taking political efforts of institutional strengthening of the *Principalities*' Union creates, necessarily, a reason for the speaker to perform the promised actions, and sufficient reason for his faith that he will achieve it.

The political discourse as a specific form of communication, takes its essence and it establishes as a force producing meaning, and also reality. Partisan political message conveyed through speech must be repeated constantly, but at the same time, it we must exclude the possibility of the alternative or contradictory messages (Arsith, 2005, p. 238), in order to ensure the sustainability of influence.

5. Conclusions

Through this approach, inspired by the theory of speech acts, we aimed at proving that, by valorification, on the level of discourse, the illocutionary force components at the level of the speech is pointed out as the actional function of the language and, from this perspective, all human reasoning on the facts, decisions, beliefs, opinions and values are no longer regarded as "listening the logic of the Absolute reason, but they are seen in their actual liaison with affective elements, with historical valuations and practical motivations." (Eco, 1982, p. 199)

References

Arsith, M. (2005). *Semiotica discursului politic/Semiotics of political discourse*. Iasi: Editura Stefan Lupaşcu.

Austin, L. (2003). *Cum să faci lucruri cu vorbe/How to do things with words*. Bucharest: ĂParalela 45.

Eco, U. (1982), *Tratat de semiotică generală/Treaty of general semiotics*. Bucharest: Editura Ştiinţifică şi Enciclopedică.

Ricoeur, P. (1999). *De la text la action/From text to action*. Cluj-Napoca: Echinox.

Searle, J.R. (1972). *Les actes de langages/The acts of language*. Paris: Hermann.

Searle & Vanderveken (1985). *Foundations of Illocutionary Logic.* Cambridge: Cambridge University Press.

The corpus of used texts

Gaulle, de, Ch. (1970). *Discours et Messages. Pendant la Guerre (Juin 1940 – Janvier 1946)/Discourse and Messages. During the war (June 1940 – Jan. 1946)*. Paris: Librairie Plon.

Iorga, N. (1981). *Discursuri parlamentare/Parliamentary speeches*. Bucharest: Editura Politică.

Mihail Kogălniceanu (1967). *Texte social-politice alese/Chosen social - Political texts.* Bucharest: Editura Politică.

Urofsky, M.I. (coord.) (2000). *Texte fundamentale ale democraţiei americane/The fundamental texts of the American democracy* Bucharest: Teora.

9

Political Party Funding in Romania - One Step Forward, Two Steps Back?

Iulian Georgel Savenco[1]

Abstract: Within political life, the determining role is given to political parties in their capacity as actors in the electoral campaign and in the race for political power. This is the reason for which we believe that the means of financing political parties and the electoral campaigns in which they partake is an important aspect within the electoral reform, as without an adequate funding their chances of winning the electoral race are drastically reduced. On the other hand, funding of political parties is of great interest as the lack of transparency which usually encircles this process can lead to a dangerous phenomenon, namely corruption. Throughout this article we present the current situation and critically analyze the changes which the Romanian legislature plans to apply to the political party financing law.

Keywords: political party; funding; Romanian Constitution; freedom of association

1 Introduction

Throughout time, myriad of definitions were issued on the term "political party". Currently as we try to define this concept we must start from the idea stipulated in the doctrine (Muraru & Tănăsescu 2013, p.24), namely that "the party is an association, thereby expressing the means of formation (through the exercising of the citizens' right of association) and its composition (it is a grouping of citizens, a collective)". This expression of the citizens' free will to associate themselves in order to form a political party also results from the provisions of the Romanian Constitution[2] that in the art. nr. 40, paragraph 1 states that citizens may freely associate in political parties, trade unions, employers' associations and other forms of association.

In regards the concept of political party we should note that, in a broad sense, the specialized literature (Ionescu, 2008, p.403) believes that the political party is "a permanent group or association of individuals freely inter-united through ideological affinities and common political beliefs, created at

[1] Senior Lecturer, PhD, Faculty of Law, "Danubius" University of Galati, Address: 3 Galati Boulevard, 800654 Galati, Romania, Corresponding author: iuliansavenco@univ-danubius.ro.

[2] Romanian Constitution published in the Romania's Official Monitor, Part I, no. 233 from November 21, 1991, came into effect after its approval through the national referendum of December 8, 1991. Subsequently, it was amended and supplemented by the Law for the revision of the Romanian Constitution, namely Law no. 429/2003, published in the Romania's Official Monitor, Part I, no. 758 from November 29, 2003, republished by the Legislative Council, pursuant to the art. 152 from the Constitution, the terms being updated and the texts renumbered (art. 152 became, in its revised form, art. 156).

the local level based on strict principles of organization and discipline, designed, the stipulations being listed in a program or status, to promote and participate in electoral and parliamentary campaigns with other parties of a particular doctrine or with political views on the development and management of a given society."

In our case we will concur to the view (Dănişor, 2003, p.304) according to which the political party is defined as "a form of structure, initially based on an ideology, which links the state and the civil society, aimed to order and to participate or at least to direct the public power, in the public interest and using constitutional means." The same author states that if the means provided by the constitution are not followed in order to accede to power, we are no longer talking of a political party but of a group which wants to stage a coup.

The legal definition of the political party is given by art. 1 from Law no. 14/2003 of political parties[1]. Thus political parties are considered to be associations of a political nature of Romanian voting citizens, freely participating in the materializing and in the exercising of their free political will, fulfilling a public mission guaranteed by Constitution. We believe that this definition should be supplemented with the provisions of art. 2 of the same law which stipulates that by their activity, political parties promote national interests and values, political pluralism, contribute to the shaping of public opinion, participate with its candidates in elections and to the establishment of public authorities and stimulate the participation of citizens in the polls, according to the effecting legislature.

The main purpose of political parties is totally different from that of other associations and consists in the conquest of power, and the manner in which they can achieve this goal is represented by the electoral process. Following the unfolding of the electoral campaign some parties will come to power, others will find themselves in the opposition. The role of the opposition parties in the political arena should not be minimized because they continue their struggle for power by means of constructive criticism to the parties that hold the majority in the parliament.

Based on the role that the Constitution[2] assigns to political parties or their contribution to the definition and expression of the political will of the citizens we conclude that their presence in the political arena is vital. However, in order to be able to "play" their role in this competition, the political parties need funding.

In the present study we will try to present the changes[3] that the legislator wishes to bring to the political party funding law, amendments explained by the fact that the effective regulations are too permissive, giving political parties the opportunity to obtain funding outside the legal framework.

2 A New Source of Funding

The topic of political party funding is of utmost interest in our country given that, in recent years, the political scene has been afflicted by scandals that had as a starting point the corruption revealed within the process of funding various political parties. Moreover, in the explanatory memorandum to the

---

[1] Political parties Law no. 14 published in the Official Monitor no. 25 from 17.1.2003, republished on Official Monitor no. 347 from 12.05.2014.

[2] Art.8 paragraph 2 from the Constitution of Romania.

[3] The legislative proposal entitled Law for the amendment and the completion of Law no. 334/2006 on the financing of political parties and electoral campaigns was adopted by the Chamber of Deputies on 18.03.2015 and on 25.03.2015 the law was sent for promulgation to the President of Romania - http://www.cdep.ro/pls/proiecte/upl_pck.proiect?idp=13537 accessed on 27.03.2015.

legislative proposal the initiators argued the implementations of the recommendations of the Group for Fighting Corruption (GRECO).

Currently the funding of political parties is regulated by the Law on financing of political parties and electoral campaigns[1] that mention from its beginning (Article 1, paragraph 1) that its purpose is to ensure equal opportunities in political competition and transparency in funding. Likewise, the law states that according to the source, we can talk about two types of funding:

a) public funding - is accomplished by subsidies from the state budget;

b) private funding - its sources of funding are: party membership quotas, donations, legacies and other liberties, income from their own activities (editing, writing publications, organizing meetings and political seminars, economic activities, sports activities, entertainment, domestic service, renting their owned premises for conferences, parliamentary offices, sublease, etc.)

The new proposed amendments provide, among others, a new source of funding for political parties namely borrowing money from natural and legal persons. The loans can be contracted by political parties only through authentic notarial papers, under the penalty of nullity, accompanied by the delivery-receipt documents, in the agreement being provided the manner and due date of their refund. The loans that have a value greater than 100 minimum gross basic salaries per country are subject to the terms of publicity set out in the law. Likewise, lending by political parties, political or electoral alliances and by independent candidates to natural or legal persons is prohibited.

The matter which needs clarifying is whether in this new source of political parties funding - the loan in cash – there will be the possibility to "hide" certain "suspicious" transactions, especially in the absence of a maximum term of loan repayment. Natural or legal persons[2] can lend to a political party stipulating a small interest rate or less than that of the banks as to subsequently acquire certain advantages from that political party. The persons who do not want to give their support for certain parties public can lend them sums of money that have lesser value than 100 minimum gross salaries without having to disclose their name, thus maintaining the lack of transparency. What will happen if a party cannot repay the loan and the related interest given when not all political parties have valuable real estate? What kind of "services" will that party provide in exchange for that debt? The legislator's proposal to amend the legal provisions is seen as beneficial in what concerns the support given to political parties, which require funding, but it is thought that the law's text should be rephrased in order for political parties to be able to receive loans only from Romania's lending institutions[3], with responsibilities in the field and with the condition that the granting of loans should not be made following preferential conditions. Thus the political parties will solve the issue of funding and the suspicions that may arise with crediting of a loan will vanish.

3 Financing the Electoral Campaign from the State's Budget

Another amendment that is intended to be brought to the law of political parties funding refers to the refunding of sums of money spent by the political parties during the electoral campaign. Thus, within 90 days from the date of the elections for the Chamber of Deputies and the Senate, the Permanent

---

[1] Law no 334 from the 17th of July 2006 concerning funding of the political parties' activities and electoral campaigns, republished in the Official Monitor, Part I, no. 510 from 22.07.2010.

[2] The proposed amendments provide that the amounts of money related to the received loans by a political party from a natural person in a year can be up to 200 minimum gross salaries per country and from one judiciary person up to 500 minimum gross salaries per country.

[3] Banks, lending companies, etc.

Electoral Authority must reimburse to political parties, political alliances and national minorities organizations (in accordance with the principle of non-discrimination - see extensively Maftei 2010), based on the documentary evidence provided by the financial agent within 30 days of the election date, the amounts of expenditure incurred in all electoral constituencies, as well as those carried out at the central level in the case that the political party, political alliance, electoral alliance or organization of national minorities obtained at least 3% of the valid votes, cast nationally, for each of the two chambers of Parliament. If at least 3% of the valid votes, cast on a national level, were not obtained, the Permanent Electoral Authority must reimburse those parties, on the basis of the documentary evidence provided by the financial agent, only the amounts of expenditure incurred at the level of the constituency in which at least 3% of the votes cast was obtained.

Currently, political parties are subsidized by the state budget (public financing), according to the law, the amount received by the parties having a limit of 0.04% of the income provided in the state budget. The criteria for granting the subsidy from the state budget are the number of votes received in the parliamentary elections (75% of the annual budget) and the number of votes received in local elections (25% of the annual budget). As seen in the table below the amounts that political parties that are currently subsidized is quite high, the growth not being justified.

Table 1. Total subsidy from the state budget for each political party –March 2015[1]

Criteria no.	Political party	Amount(lei)
1.	Social Democrat Party	164.731,56 164,731.56
2.	National Liberal Party	197,282.80
3.	Conservator Party	16,011.36
4.	National Union for the Progress of Romania	7,532.39
5.	Christian Democrat National Peasants' Party	1,387.34
6.	The People's Party - Dan Diaconescu	69,221.55
TOTAL		**456,167.00**

Based on the above stated we adhere to the opinion (Gilia 2012, p.68) according to which "an exclusive funding from the state budget is extremely costly, especially for a country like Romania that faces multiple financial problems and has trouble in allocating amounts of money in critical areas to the development and the evolution of a nation (e.g. education, health, development, etc.)". Professor Claudia Gilia also notes that there can be stated myriad of tools in electoral laws in order to determine a more rigorous selection of candidates, to prevent electoral bribery, to establish clear rules on principles which should govern any choice, like the eligibility conditions, the organization and development of elections, the electoral disputes, funding and control of electoral campaign accounts all these eventually leading to a clean political class.

Proving that an exclusive funding of electoral campaigns is not necessary we will to show the fundamental role of other sources of funding in the election campaign of the President of Romania, namely the donation.

[1]http://www.roaep.ro/finantare/wp-content/uploads/2015/03/PAGINA-TOTAL-SUBVENTIE-LUNA-MARTIE-2015_SITE1-EX.pdf, accessed on 7.04.2015.

Centralizer for the received and declared donation by political parties, electoral alliances and independent candidates for the presidential election campaign in 2014[1]

ELECTION CAMPAIGN - TOTAL

I.	Political party	Total donations		
		Legal persons	Natural persons	Total
1	Electoral Alliance PSD-UNPR-PC	768,794	2,961,175	**3,729,969**
2.	Christian Liberal National Liberal Party - Liberal Democratic Party Alliance	622,140	3,035,099	**3,657,239**
3.	Popular Movement Party	96,000	721,510	**817,510**
4.	Democratic Union of Hungarians in Romania	0	67,302	**67,302**
5.	The People's Party - Dan Diaconescu`	1,000	17,714	**18,714**
6.	The Socialist Alternative Party	0	0	**0**
7.	Hungarian People's Party of Transylvania	100	19,800	**19,900**
8.	Romanian Green Party	0	0	**0**
9.	PRODEMO Party	0	0	**0**
10.	Great Romania Party	0	4,393	**4,393**
	Total donations for political parties	**1,488,034**	**6,826,992**	**8,315,026**

II.	Independent candidate	Total donations		
		Legal persons	Natural persons	Total
1.	Teodor - Viorel - Meleşcanu	0	164,960	**164,960**
2.	Călin - Constantin - Anton Popescu Tăriceanu	50,300	785,968	**836,268**
3.	Monica - Luisa Macovei	78,892	218,028	**296,920**
4.	Gheorghe Funar	4,400	4,200	**8,600**
Total donations for independent candidates		**133,592**	**1,173,156**	**1,306,748**

As shown in the table above the amounts received as donations by political parties, independent candidates, political and electoral alliances for the presidential electoral campaign in Romania are quite consistent and can relieve the state budget from additional subsidies for political parties. In our case we believe that the exclusive financing of electoral campaigns from the state budget is not the solution, the real solution means creating a set of clear and stable rules and procedures that prevent the apparition of "black money" in election campaigns. For example, maintaining the confidentiality of donations (amounts below 10 minimum gross salaries per country) continues to raise suspicions and leads to criticism about the lack of transparency etc.

4. The Danger of External Funding

Another important aspect of the legislative proposal that must be debated is the amendment of provisions regarding the possibility of funding the electoral campaign from external sources. The current provisions[2] prohibiting funding by natural or legal persons from abroad are still kept, but an

[1] http://www.roaep.ro/finantare/wp-content/uploads/2014/11/21-noiembrie-2014-FINAL.pdf, accessed on 7.04.2015.

[2] Currently the law states that campaign funding by foreign natural or legal persons, be it direct or indirect, is illegal (art. 24 paragraph1). Likewise, accepting donations from other states or foreign organizations as well as from foreign natural or legal persons is prohibited (Article 11 paragraph 1) - Law no 334 / 2006 concerning funding of the political parties' activities and electoral campaigns.

exception is introduced namely that funding from Member States of the European Union citizens, residing in Romania, who hold political party membership to whose electoral campaign they financially contribute, is accepted.

Funds from external sources of the electoral campaigns is a vulnerability of the entire electoral process because if that party wins the elections or is in a position to influence the government the possibility that it will be "constrained" to make some "concessions" (contrary to the national interest) by and to the external sponsors.

We understand the desire of the legislator to amend the law in the spirit of the European Union, but we believe that there are several aspects that remained unclear. According to the proposed amendments donations from citizens of the European Union Member States which meet the conditions relating to residence and party membership are accepted but their mere membership in a European Union Member State is not a sufficient guarantee, they still being citizens of a foreign state.

Likewise, the proposed amendment being unclear, there is a possibility that political parties will be externally funded through donations or through the new source of funding - the loan. Romanian companies can finance electoral campaigns even if foreigners or stateless persons or other foreign firms are amongst their shareholders. In these circumstances we believe that it is necessary that the text of the law should provide in the case of these companies a limitation of foreign participation to 20-30% or a more radical solution, eliminating legal entities with foreign or mixed capital from the list of potential donors or from those who can lend money to political parties. In order to endorse this idea, we mention the recent suspicions aroused by a loan given by a Russian bank to the National Front Party (FN) in France given the fact that the Marine Le Pen (the party's leader) constantly praised Russia's actions in Ukraine and blamed the West for the crisis, the FN Members of the European Parliament voting against an European Parliament resolution condemning Russia[1].

5. Conclusion

The present realities have shown that it is no longer possible to fund political parties solely from quotas paid by party members, multiple sources of funding being required for their activities to function normally. Under these circumstances it is imperative to diversify the sources of funding (public and private) and also to ensure transparency thereof in order to avoid any further suspicions.

The proposed amendments to the law on funding of political parties solves some of the current problems (the so-called "electoral charity" etc. being eliminated), but as was shown throughout this article, it does not eliminate them completely, there still being the possibility that the funding will convert itself into corruption. Funding of election campaigns exclusively from the state budget will not solve the problem of corruption, on the contrary there being the possibility that the subsidies managers will not behave like "good managers" which will lead to corruption and create discontent among the population. Keeping the confidentiality of donations and loans, maintaining law vulnerabilities throughout its content by permitting external funding, allows us to conclude by saying that although the modernization of the law was wanted through the proposed amendments, it was not accomplished. We still need clear provisions that cannot be subjected to interpretations and more transparency in the process of funding of political parties.

---

[1] http://www.hotnews.ro/stiri-international-18652783-frontul-national-partidul-extremist-din-franta-imprumutat-9-milioane-euro-banca-apropiata-kremlin.htm, accessed on 7.04.2015.

6 References

Dănişor, D.C. (2003). *Actorii vieţii politice / The actors of the political life*. Craiova: Sitech.

Gilia, C. (2012). Sisteme de finanţarea ale partidelor politice în dreptul comparat / Financing Systems Of Political Parties In Comparative Law. *Sfera Politicii / The Sphere of Politics*. No. 3 (169), pp. 65-81, at www.ceeol.com.

Ionescu, C. (2008). *Tratat de drept constituţional contemporan / Contemporary constitutional law treaty*. 2nd Ed. Bucharest: C.H. Beck.

Maftei, J. & Coman, V.L. (2010). Principle of Non Discrimination and the Protection of National Minorities in the European Judicial Space. *Agora International Journal of Juridical Sciences*, No. 01, on www.researchgate.net.

Muraru, I. & Tănăsescu, E.S. (2013). *Drept constituţional şi instituţii politice, vol.II / Constitutional Law and Political Institutions, vol.II*. 14th Ed. Bucharest: C.H. Beck.

Legislation

Romanian Constitution published in the Romania's Official Monitor, Part I, no. 233 from November 21, 1991, came into effect after its approval through the national referendum of December 8, 1991. Subsequently, it was amended and supplemented by the Law for the revision of the Romanian Constitution, namely Law no. 429/2003, published in the Romania's Official Monitor, Part I, no. 758 from November 29, 2003, republished by the Legislative Council.

Political parties Law no. 14 published in the Official Monitor no. 25 from 17.1.2003, republished on Official Monitor no. 347 from 12.05.2014.

Law no 334 from the 17th of July 2006 concerning funding of the political parties' activities and electoral campaigns, republished in the Official Monitor, Part I, no. 510 from 22.07.2010.

The legislative proposal entitled Law for the amendment and the completion of Law no. 334/2006 on the financing of political parties and electoral campaigns was adopted by the Chamber of Deputies on 18.03.2015 and on 25.03.2015 the law was sent for promulgation to the President of Romania - http://www.cdep.ro/pls/proiecte/upl_pck.proiect?idp=13537 accessed on 27.03.2015.

10

Considerations on the Improvement of the Legal Framework Necessary for Preventing and Combating Violence against Women in the European Union

Tache Bocanială[1]

Abstract: Violence against women is a common phenomenon in all social layers and in all society, regardless of their stage of development, political stability, culture or religion, with particularly negative consequences. Combating violence against women requires, besides the sanctioning, repressive measures against perpetrators, and also a series of preventive protection measures and services for victims. Reforming the criminal law of Romania, but also a number of regulations adopted by international organizations, especially the European ones, be it European Union or the Council of Europe, attest encouraging legal developments in this area. The conclusions drawn in this paper from the daily practice of judicial bodies, as well as specialized studies highlight the need for improvement and adaptation of specific legislation in order to prevent and combat crime and violence targeting women, highlighting a few directions in this regard.

Keywords: gender violence; domestic violence; reporting acts of violence; law enforcement agencies

1. Introduction

Despite the fact that domestic violence and, in particular, violence against women represents a subject of debate for decades, the international community has failed, so far, to end this form of violence extremely destructive.

Violence and fear of being victimized undoubtedly affect the quality of life of any person. In practice it has been found, however, that different groups, such as women, children and elderly persons, are usually regarded as the favorite targets of violence, as evidenced by statistics and judicial bodies. With regard to scientific interest on the domestic violence phenomenon, especially against women, it did not know the proportion according to its dimension, especially on the need to identify the best ways and means to prevent, control and mitigate its extremely harmful effects. The specialized literature records only a few studies based on prevalence data regarding gender-based violence, and less on procedures and mechanisms of accountability of the perpetrators.

A general definition of violence, as formulated by the World Health Organization, is "the intentional use of physical force, on oneself, to someone else or on a group or community, resulting in physical or psychological trauma."

[1] Senior Lecturer, Faculty of Law, "Danubius" University of Galati, Romania, Address: 3 Galati Boulevard, 800654 Galati, Romania, Corresponding author: tache.bocaniala@univ-danubius.ro.

Violence against women includes crimes that disproportionately affect women, such as sexual assault, rape and "domestic violence", the most frequent cases encountered in the practice as those in which the physical, brutal, violence combined with violence or sexual assault in domestic violence. We can speak of the fact that, most often, in such cases we are dealing with a violation of women's fundamental rights regarding dignity and equality. In fact, female genital mutilation - one of the most brutal forms of gender violence, is still common in different regions of the world, it is recognized internationally as a human rights violation, a form of torture against girls and women and it reflects an inequality deeply rooted between genders.

In the specialized literature, domestic violence is defined as "a threat or production of physical injury, in the past or the present in the cohabitation with a partner. Physical or sexual assault may be accompanied by intimidation and verbal abuse; destruction of personal property of the victim; her forced isolation from the rest of the family or friends or other people who could be a potential aid for the victims, including children; spreading threats and terror around the victim; controlling access to money or personal items, food, means of transportation, telephone and other sources of protection and care that the victim-women could benefit from". (Stark & Flitcraft, 1996)

In turn Directive 2012/29/EU of establishing minimum standards on the rights, support and protection of the victims of crime, gender violence is defined as " the violence directed against a person due to gender, gender identity or his gender expression, or affecting people of a particular gender disproportionately; as it can cause to the victim physical, sexual, emotional and psychological trauma and economic damages and it is understood as a form of discrimination and violation of the victim's fundamental freedoms and it includes violence in close relationships, sexual violence (including rape, sexual assault and harassment), human trafficking, slavery and different forms of harmful practices such as forced marriages, female genital mutilation and the so-called "honor killings".[1]

2. Knowing the Exact Dimensions of Violence Phenomenon against Women

According to Eurobarometer data from 2010, 72.3% is "Domestic violence against women" coordinated by the European Commission, in Europe, one woman out of four is a victim of domestic violence at some point in life. Between 6% and 10% of the female population of Europe are affected by domestic violence within a year.

According to preliminary results of a European survey on violence against women conducted by the Agency for Fundamental Rights[2] in March 2013 it resulted, inter alia, that: four out of five women have not resorted to any services, such as healthcare, social services and support for victims, after the worst incidents of violence of people, other than their partners; women who reached for support have benefited most likely of health care, emphasizing the need to ensure that health professionals can address the needs of the victims of violence; two in five women did not know the law or police initiatives that may protect domestic violence cases and half of them did not know of any law or preventive initiative.

A serious fact that can be established today is that most women who are victims of violence do not report their experiences, neither to police nor any organization supporting victims. Fear, shame,

[1] Directive 2012/29/EU of the European Parliament and of the Council of 25 October 2012 for establishing the minimum standards on the rights, support and protection of victims of crime and replacing Council Framework Decision 2001/220/JHA (OJ L 315, 14.11.2012, p. 57).

[2] Established by Regulation (EC) no. 168/2007 of 15 February 2007 on the establishment of the Agency for Fundamental Rights of the European Union.

partner commitment, hope that the situation will change, keeping the family image are barriers that stand in the way of going to the police or to the judicial bodies. To these are added often a series of pressures from the family, the aggressor and / or children and some community obstacles emphasizing the vulnerability of women such as insecurity, bureaucracy (Savenco, 2011, pp. 103-111), lack of financial resources, poverty and lack of social resources.

Worse is the fact, unacceptable nowadays, as most women do not report violence and do not feel encouraged to do so by law enforcement agencies, often seen as uncaring, which has as consequence the records of official data in the criminal justice system, very few reported cases compared with the actual crime in the area.[1]

Thus, regarding the cases of violence against women, other than domestic, we can speak of a more appropriate and sort of non-discriminatory one, the general perception of women in situations of domestic violence is that the answer of law enforcement agencies is fragmented; each episode of violence is treated as an isolated event, without taking into account its repetitive feature. Moreover, even when the police are asked several times, and the acts of violence worsen, the police's answers often remain inefficient, i.e. fine or warning. In most cases the implementation of these measures is ineffective in that it does not determine the abuser's liability, and often not even the cease or deter further violence or even diminish it.

In reference to the stage of criminal prosecution, in order to ensure criminal liability of the perpetrators, the women victims of various forms of violence are often unable to access the judicial system due to the conditioning of the receipt of complaints and for starting inquiries, having difficulties in obtaining evidence, given its specific environment, usually private, where such acts are usually committed, lack of witnesses or their lack of involvement in supporting the charges. Last but not least it should be mentioned among the obstacles that hinder or sometimes makes it even impossible to precede a trial it is also the difficult access, including monetary costs that must be incurred at the forensic institutions to obtain the medical certificates attesting the injuries or the wounds or their seriousness.

As a result, most women who are victims of violence do not come into contact with the judiciary system and other services that may mitigate the suffered prejudice.

To close a real vicious cycle, previous failures regarding the liability of the aggressor can lead to greater distrust of women victims of violence in the criminal justice system, namely the renunciation to further address the prosecution or courts in such cases.

For the references on the context of reporting by women victims of violence and their registration by the judiciary bodies in order to handle the aggressor's liability, we should add the huge justice gap[2], which we are currently experiencing. Many are lost cases or do not have a proper finality, at different levels of the criminal justice system, with negative consequences especially in terms of proliferation phenomenon on the one hand, but also in terms of the impossibility of dimensioning the judicial, legislative measures for preventing and combating the effectiveness of this phenomenon. Thus, to increase the degree of addressability of victims to law enforcement agencies with responsibilities in the field, but also to reduce this judicial gap, there are necessary obvious changes at all levels, those of

---

[1] Even in Romania the situation is not better in this regard, but it could be pointed out some progress. Thus, for example in 2011, at the level of the General Inspectorate of Romanian Police there were notified by 9.46% more domestic violence offenses compared to 2010, which shows some increase of the public trust in the police.

[2] Justice gap - the difference between the number of offenses recorded and the number of perpetrators who are brought to justice, the key measure of the effectiveness of the criminal justice system and a key indicator of success in reducing crime (The Crown Prosecution Service, UK).

ruling and those of intervention, on individual background (becoming liable the individual) and also for policies and methodologies that govern the criminal justice system.

Basing on a series of statistical data, and for the reasons stated above, they are far from reflecting the reality, as for the practical answers and the level of policies that have as aim combating violence against women, they are not always the most appropriate. This highlights the need for the EU and some Member States and their research institutions to conduct surveys and other research on violence against women in order to cover the lack of comprehensive and comparable data in this field which maintains compared to other areas as employment where most Member States collect data according to gender.

3. The Current European Legal Framework on Violence against Women and its Prospects

Despite the many efforts made so far to ensure a climate of equality between men and women in the public sphere, a more careful analysis on family, the relationships within the family and of couple may further highlight the contrasts and the dysfunctional realities.

The fight against domestic violence is placed under the paradigm of child's fundamental rights and human rights protection, as they are stated and recognized by the UN Convention on the Rights of the Child, the Universal Declaration of Human Rights or the Charter of Fundamental Rights of the European Union.

From the human rights perspective, the family is no longer perceived as a long private domain with patriarchal rules, where the man has absolute power and therefore the family is no longer outside the legal regulations and social control. On the other hand, the legislation currently adopted continues to reflect a series of norms and social structures, which perpetuate the inequalities of power in the society.

Although in the recent decades there have occurred changes at the legislative level, both at national and European level, the phenomenon requires continuous attention in order to achieve the most effective approaches for preventing and combating violence against women, and to achieve that is, on the one hand, the actual material impact of the legislation, by its actual effect brought in the life of women in the situation victims of violence and with what measures and steps of complementary actions must be supplemented in order to achieve this goal.

The Istanbul Convention, adopted by the Council of Europe in 2011[1], is the first regional instrument with compulsory legal force in Europe that comprehensively deals with the many forms of violence against women. It is addressed both domestic violence and other forms of violence against women: physical; psychological, sexual (including rape) violence; sexual harassment; forced marriage; female genital mutilation; abortion and forced sterilization.

Preventing violence, protecting the women victims and prosecution of perpetrators of such violent acts are key points of the Convention. Based on the finding that violence against women has its origins in the inequality between women and men in society, it manifests a perpetuated culture of tolerance and denial, this instrument with a regional character, trying to change the mentality and feelings of individuals, being practically a call to society, especially men and boys, to change their attitude.

[1] Council of Europe Convention on preventing and combating violence against women and domestic violence (Council of Europe Treaty Series - No. 210/2011).

Beyond the direct impact of violence on women victims than on their intimates, children or other relatives, it is also emphasized the harsh economic impact upon society. The annual cost to the EU of gender violence against women was estimated at 228 billion in 2011 (equivalent to 1.8% of the EU GDP), of which 45 billion annually for public and state services and 24 billion EUR to lower the economic output.

According to EU statistics, in 2012, about 13 million women in the EU have been subjected to physical violence which corresponds to a percentage of 7% of women aged between 18 and 74 years in the EU.[1]

Based on these realities, through its main bodies, particularly the Parliament, the Council and the Commission, the European Union has expressed clearly and supported a clear political will to consider women's rights as a priority and to take long-term measures in this field. There are particularly regarded preventing and combating gender violence, the development of a network of institutions and organizations, both governmental and non-governmental to collaborate, in order to aid and assist women victims of violence and not least, achieving a coherent and efficient data collection targeting violence against women that represents a good basis for directing political, legal and administrative efforts in the field.

The rejection by the European Parliament on 12 December 2012 the Commission proposal for a Regulation of the European Parliament and of the Council regarding the European statistics on safety against crime emphasized the need for a new EU legislative proposal that would establish a coherent system for collecting statistics on violence against women in the Member States; the Council in its conclusions of December 2012 called for the improvement of data collection and dissemination of comparable, reliable and regularly updated data on all forms of violence against women, both at national and EU level.[2]

Consequently, by the resolution adopted on 25 February 2014, the European Parliament called on the Commission to present an EU strategy and an action plan to combat all forms of violence against women, as it was set out in the Action Plan 2010 for implementation the Stockholm Programme[3], in order to protect the integrity of women, equality[4], and welfare[5], concretely and effectively in an area of freedom, security and justice, with particular emphasis on prevention, by informing women about their rights and the awareness of men and boys, from an early age to respect the physical and psychological integrity of women. The strategy and action plan must insist on adequate training of staff in police and judicial services, which would take into account the specific nature of gender-based violence and encouraging the Member States to consider supporting victims, for rebuilding their lives and to regain self-confidence, so they would not get back to vulnerability or dependency situations. The strategy should include measures to support children who have witnessed violence and to recognize them as victims. Last but not least, the European Parliament called on the Commission to submit a revised proposal for a Regulation on European statistics on violent crime, including a coherent system of

---

[1] According to Eurostat online database, 186 590 848 women aged between 18 and 74 years living in the EU-28 on 1 January 2013, see: http://epp.eurostat.ec.europa.eu/ portal / page / portal / statistics / search_database (demo_pjan data code, data extracted on 16 August 2013).

[2] European Parliament resolution of 25 February 2014 with recommendations to the Commission on combating violence against women (2013/2004 (INL))

[3] The Stockholm Programme has set the priorities of the European Union (EU) for the area of justice, freedom and security for 2010-2014.

[4] Article 2 of TEU.

[5] Article 3, paragraph (1) of TEU.

collecting statistical data, relevant and comparable information on gender-based violence in the Member States.

4. Elements of Specific Measures regarding Combating Violence against Women in Romania

The general framework for preventing and combating violence against women at national level is legally ensured by the new Criminal Code (NCC) and especially by the Law no. 217/2003 on preventing and combating domestic violence, republished.[1]

Although as the previous legislation, the new Criminal Code of Romania does not regard distinctively the offenses that have as victims the women, we find a breakthrough achieved by the delimitation in the Chapter III of Title I of the Special Part a distinct category of facts under the title "Offenses committed against a family member". According to article 199 of the NCC, the offenses consisting of violent acts committed on a family member are considered as aggravated and sanctioned form, by increasing with a quarter of the maximum for the punishment provided by the law.

In turn, Law no. 217/2003 on preventing and combating domestic violence, republished, establishes since the first article that "Preventing and combating domestic violence are part of an integrated policy for protecting and supporting the family and it represents an important public health problem"[2] and "The Romanian State, through the competent authorities, develops and implements policies and programs aimed at preventing and combating domestic violence and it protects victims of domestic violence."[3]

The many changes, including the emergency procedure[4], the completions and republishing suffered by this legislative act testify the Romanian legislator's concern for improving the regulatory framework in the field, in order to meet the demands of social evolution, but also those imposed by the European standards.

An important addition represents the provisions on the possibility of requesting and obtaining a protection order for the victim of violence, by which the court to decides, provisionally, one or more measures or obligations or prohibitions for the aggressor. This legal institution represents an absolute novelty for the Romanian legal system, as well as for specialized institutions to execute it. Violation of any of the measures ordered by the protection order constitutes the offense of not complying with the judgment and he shall be punished with imprisonment from one month to a year. In case of conviction, he cannot be released on parole.

Pursuant to article 108 of the Constitution of Romania, republished, and article 8, paragraph (5) of Law no. 217/2003 on preventing and combating domestic violence, republished, the Romanian Government approved the National Strategy for preventing and combating domestic violence for the 2013-2017 period and the Operational plan for implementing the National strategy for preventing and combating domestic violence in 2013-2017.[5]

---

[1] Official Monitor, Part I, no. 205 of 24 March 2014.
[2] Article 1, paragraph (2) of Law no. 217/2003 on preventing and combating domestic violence, republished.
[3] Article 1, paragraph (3) of Law no. 217/2003 on preventing and combating domestic violence, republished.
[4] Last update was brought to Government Ordinance no. 6/2015 amending and supplementing Law no. 217/2003 on preventing and combating domestic violence, published in Official Monitor, Part I, no. 78 of January 29, 2015.
[5] Official Monitor, Part I, no. 819 of December 6, 2012.

5. Short Conclusions and Proposals for Measures Limiting the Phenomenon

The impact of violence against women is felt beyond those women who are victims themselves, as it seriously affects in different ways also their families, friends and society as a whole. This requires a critical analysis of how the society and law enforcement agencies respond to this abuse. Therefore, measures are needed to prevent and combat violence against women; there are required services for victims both in the European Union (EU) and at national level.

Stopping violence against a woman can be achieved effectively only through the liability of the actual perpetrator and increasing the victim's confidence that she will be protected and supported in order to reach a safe life.

Given the extent of the violence against women, the European Union context in the field of justice and internal affairs in the future will have to ensure that violence against women is recognized, dealt with and addressed as a serious violation of fundamental rights in the EU positioning on crime and victimization after the offenses.

The legislation should be amended permanently in order to respond to the new form or the newly recognized forms of violence against women, such as stalking for the purpose of harassment or abuse through new technologies such as the internet.

Prostitution may be recognized as a form of violence against women due to its effects on physical and mental health, especially in cases of forced prostitution and trafficking in women for prostitution.

European Union, together with all 28 Member States should urgent the adherence to the Council of Europe Convention on preventing and combating violence against women and domestic violence (Istanbul Convention). Nowadays one can see that this is the most comprehensive regional instrument that deals with violence against women.

All EU Member States should be encouraged and determined to develop specific action plans of action at national level regarding the violence against women, by engaging the civil society actors working with women victims of violence by involving them effectively in developing these strategies and action plans in order to help ensure victims obtain practical results, and also the sustainability of these plans.

The EU policy on employment, education, health and information technology and of communications should address the impact of violence against women in those areas. This should be reflected at the level of Member states in the specific interventions form the political point of view and national action plans in these areas.

A victim-oriented approach and focus on the rights of women victims of violence needs to be strengthened at the level of the EU and Member States by generalizing the recognition of violence "domestic" or " in a couple" as a problem that requires the state's intervention more strongly.

It is striking the need for the EU and the Member States to adopt compulsory rules for data collection on a regular basis, on various forms of violence against women, to compile the answers at policy level and action on site. This process could be supported by Eurostat and its relevant expert groups and it could be used to provide data to specific monitoring bodies of the UN and Council of Europe and the European Institute for Gender Equality between Women and Men.

It is obvious the need for a European Observatory on violence against women and girls, based on the existing institutional structures (the European Institute for Gender Equality EIGE) and under the direction of an EU coordinator for violence against women and girls.[1]

6. Bibliography

Resolution of the European Parliament of 26 November 2009 on eliminating violence against women http://www.europarl.europa.eu.

***(1995). United Nations, The Beijing Declaration and the Platform for Action, *Fourth World Conference on Women*, Beijing, 4-15 September 1995. New York.

The Council of Europe Convention on preventing and combating violence against women and domestic violence (Council of Europe Treaty Series - No. 210/2011).

Recommendation of the Council of Europe No R (2002)5 on the protection of women against violence.

United Nations General Assembly Resolution no. 61/143 on the intensification of efforts in order to eliminate all forms of violence against women of 19 December 2006

Council of Europe Resolution no. R (2007) 1582 "Parliaments united in combating domestic violence against women".

Convention on the Rights of Persons with Disabilities, adopted by the United Nations General Assembly on 26 September 2007.

European Parliament resolution of 26 November 2009 on the elimination of violence against women (2010/C285 E/07).

European Parliament resolution of 5 April 2011 referring to priorities and the structure of an EU policy framework to combat violence against women [2010/2209 (INI)].

Council of Europe Convention on preventing and combating violence against women and domestic violence (Council of Europe Treaty Series - No. 210/2011).

Law 217/2003 on preventing and combating domestic violence, republished in the Official Monitor no. 205 of 24 March 2014.

G.D. 1156/2012 on approving the National Strategy for preventing and combating domestic violence for the period 2013-2017 and the Operational plan for implementing the national strategy for preventing and combating domestic violence for the period 2013-2017, Official Monitor no. 819 of December 6, 2012.

Government Ordinance no. 6/2015 amending and supplementing Law no. 217/2003 on preventing and combating domestic violence, published in Official Monitor, no. 78 of January 29, 2015.

Ogien, Albert. (2002). *Sociologia devianţei/The Sociology of Deviance*. Iasi: Polirom.

Savenco, Iulian (2011). Bureaucracy – Angel or Demon? *Acta Universitatis Danubius. Administratio*, Vol 3, No 1, pp. 103-111.

Stark, Evan, Flitcraft, Anne. (1996). *Women at risk*. New Delhi, London: Sage Publication.

[1] Institutions of this type have proven their particularly usefulness in other "hot" areas such as the European Monitoring Centre on Racism and Xenophobia (OEFRX) or the European Monitoring Centre for Drugs and Drug Addiction (EMCDDA).

11

E-Cohesion – a Simplification Method within European Union Rules

Paul Zai[1], **Cristina Nicoleta Caranica**[2]

Abstract: The e-cohesion is according to European Commission (EC) a set of common rules for simplifying the accountancy and more precise reporting for European structural funds and European investment funds by using the digital technologies and public databases for all exchanges of information between the beneficiaries of projects financed with European funds and audit authorities, intermediate bodies, certifying authorities, managing authorities. The budget allocated for investments of the European Union (EU) for period 2014-2020 is of approximately a trillion Euros for sustainable growth, new jobs and competitiveness, solidarity and cohesion for an important role of EU in world. One of the ten points of reforms related with the cohesion politics refers to e-cohesion. The article outline the EU and Romania regulations prepared for e-cohesion target that is established for all EU countries in 2016. The paper is presenting the main opportunities and limits in the e-cohesion process for the horizon 2014-2020 using as methodology of study the computing and analysis based on the documentation published by EU, Netherlands and Romanian regulators. The study is also presenting the stage of e-cohesion changes reported by Netherlands and Romania.

Keywords: EU member states; sustainable growth; e-cohesion; digital technologies

1. Specific Regulation Related to E-cohesion Rules

The "history" of the process of adopting the e-cohesion into European Union (EU) regulations for the framework 2014-2020 began on 29 June 2011 when the European Commission (EC) presented a proposal for making the EU funding simpler, more transparent and fairer.

On 8 February 2012, the EC launched the Simplification Agenda for the Multiannual Financial Framework (MFF) 2014-2020. The Simplification Agenda was built from two parts of simplification: the reviewed financial regulation and 57 sectorial proposals for specific programs. After consulting with citizens and stakeholders for designing, the programs were released on 1 January 2013. On 26 February 2013 was released the 2nd Simplification Scoreboard. (European Commission, 2013)

By using the digital technologies is considered by EU to reduce amount of work with 11% and to reduce the risks in the process of funding. The applications for e-cohesion are considered to permit the

[1] Senior Lecturer, PhD, University Babes-Bolyai, Romania, Address: 1 Mihail Kogălniceanu Str., Cluj-Napoca 400084, Romania, E-mail: zai@fspac.ro.
[2] PhD Student, Department of Management Information Systems, The University of Economic Studies, Romania, Address: Piața Romană 6, Bucharest 010374, Romania, Corresponding author: cristina.caranica@gmail.com.

interchange of papers only electronically, reducing the burden of the administration costs for the funds beneficiaries. The main challenges for the period 2014-2020 are presented schematically in Appendix 1.

According to the article 125.2.d from the EU regulation no. 1303/2013 is necessary to establish technical specifications for the applications used for registering and storage of data for the operations with European funds in this way to be at disposal for monitoring, evaluation, financial administration, control and audit. Within EU Regulation no. 1303/2013 the minimum requirements on e-Cohesion are:

- Minimum technical requirements: authentication of the sender, data integrity and confidentiality (also according with the EU Directive 1999/93/EC) and the storage must comply with the retention rules (article 140) → E-submission component
- Electronic audit trail (article 122 and 140 and other requirements referring at the document availability) → E-signature component
- 'Only once' submitting of all information using same Operational Program (article 122.3) also it will be assured electronic exchange for post-award processes (article 122.3) and no technical requirements on software platforms and protocols are yet established (article 122.3)→Security web portal (EIPA & ECORYS & PwC, 2014)

An important administrative burden for the period 2007 – 2013 was the administrative cost (for the implementation of the projects financed by EU national and regional), related to projects selection and management of verification (because these are repetitive actions and executed throughout all the period of the projects). (European Commission & SWECO, 2012)

The economic crisis, not yet overcome (according to Janusz Lewandowski, member of EC responsible with the financial and budget programs) has impact into the MFF 2014-2020. The EC considered also other facts to reduce the costs with management and control as complementary to the e-cohesion tools (European Commission & SWECO, 2012):

- Existence of one responsible organism for administration and control (accredited body) and just one authority of accreditation, an annual closing of accounts;
- Ex-ante evaluation of system administration and control: the replacement of the conformity evaluation with a national accreditation together with a proportional revision by the EC;
- Final closure at the end of the programming period with a rolling process for each annual closing of accounts.

The below numbers are presenting the diminishing of the EU budget from MFF for period 2007-2013 to MFF period 2014-2020:

Table 1. Comparison of engagements and payments in billion Euros in 2011 prices for the funding period 2007-2013 vs. 2014-2020

Prices in 2011		2007-2013	2013	2013*7	2014-2020
Commitment appropriations	In billion Euros	993.60	146.40	1,024.80	959.99
	% of GNI	1.12%	1.12%		1.00%
Payment appropriations	In billion Euros	942.80	137.80	964.40	908.40
	% of GNI	1.06%	1.05%		0.95%

Processed data with primary data retrieved from: http://www.fonduri-structurale.ro

For the new period the EU budget allocation is 1025 billion Euros, from which 336 billion is dedicated for the cohesion policies, and 40 billion is facilitating the programs for European connections like information technology projects together with energy projects and cross border projects. (The budget of the Cohesion policy 2014-2020, 2015)

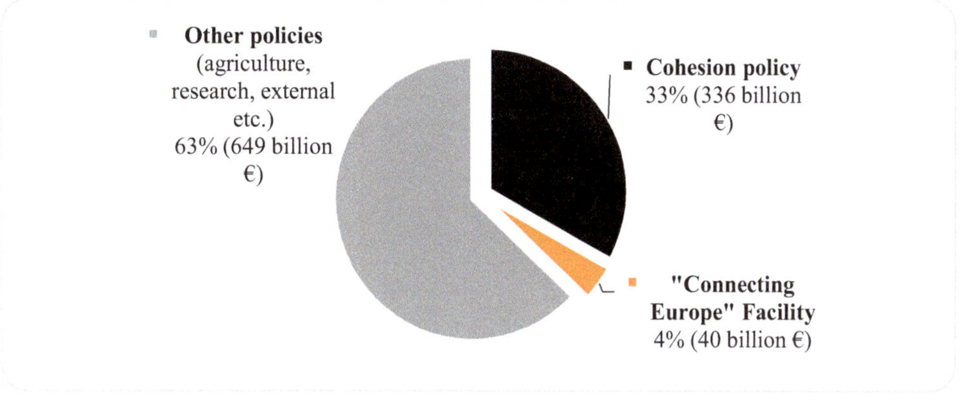

Figure 1. The EU budget allocation by policy for 2014-2020 period

Source: The budget of the Cohesion policy 2014-2020 (2015) retrieved from http://www.fonduri-structurale.ro/detaliu.aspx? eID=10117&t=fs2014-2020

Elements not yet analysed in the design of MFF 2014-2020 budget, which impact the administration cost analysis and the allocation of the budget (European Commission & SWECO, 2012):

- The changes related to the programs proposed for the period 2014-2020 that are different organized than the ones from 2007-2013, this effect was not measured as impact into the new budget;
- Reduction of the functions and responsibilities that overlap in the systems of administration, control and motorization;
- A proportional use of audit according with the risks and operations dimension for reducing the administrative costs;
- Introduction of common plans of action for diminishing the administrative costs through the simplification of financial management

In the Partnership Agreement 2014-2020 signed by Romania with EU (2014) at the point 1172 the „Mechanisms to ensure effective implementation of ESI funds" was presented by the evaluators the importance of using the new technologies in order to obtain: less administrative tasks, easy access of data, quality and security of data, make queries for research of data.

2 Research Methodology

The methodology of the study conducted is represented by the analysis of the documentation and data published by the EU and the two countries regulators, on this topic. The analyzed data was presented using tables and graphics for presentation by comparison of the systems used in the e-cohesion process. The paper aims to present the status of the e-cohesion process for the horizon period 2014-2020, reported until this moment by two EU countries (Netherlands and Romania) taking into consideration the main limits and the opportunities of this process.

3 The E-cohesion Status in Netherlands and Romania – Case Study

The web design of systems used in Romania for the period 2007-2013 according with the Partnership Agreement 2014-2020 signed by Romania with EU (2014) is described in the figure below (applications and functions):

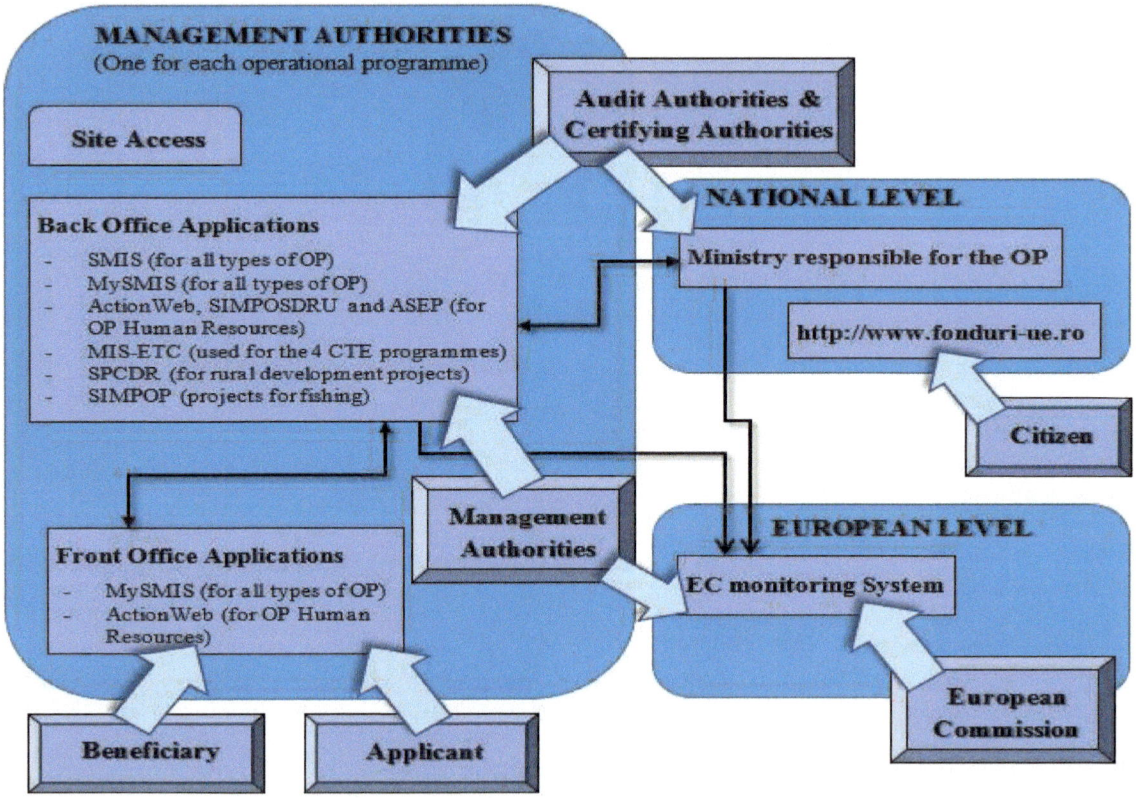

Figure 2. System Overview 2007-2013 for Romanian Operational Programmes

Source: Processed data with primary data from Partnership Agreement 2014-2020 (2015), retrieved from http://www.fonduri-ue.ro/res/filepicker_users/cd25a597fd-62/2014-2020/acord-parteneriat/Partnership_Agreement_2014RO16M8PA001_1_2_ro.pdf

As it can be seen from the above representation SMIS web application and the MySMIS application can be used for all OPs, the last one being also able to ensure the contact with beneficiaries.

In the same figure 2 we can notice that for the period 2007-2013, 6 applications were used for data input and reporting and other 2 applications only for reporting in Romania. The Action Web application and My SMIS application were the front office applications. Taking into consideration the last fact, the Action Web application was the first in being developed in the new period in order to become a useful electronic tool in facilitating the transmitting of electronic information (Annex 2 of the Action Web manual, 2014).

Already in June 2014 Netherlands reported more than 57.000 electronic documents regarding funds administrated by one of the OP's, OP West for a total of 45 GB of data. In the new period (2014-2020) Netherlands will use a more centralized model for inputting and reporting data (see below figure), where all involved parts in the process respectively citizens, beneficiaries, management authorities from each OP, audit authority and certifying authority will have access to the same back office application that will be enquired also by SFC2014 administrated by EU and will have data available from the national authorities such as Chamber of Commerce of Netherlands. (EIPA & ECORYS & PwC, 2014)

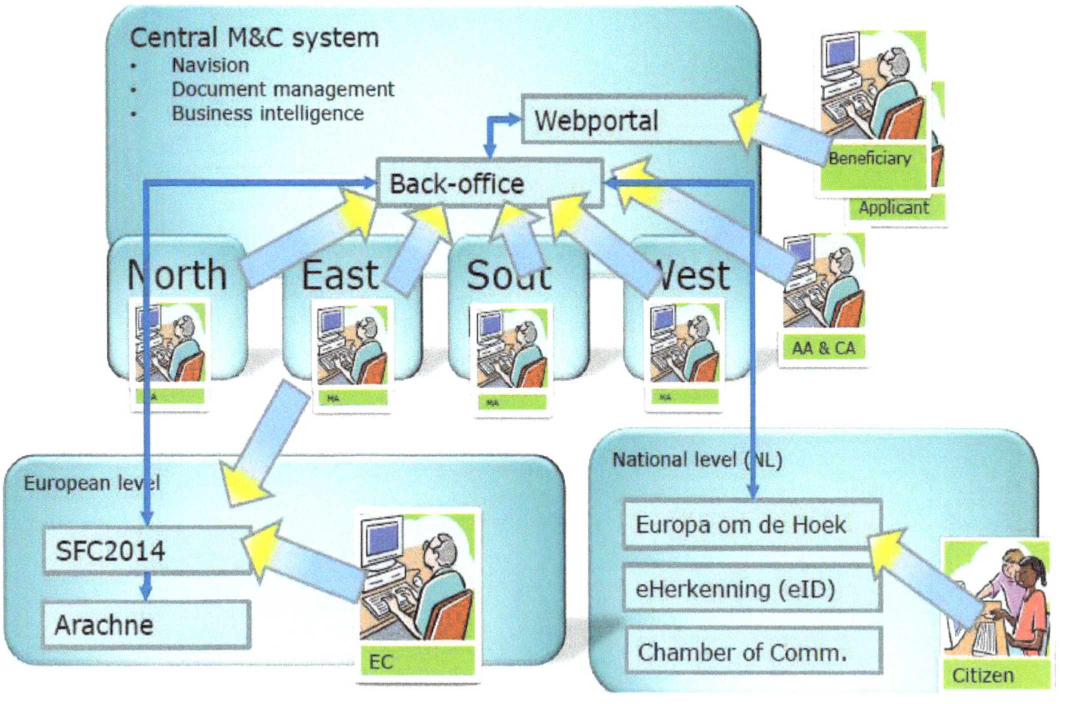

Figure 3. System Overview 2014-2020 for Netherlands Operational Programmes

Source: Fulfilling e-Cohesion requirements, retrieved from http://www.eipa.eu/files/DGREGDay%201-5%20e-cohesion.pdf

For the period 2014-2020 OP West reported the development of a Dutch system for hosting the components of e-cohesion (EIPA & ECORYS & PwC, 2014):

➔ E-submission component : application forms, authentication by login and user, use of Excel file for mass-upload of documents referred to hours spent and invoices, refuse for physical paper documents;

➔ E-signature component: use of national signature;

➔ Security web portal component: to login with user and password, possibility of management of users for the beneficiaries and secure connection with the My-site;

➔ E-storage component: online real-time data, storage of documents in a Document Management System (for different type of document extension), complete digital dossier, no maxim of documents for store, all documents can by accessible for audit reasons;

➔ Only once encoding 2014-2020, it is considered useful the pre-filled html forms, for reports that are using the previous reported data and JavaScript validation and connection with the Commerce Chamber for data regarding beneficiaries;

➔ Interoperability assured by EC monitoring system and MA Control System through xml file exchange.

➔ Audit trail assured by work flows for the MA and need to do, chronological view of the documents, strong authorization in the system.

The Romanian strategy for the next period is to use the MySMIS application for e-cohesion scope and is considered that the Romanian laws regarding the electronic signature, archiving electronic data, data registration on electronic documents and protection of personal data are matching with e-cohesion policy. The users' necessity in Romania is considered to be of predefined reports, functions and data contain (Partnership Agreement 2014-2020 signed by Romania with EU, 2014).

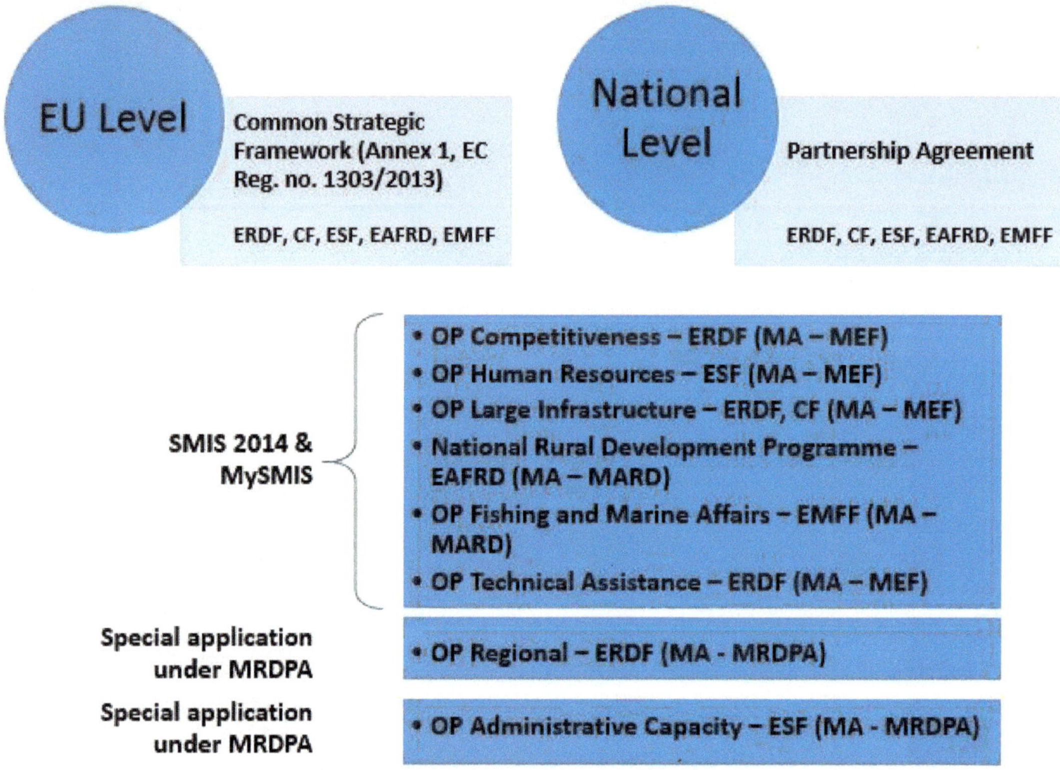

Figure 4. Web applications used for each OP for the period 2014-2020 in Romania

Source: Processed data with primary data from Partnership Agreement 2014-2020 (2015) retrieved from http://www.fonduri-ue.ro/res/filepicker_users/cd25a597fd-62/2014-2020/acord-parteneriat/Partnership_Agreement_2014RO16M8PA001_1_2_ro.pdf

Only two types of applications will be used for 6 of the OPs (SMIS 2014 and MySMIS). The MySMIS application was reported as implemented but not used so the new applications will be tested and implemented for the new OPs. At the national level, MRDPA will develop and implement two special applications for the OP Regional and OP Administrative Capacity, two applications that will be implemented according to new requirements of these two OPs.

The new applications must assure according with the deficiencies reported a simpler process. In this matter we recommend online submission of projects, computerization and simplification in public procurement process, auditing, reimbursement, computerization process of implementation, giving up paper format, use of electronic signatures, creating databases, storing project documents on electronic media with low accessibility and applications use in decision making. Other measures related to automating release or availability of fiscal information of applicants for funding to improve the efficiency of submitting project applications for funding and reducing the administrative burdens and the number of documents to be transmitted, electronic archiving.

Limits and opportunities of the e-cohesion process identified through documentation analysis:

- A broad framework of documentation of the OPs is diminishing the total impact of the e-cohesion policy;

- Frequent changes of the regulation can increase the costs of implementation and to update the applications for e-cohesion;
- Using applications cross-border can diminish the costs of development of the applications for e-cohesion;
- Using the application for a big sector of programs for convergence can diminish the cost reported for each OP;
- The number of the authorities and the control system can influence the costs of the implementation and update;
- The cultural and organizational conditions of each state member can influence the costs of training and familiarization with the applications for e-cohesion.

4. Conclusions and Limits of the Analysis

Increasing the level of the information integration is used for facilitating compliance, monitoring and audit of the projects funded with European funds. The EU requirements must be followed by both EU countries, Romania and Netherlands, as presented in our study.

In case of The Netherlands, the applications already using electronic documentation are mixed into a single system that is subject of additional development.

In Romania, the applications used in the first period after EU adherence (2007-2013) are now analysed and developed in order to comply with the e-cohesion components presented in our study that will be used in period 2014-2020.

The development process for the application using electronic documentation began in Romania in 2014. First documents are available on one of the web applications, but currently the application is under new developments in order to be successfully used for the new period. In case of Romania the applications will be reduced to two systems that will be used for 6 of the most important OPs and other two applications under MDRPA minister for 2 other OPs.

The European countries are now in a process of analysing the past period experience (2007-2013) and making decisions for the new period 2014-2020. Using an application that can diminish the administration costs of the projects for beneficiaries but also for the management authorities is consider to be a powerful tool for impel the funds absorption process.

The article has some limitations regarding the number of the systems of e-cohesion analysed and regarding the period of the analysis as we are referring to one of the further developments of those systems. When more documentation will be available related to the implemented development further analysis is strongly recommended in order to facilitate the understanding of the e-cohesion process strengths.

5. Glossary of Terms and Acronyms

ARACHNE – Operational tool to identify the most risky project

CF – Cohesion Fund

EAFRD – European Agriculture Fund for Rural Development

EHerkenning (eID) – e-Recognition authentication for companies and government

EMFF-European Maritime and Fisheries Funds

Europa om de Hoek – site for publicity

ERDF – European Regional Development Fund

ESI – European Structural and Investment Funds

ESF – European Social Funds

GNI – Gross national income

MA – Management Authority

MARD – Ministry of Agriculture and Rural Development

MEF – Ministry of European Funds

MRDPA – Ministry of Regional Development and Public Administration

Navision – Accounting application

OP – Operational Programme

SFC 2014 – System for Fund Management in the European Union

6. Appendix 1. Key differences between the 2007-2013 and 2014-2020 programming periods (European Parliament & European Council, 2014)

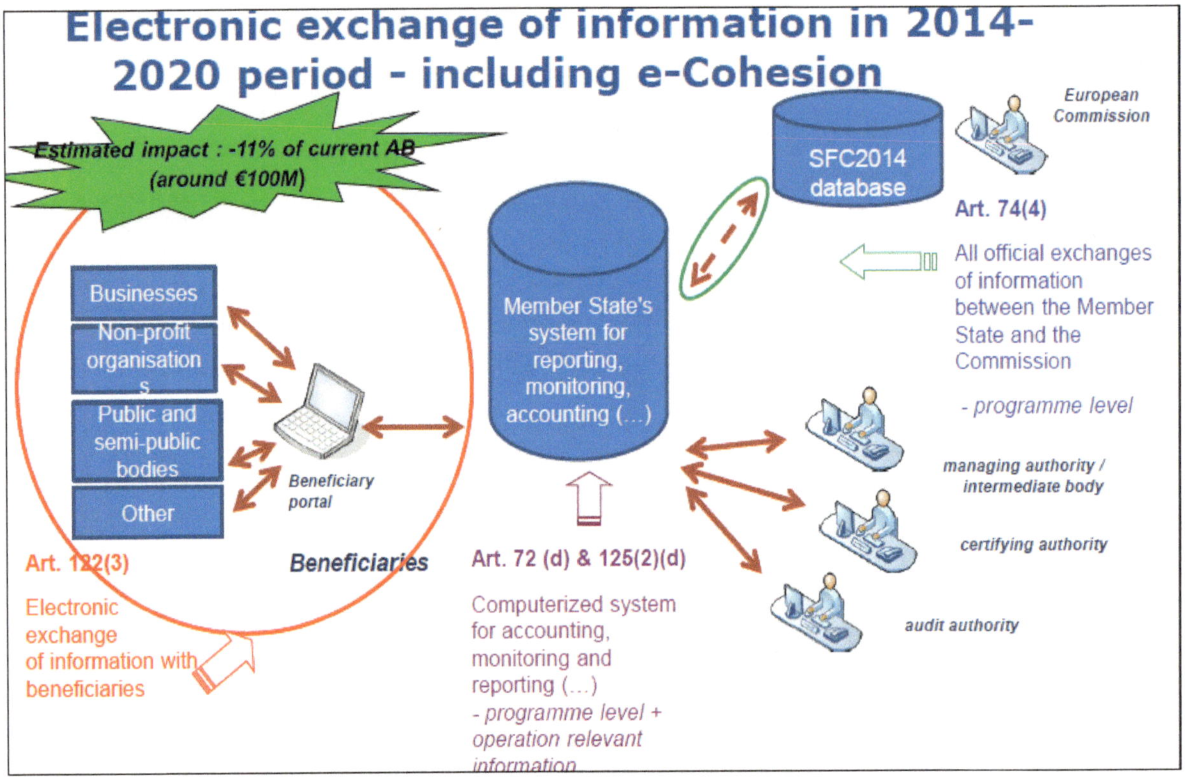

7. Acknowledgement

This work was co-financed from the European Social Fund through Sectorial Operational Programme Human Resources Development 2007-2013, project number POSDRU/159/1.5/S/142115 “Performance and excellence in doctoral and postdoctoral research in Romanian economics science domain”.

8. References

Annex 2 of the Action Web manual. (2014, November 26). Retrieved from fonduri-ue.ro: http://www.fonduri-ue.ro.

EIPA & ECORYS & PwC. (2014). *Fulfilling e-Cohesion requirements.* Retrieved from eipa.eu: http://www.eipa.eu/files/DGREGDay%201-5%20e-cohesion.pdf.

European Commission & SWECO. (2012, July). *Measuring the impact of changing regulatory requirements to administrative cost and administrative burden of managing EU Structural Funds (ERDF and Cohesion Funds).* Retrieved from ec.europa.eu: http://ec.europa.eu/regional_policy/sources/docgener/studies/pdf/measuring/measuring_impact_report.pdf.

European Commission. (2012, February 8). *Simplification Agenda for the Multiannual Financial Framework (MFF) 2014-2020.* Retrieved from ec.europa.eu: http://ec.europa.eu/budget/library/biblio/documents/fin_fwk1420/com_2012_42.5_annex1_en.pdf.

European Commission. (2013, November 19). *Refocusing EU Cohesion Policy for Maximum Impact on Growth and Jobs: The Reform in 10 points.* Retrieved from europa.eu: http://europa.eu/rapid/press-release_MEMO-13-1011_en.htm.

European Commission. (2013, February 26). *Second Simplification Scoreboard for the MFF 2014-2020.* Retrieved from ec.europa.eu: ec.europa.eu/budget/library/biblio/documents/fin_fwk1420/COM_2013_98_en.pdf.

European Parliament & European Council. (2014, March 24). *ESIF Regulations published in OJ 347 of 20 December 2013, version 2.* Retrieved from ec.europa.eu: http://ec.europa.eu/regional_policy/sources/docgener/informat/2014/implementation_ecohesion.pdf.

Partnership Agreement 2014-2020 signed by Romania with EU. (2014, July 22). Retrieved from fonduri-ue.ro: http://www.fonduri-ue.ro/res/filepicker_users/cd25a597fd-62/2014-2020/acord-parteneriat/Partnership_Agreement_2014RO16M8PA001_1_2_ro.pdf.

The budget of the Cohesion policy 2014-2020. (2015, March 1). Retrieved from fonduri-structurale.ro: http://www.fonduri-structurale.ro/detaliu.aspx?eID=10117&t=fs2014-2020.

12

The European Projects in the Support of Albanian's VET

Ermira Sela[1]

Abstract: The main objectives of Albanian society are economic development and integration into the European Union. These aspirations need the acceleration of structural reforms that will allow to Albania to be adapted to modern societies. In this contest, the improvement on the role played by education, especially by VET system, is very important for the economic and social development of the country. Generally, VET is seen as a key factor in the economic growth because he equips people with the skills needed to be protagonists in the labor market. This system in Albania has undergone toward many changes in structure and content, with the aim of improving his approach to the requirements of the labor market. However, to provide a vocational education of high quality it's important to invest more in it, but the Albanian investments in this sector are among the lowest. In these conditions, the partnership with EU offers a great opportunity for the country to develop the VET system. This paper tries to show how has Albania used the opportunities that derive from integration process. The method used is qualitative. In consideration are taken the reports, studies and statistics get into the sector of vocational education.

Keywords: vocational education; unemployment; labor market; European Union

1. Introduction

The development of globalization and changes in technology has transformed the world of work. In order to be competitive in the global market a country needs qualified workforce. So, more and more the emphasis is placed on the importance that human capital has on the economic growth. For these reasons, it is given greater significance to vocational education. He represents a field of education, which includes all those programs that are related to the development of specific skills for work. (Billet, 2011, p. 6). Precisely this is his main purpose the identification of the necessary knowledge, which increases effectiveness in a particular profession. Numerous studies have shown its positive effects. Within the socioeconomic dimension the benefits that vocational education brings to society are associated with: reducing unemployment, improving labor market, improving social cohesion, increasing productivity, improving the quality of life, etc.[2]

VET help in the sustainable youth employment, because in comparison with other education and training systems, is closest to the labor market, something that facilitates the transition of young people at work. So, it is seen as a tool to mitigate youth unemployment, which constitutes one of the main problems of the current societies. The latest data onto the European level indicate that, graduates

---

[1] Student, University of Tirana, Albania, Address: Bulevardi Zogu I, Tiranë, Albania, Corresponding author: ermirasela@hotmail.com.

[2]Cedefop. (2011). Research paper no 10, The benefits of vocational education and training. pg.7 file:///C:/Documents%20and%20Settings/Internet/My%20Documents/Downloads/5510_en.pdf.

from vocational education are more successful in finding a job and better paid than candidates coming from general education[1].

Also, for Albania the reformation of VET system has a great importance for economic growth and social development of the country. However, the system in Albania is problematic and fails to play the proper role in the current developments in the labor market. With the aim of improving it in recent years they have been carried out some changes in its structure and contents. Changes are set to reach some targets; to create a system that will allow young people to gain a basic profession, to provide the possibility for further training and education and also to establish a large and continuous contact with the world of work. To achieve these goals, vocational education should optimally utilize financial, human and infrastructural, resources. In this circumstance, the cooperation with the European Union is a great opportunity to increase the quality offered.

2. Actual Problems of Vocational Education in Albania

Youth unemployment is a concern for Albania. This problem is often associated with unprepared individuals in comparison to the needs of the labor market. Youth (15-29 years old) unemployment rate in 2014 was 32.5%, (35.6% for males and 27.4% for females). Compared to the previous year, youth unemployment rate was increased by 5.3 percentage points[2]. So it is important to develop the labor market with the aim to reduce the unemployment rate.

One of the solutions is to improve vocational education schools, which aim to prepare technicians and skilled workers. But, contrary to the rest of Europe the data show that vocational education in Albania faces many difficulties. This is worrisome if we consider that qualified human resources are indispensable factors to face the challenges of an increasingly competitive world. In fact, Albania's competitiveness in the regional arena is still very low and is based mainly on the factors of production costs. As we said above, the collaboration with the EU is a great opportunity to fill the gaps that VET has, in order to enhance the quality of education and training offered.

The vocational education system in Albania has undergone toward many changes in structure and content, with the aim of improving his approach to the requirements of the labor market. However, it should be noted that it continues to face a number of shortcomings which affect its quality level.

If we make a comparison with other European countries the percentage of students attending vocational schools continues to be very low. The statistics for 2007-2008 show that the percentage of students in secondary vocational schools in Albania were 19% and at European level was 62.7%[3]. Suffice it to recall that for the 2009-2010, students graduated from vocational schools were only 4839 compared with 29 984 students graduated from general schools[4].

Researchers have shown that there are significant differences in the level of infrastructure construction, environment and teaching tools. The quality of specialist teachers remains a problem for many schools. Another problem of vocational education in Albania is the lack of basic criteria in determining student admission. Usually students enrolled in vocational education have very low scores school.

---

[1] Commission Staff Working Document. (2012).*(Vocational education and training for better skills, growth and jobs). pg.2* http://eur-lex.europa.eu/legal-content/EN/TXT/PDF/?uri=CELEX:52012SC0375&from=EN.

[2] INSTAT, http://www.instat.gov.al.

[3]*Strategjia Kombetare e Arsimit Parauniversitar 2009-2013/ National Education Strategy 2009-2013.* http://planipolis.iiep.unesco.org/upload/Albania/Albania-Strategy-Pre-university-2009-2013-alb.pdf.

[4] Source, INSTAT, http://www.instat.gov.al.

About 69% of the students attending VET are boys, with a decrease in the number of girls. In fact, vocational education serves as a very simple way to get access to University for at least 50% of its graduates. In most cases are girls who use VET as a path to higher education, while boys mainly enter the labor market.

Investments in this sector are lower than in other countries. Mostly its financing is done from the state budget for education, while schools, economic activities or business sponsorships are negligible. The majority of the cost of education is taken by primary schools with 61% and vocational education has the lowest with only 5.9% of spending[1]. Most of the vocational education funds are used to pay staff, leaving limited resources for the improvement of work equipment.

And also it should be noted that the fragmentation of the labor market is an obstacle to the development of VET system. The private sector in the country is dominated by the economic activities of small and medium size (99.2%), of which approximately 95.7% of them have from 1 to 9 employees[2]. These businesses are less cooperative with vocational education schools, e.g. about students' practices. This position does not help vocational education to improve the quality of their programs so that they would be important to the labor market. In fact, VET in Albania is not oriented toward labor market demands, 1/3 of his pupils attend programs for which there does not exist a suitable employment market. As stated above, obviously it affects the quality of the labor force in terms of qualifications and skills.

Various surveys of business climate have shown that a significant proportion of firms admit that the lack of a skilled work force constitutes a major obstacle to business development. There are discrepancies between the skills required by businesses and graduate fields of study. For more qualifications there is little or no training, while other courses are followed up and graduates have difficulty finding work. These are the main issues to be resolved.

3. European Assistance on VET

As we noted above, integration into the EU is one of the goals of the Albanian society. In this way, the main achievement has been receiving candidate status in June of 2014. On the whole the process carries a set of criteria and conditions that must be met to become a full member. One of them is to bring Albanian legislation with the EU. Now, this condition is reflected on the new rules of the IPA (Instrument for Pre-Accession) adopted in March 2014.

A new base law is set for financial assistance instruments, in order to make sure that "assistance for pre-accession will be closely linked to the priorities of enlargement, and will be based on a more strategic approach oriented towards results of key reforms in the countries that are candidates for expansion[3]". Their main demand is "decentralized management" or more accurately the full responsibility of the candidate countries for funds management. Another characteristic is that funds can be spent only in areas that have been designated by the EU as appropriate with European accession strategy. The more a candidate country approaches to the membership, the more the focus should be on projects related to areas belonging to the European acquit. Among other things, social

[1] Final Report, (2014). *Baseline Survey of Public VET Providers in Albania.* http://www.sociale.gov.al/files/documents_files/ALB-Report-Survey-Public-VET-Provider_20_06_14_FINAL.pdf.

[2] Source, INSTAT, http://www.instat.gov.al.

[3] Koeth, Wolfgang. (2014). *The new Instrument for Pre-Accession Assistance (IPA II): less accession, more assistance? p. 4,* http://www.eipa.eu/files/repository/product/20140507143645_WorkingPaper_2014_W_01.pdf.

welfare services, vocational education and training and the labor market, are priority areas to be financed by IPA funds.

In the EU-Albania partnership documents are always stated that the Albanian government should improve the education system and create a modern vocational education system. According to the Stabilization and Association Agreement (2009), in the chapter on education and training, is determined that the parties should cooperate in order to raise the level of education and training in Albania, also improve policies on youth employment.

As we have shown in this paper, youth employment is a major challenge for the country. Young people should be helped to be ready for the labor market, possessing the skills required from him. In this way, vocational education is the instrument to face this challenge and partnership with the EU is a great opportunity. The investment in construction and rehabilitation of schools is the first step to transform and improve the structure of VET. At this point, donor projects have had an important role.

Major European projects until 2008 included technical assistance for the reform in the VET system and the reconstruction of vocational schools. During this period the European Union has provided support to complete the legislation of VET and Albanian Qualifications Framework. The Albanian Qualification Framework is fully in line with European framework and giving in this way the possibility of education system in Albania to be compared with most education systems in Europe.

Various European agencies, in particular the European Training Foundation (ETF) has supported initiatives in Albania in VET sector through qualifications, guides for career, support initiatives aimed at developing human resources, etc. While through IPA funds is made possible the reconstruction and rehabilitation of many vocational schools equipped with the necessary infrastructure.

To be mentioned, during 2008 they were reconstructed 5 schools and in 2011 were rehabilitated 3 other schools in Lezha, Fier and Cerik. At a cost of 2.2 million Euros, the goal was to improve learning conditions for the students of these schools. Another IPA project in 2010 has provided technical support for the reform in the vocational education system, particularly in the preparation of national strategy in VET and the strengthening of services provided by the national employment service. This project was implemented with ILO's assistance[1]. The overall IPA support over the period 2007-2013 amounts to over 24 million Euro[2]. Other donors assisting the sector are Germany, Austria, Italy and Switzerland.

For the years 2014-2020 European assistance to Albania will focus on seven priority sectors: democracy and governance; rule of law and fundamental rights; environment; transportation; competition and innovation; education, employment and social policies; agriculture and rural development. Strategy for Albania, confirmed that IPA funds will continue to co-finance projects in strategic sectors and the negotiating chapters of membership. For example; participation in EaSI program (Program for Employment and Social Innovation) – will support government initiatives and strategies to modernize the labor market and social security, to increase the proportion of employment and social inclusion, in particular for the younger generation.

---

[1] European Commission, (2012). *National Programme for Albania under the IPA - Transition Assistance and Institution Building component for the year 2011.* http://ec.europa.eu/enlargement/pdf/albania/ipa/2011/1_en_annexe_part1_v3.pdf.

[2] Instrument for Pre-Accession Assistance (IPA II) (Indicative Strategy Paper for Albania 2014-2020). http://ec.europa.eu/enlargement/pdf/key_documents/2014/20140919-csp-albania.pdf, p. 30.

The effective implementation of European programs is provided through service contracts, TAIEX or may be implemented in combination with other donors' funding[1]. The aim is to support the management capacities of Albanian institutions in order to benefit as much as possible from European initiatives.

4. Conclusions

Albania's aspiration to be part of the European family is generally based on the approximation approach to European standards; one of the most important aspects is the education. To be developed economically, to be competitive and to attract foreign investment, Albania needs a population equipped with the knowledge and skills required by the labor market. The Reformation of the vocational education system has a huge impact on economic growth and social development of the country. However, from the above, the VET system in Albania continues to be problematic.

It should be noted that VET schools do not offer an attractive environment to the students because they do not possess the necessary resources both material and human. In the vocational schools are mainly enrolled students who have not been enrolled in other high schools, as a result the quality of this sector is weak. The lack of qualified teacher and administrators has negatively affected the quality of VET. Financial dependency, has become an obstacle for proper implementation of professional practices. The relationship between vocational schools and the business is weak, etc.

Researches done in this area show that the VET system needs changes to increase its quality. This requires close cooperation between the various levels of the education system and society. Objectives are clear: we need to invest in human resources, improving vocational policies, investing in construction and rehabilitation of schools, etc. In this context, cooperation with the European Union is an important factor for the development of rapid and sustainable VET.

As we said above, despite the progress made, the challenges in this sector are numerous. In order to improve access and quality of education and training for young people is necessary that the objectives set in VET system must be linked with economic and regional development goals.

In this work we have tried to show what Albania has benefited from European investments in this sector. We have made a brief description of the main European projects, but obviously this paper is not exhaustive. Other works are needed to be carried out in order to assess the results achieved and recognize other issues that require solutions.

5. References

Commission Staff Working Document. (2012). *Vocational education and training for better skills, growth and jobs.* http://eur-lex.europa.eu/legal-content/EN/TXT/PDF/?uri=CELEX:52012SC0375&from=EN.

Instrument for Pre-Accession Assistance (IPA) /Multi-annual Indicative Planning Document 2011-2013. http://ec.europa.eu/enlargement/pdf/mipd_albania_2011_2013_en.pdf.

European Commission, (2012). *National Programme for Albania under the IPA - Transition Assistance and Institution Building component for the year 2011.* http://ec.europa.eu/enlargement/pdf/albania/ipa/2011/1_en_annexe_part1_v3.pdf.

Strategjia Kombetare e Arsimit Parauniversitar 2009-2013/National Education Strategy 2009-2013. http://planipolis.iiep.unesco.org/upload/Albania/Albania-Strategy-Pre-university-2009-2013-alb.pdf.

[1] Instrument for Pre-Accession Assistance (IPA II), (Indicative Strategy Paper for Albania 2014-2020). http://ec.europa.eu/enlargement/pdf/key_documents/2014/20140919-csp-albania.pdf, p. 31.

http://www.instat.gov.al.

Cedefop. (2011). Research paper no 10 *The benefits of vocational education and training.* file:///C:/Documents%20and%20Settings/Internet/My%20Documents/Downloads/5510_en.pdf.

Billet, S. (2011). *Vocational Education; purposes, traditions and prospects.* Publisher Springer.

Final Report (2014). *Baseline Survey of Public VET Providers in Albania.* http://www.sociale.gov.al/files/documents_files/ALB-Report-Survey-Public-VET-Provider_20_06_14_FINAL.pdf.

Koeth, W. (2014). *The new Instrument for Pre-Accession Assistance (IPA II): less accession, more assistance?* http://www.eipa.eu/files/repository/product/20140507143645_WorkingPaper_2014_W_01.pdf.

Stabilization and Association Agreement (2009). http://ec.europa.eu/enlargement/pdf/albania/st08164.06_en.pdf.

Instrument for Pre-Accession Assistance, (Indicative Strategy Paper for Albania 2014-2020). (2014). http://ec.europa.eu/enlargement/pdf/key_documents/2014/20140919-csp-albania.pdf.

13

The Briand Plan of European Union Commented by the Interwar Romanian Press

Fanel Teodorascu[1]

Abstract: With each passing day, the construction called the European Union presents increasingly clear signs of disease. Something is not working and it is likely not to work anymore. For this reason, more and more resounding voices announce the decline of Europe. The Greek crisis, the Ukrainian crisis, the refugee crisis are just some of the issues that shows that countries that make up the European family (28 countries) find it difficult to act as a whole. After the completion of the Second World War, Romania did not matter in any way in achieving the European family plans, entering in the sphere of influence of the Soviet Union. Things were not always this way. The plans for a federal state comprising the European countries have existed before the interwar period, as we shall see below. The years between the two world wars were marked by political debates on this theme, which have not been seen before.

Keywords: federalization; speech; press; crisis; European Union

1. Introduction

In Romania, the interest for this topic was as high as in any other European country that emerged from war with some territorial gains and unwilling outbreak of a new world cataclysm. It is understood that the Romanian state people have addressed the issue of uniting the European states into speeches both at home and abroad. What interests us, however, is how the theme "federalization of Europe" was analyzed in the interwar media.

European Union as it stands today has as its starting point year 1951, when it was created the European Community of Coal and Steel (ECSC). Until reaching to this point, the European political leaders had to go through a long and arduous path. Among those who supported the idea of a united Europe was the French statesman Aristide Briand. His plan was, however, considered by some authors as being inaccurate. (Judt, 2000, pp. 136-139)

Despite this "defect" of the thought plan of Aristide Briand, the Romanian journalists, more or less skilled in such matters, reacted promptly to the idea of the emergence of a political construction that is able to guarantee peace in Europe. Many claimed the idea of building a European federal state, showing that this is the only way it can be achieved an economic balance between the European countries. There were, of course, and challengers of the idea that, at that time, that the federalization of

[1] Senior Lecturer, PhD, Faculty of Communication and International Relations, Danubius University of Galati, Romania, Address: 3 Galati Blvd., Galati 800654, Romania, Corresponding author: teodorascu.fanel@univ- danubius.ro

Europe could be achieved. The theme of federalization Europe was not debated only in the Bucharest press. Provincial newspapers, more or less important, reserved gencrous space for this issue.

2. Economic and Moral "Federalization"

In June 1930 in the pages of the Sibiu publication *Revista economică/The Economic Review* it was published, signed by Dem. I. Georgescu, a consistent article about the need to reorganize Europe. According to the mentioned author in order to achieve a federal state encompassing all European countries it was necessary to act in two directions: one economic and the other moral. Creating the Federal European Union would have solved two major issues: strengthening worldwide the economic position held by Europeans and eliminating the fears regarding the possibility of an outbreak of a new World War:

"*The key word in the current political and economic state Europe is Union in order to live and prosper in the common interest. The dictum "unity is strength" has never been more proper than now. The "Federalization of the European States" will bring to the whole Europe the much needed peace and a real improvement in the international economic life.*" (Georgescu, 1930, pp. 219-221)

Regarding the *political union*, it "*will be achieved only if needed and only after the people will be convinced of the benefits it will have the economic, moral, social, intellectual, etc. union.*" The outcome of Aristide Briand's action was everything but what the author hoped in the above text. The European states have failed to find the way of fulfillment of the federalization plan of Europe, and the biggest fear of the European political leaders of good faith was the outbreak of a new World War, which later would have become reality.

3. The Need to Achieve an Economic Balance between the European States

In November 1930, the *Revue Economique Internationale/The International Economic Journal* published a study of Mihail Manoilescu, the Minister of Industry and Commerce at the time. The text will be duplicated, a month later, in the newspaper *Adevarul/The Truth*. From the mentioned study, we will highlight only two fragments, the most conclusive ones, in our opinion. In the first passage, Manoilescu talks about the need to achieve economic balance between the European states. Without this economic balance, the same author stated, the European civilization itself was in danger of extinction:

"*It was discussed a lot before the war, the European balance, but in a strictly political sense. It was then a continental interior balance between the various political powers of Europe.*

Quite to the contrary of what the European balance means today. It is about an economic balance and not an interior balance, but also the equilibrium determining the Europe's position towards other continents and which keep Europe in its current situation.

What is, in truth, the current situation of Europe?

Today, Europe is a high placed and the major problem for it is to keep its position, of not to going down and, if I may use a more serious expression, not to collapse.

Facing this hypothesis, the question arises: is there truly a danger for Europe?

Is Europe threatened? The civilization which we represent is on the verge of a true catastrophe? (as in the day that Europe's economic superiority would not be able to maintain, its political supremacy would be in danger)." (Manoilescu, 1930, p. 3)

In support of his statements, Manoilescu comes with the following arguments:

"*In China, for example, the productivity of today is only about 250 Swiss francs per worker, per year.*

If so, if it would start today to introduce new industries in China, those industries, even working with the lowest output possible, it would achieve a much higher productivity, therefore the purchasing power of part of the Chinese population would increase.

What force could prevent this irrepressible trend? Even if the coercion could no longer continue its course. And on behalf of what principle could such a development be prevented?

Our conclusion is that the danger which Europe is going through is not transient. Deep causes lead to a sustainable economic development.

A new adaptation will be necessary for Europe to retain still a predominant position in mankind." (Manoilescu, 1930, p. 4)

Details of the difficult situation, in which the strong economies of Europe were in, were presented by Costin Stoicescu at a conference organized on 14 February 1932 by the Romanian Social Institute (ISR). The text of the lecture was then published in the *Arhiva pentru știință și reformă socială/ The Archive for science and social reform,* ISR publication. We will mention only a short excerpt of which it can be detected, despite the optimism displayed by the author, the bleak atmosphere that reigned over Europe:

"*The sinister predictions of some philosophers and others who, if they are not philosophers, are bad croakers, predictions that the organization of today's world is about to end, we expect a new state of things, where people will not never want to live better, they will not want to make progress, they will not want to feel the satisfaction of their work, these predictions prove to be unfounded. The mankind's response to these predictions was at a time when the issue was put forward, the answer of the wholesome reason: we continue to work, we continue to produce, we continue to progress.*" (Stoicescu, 1932, p. 53)

Another very interesting text on the need to complete the Aristide Briand's project can be read in the publication *Chemarea Tinerimii Române/The Call of the Romanian Youth*. In this article, however, the author states that the plan of the French state man has never had a real chance of success:

"*There are many arguments advocating for the European Federation. However the project of Mr. Briand - commented live - has little chance to succeed. Predicting results on the matter is risky. However, having a general opinion of the world press, you reach involuntary to pessimistic results.*" (Vasiu, 1930, p. 3)

A categorical position of the chances of success of the plan for federalization of Europe we find on another interwar journalist.

4. The Federalization of Europe - a Great Deception

Pamfil Șeicaru analyzed in several articles in *Cuvântul/The Word* and *Curentul/The Current* the plan of Europe's federalization launched by Aristide Briand, statesman, that some journalists claimed that he was the opposite of Benito Mussolini, the one who with his speeches feed the fears of the outbreak of a new World War. The Press influential man did not believe possible the Briand's project. In his opinion, Eastern Europe has always been ignored by the Western Europe, Westerners seeing the Eastern Europeans just good to be "*cannon fodder*". In the article titled "Patria europeană/European Homeland", the text of which was published in the period that interests us, Şeicaru argued that the failure of European statesmen to create a genuine relationship of equality between big states and small states make it impossible to achieve a *European federal state*. (Şeicaru 1929, p. 1)

In another article, "The federalization of Europe?", in May 1930, Pamfil Şeicaru showed that the project of Aristide Briand, who was only a new *comforting deception*", was intended to replace *the lost illusion of the League of Nations*. Şeicaru believed that the federalization of the old continent was possible only if it was previously achieved a *rationalization of Europe's economy*. This reorganization of Europe's economy implied that the *industrial countries* would fund the *agricultural countries* and would impose high customs duties on agricultural products from the two Americas and Australia.

In December 1930 Şeicaru showed his support for the project by Iuliu Maniu for setting up a Central - European Confederation. The Romanian statesman had made known his project in the newspaper *Neue Freie Presse* from Vienna. Maniu considered at that time, that *the integration process towards a major economic unification* could be achieved only by creating a *Central - European Confederation*. This union of states was to include the following countries: Poland, Czechoslovakia, Austria, Yugoslavia, Hungary, Bulgaria, Greece and Romania.

The idea of this confederation is the source of unfulfilled expectations of Romania to receive attention from France, which was admired and it was considered a friendly country.

The failure of Briand's approach to achieve a state building in which the European countries would stop fighting each other is announced by Şeicaru in the article "Himera egalităţii popoarelor/the illusion of equal nations." The text refers to the failure of the League of Nations and it is interesting to follow as the author brings solid arguments against those who believed that a principle as that of equal peoples could underlie a political, economic or moral construction, involving all European states. (Şeicaru, 1932, p. 1)

5. The Danger of Extinction of the European Culture

On 1st June 1930 in order to mark the end of the cycle of the conference entitled "The Contemporary social and political experience", which was organized by the Romanian Social Institute in the period 1929-1930, Dimitrie Gusti had a lecture based on the issue of European states federation. From the text of the lecture, which we will render only a fragment, would appear in the newspaper *Arhiva pentru ştiinţă şi reformă socială/The archive for social science and reform*. In his lecture, Dimitrie Gusti seeks to answer to some questions that disturbed both ordinary citizens and Romanian statesmen[1]:

"*Europe is a rational and activist idea, culminating in the scientific creations and technical applications, which dominate and absorb other human cultures.*

[1] *Is there a crisis of the European culture? From an economic perspective, can Europe compete with other continents? Is it possible the union of European states? How real is the danger of an outbreak of another world war?*

Some talk persistently about a crisis of the European culture. [...] Let's not exaggerate! When there is a science and a European Technique, which are nor the leaders of all mankind's destiny, one cannot speak of a crisis of the European culture.

But the phenomenon of Europe is interested from another point of view. Europe begins to doubt of itself; its worldwide hegemony is discussed and questioned; for the first time, the other continents are put before it as rivals.

American expansion, the awakening of the yellow race peoples, the evolution of Islamic nations towards a more active conception of the public life are reasons that impose severely in the European conscience. For Europe it is not only in danger of losing its supremacy in the world, but something more precious, its very independence!

[...] Europe is to buy! This is the economic situation.

But to the economic considerations it is added to the political situation, worse yet! Let us not delude ourselves. In Europe, as it is established today, a new war appears as something possible, nay, sometimes even as inevitable.

[...] So here it is the great peril: Europe impoverished, the vassal Europe, the barbaric Europe.

What is to be the salvation from this awkward situation that designs painful perspectives? In order to answer, we should see once again what may be causing this situation?

All European states are ill. The disease consists of their isolation. Saving them would necessarily and logically imply their union.

The union of European states is therefore necessary; but is it really possible?" (Gusti, 1930, pp. 2-7)

6. Conclusion

As soon as the European Union (EU) emerged, many would say that this last question of Gusti has found its answer. Today, however, things do not seem as certain. In the recent years, some states, through their representatives, have spoken increasingly about their intention to leave the *European family*. Also, the pressure waves of refugees from countries in conflict weaken more visibly the already fragile cohesion of the Member States of the European Union.

7. References

Judt, T. (2000). *Europa iluziilor/The illusions' Europe*. Iasi: Polirom.

Duca, I.G. (1910). Cronica externă – Politica d-lui Briand/Foreign Chronicle – The policy of Mr. Briand. *Viața Românească/The Romanian life*, year V, no. 6.

Georgescu, Dem. I. (1930). Federalizarea economică a statelor europene/Economic federalization of the European states. *Revista economică/Economic Review*, year XXXII, no. 26.

Gusti, D. (1930). Problema federației statelor europene. The problem of the European states federation. *Arhiva pentru știință și reformă socială/Archive for social science and reform*, year IX, numbers 1-3.

Manoilescu, M. (1930). Echilibrul economic european/European economic balance. *Adevărul/ The Truth*, year 43, no. 14411.

Marcu, A. (1936). Statele Unite ale Europei în programul lui Carlo Cattaneo (1801-1869)/The United States of Europe in the program of Carlo Cattaneo (1801-1869). *Arhiva pentru știință și reformă socială/Archive for social science and reform*, year XIV, Volume II.

Stoicescu, C. (1932). Politica Institutului de Emisiune al României în Epoca Depresiunii Mondiale/The Policy of the Institute of Romania's Emission in World Depression Era. *Arhiva pentru știință și reformă socială/Archive for social science and reform*, year X, no. 1-4.

Şeicaru, P. (1929). Patria europeană/European homeland. *Curentul/The Current*, year II, no. 583.

Şeicaru, P. (1930). Confederaţia Central Europeană/The European Central Confederation. *Curentul/The Current* year III, no. 1055.

Şeicaru, P. (1930). Federalizarea Europei?/The federalization of Europe? *Curentul/The Current,* year III, no. 842.

Şeicaru, P. (1932). Himera egalităţii popoarelor/ The Illusion of equal peoples. *Curentul/The Current*, year V, no. 1756.

Vasiu, A. (1930). Memoriul d-lui Briand. Un progres al pacifismului/Mr. Briand's memorandum. A progress of pacifism. *Chemarea Tinerimii Române/The Call of Romanian Youth*, year V, no. 24.

14

The Cournot Equilibrium for n Firms

Gina Ioan[1], **Catalin Angelo Ioan**[2]

Abstract: Oligopoly is a market situation where there are a small number of bidders (at least two) of a good non-substituent and a sufficient number of consumers. The paper analyses the Cournot equilibrium in both cases where each firm assumes the role of leadership and after when firms act simultaneously on market. There are obtained the equilibrium productions, maximum profits and sales price.

Keywords: oligopoly, Cournot, equilibrium

1 Introduction

For Homo Oeconomicus (the abstract concept around which Adam Smith builds scientific edifice), the ultimate goal is to achieve a maximum level of utility or profit with a minimum of effort. Regardless of the time, circumstances, or players, maximizing the effects can only get in a perfectly competitive scene, where responsibility of a efficient allocation of resources in a market have income, prices and profits, guided by an "invisible hand" or the freedom to choose.

In this scene, in which resists the strongest stands up to and where competition leads to efficiency and progress, the rules are quite tough, based both on their own actions and the anticipate the actions of other players.. The game, in its dynamics may be perceived as uninteresting to the player on stage (because he seeks only purpose), but it can also be interesting for the same player who withdraws from the scene and analyze it from the perspective of the researcher economist.

Depending on the number, the economic power of economic agents (either producers or consumers), the price elasticity of demand, the degree of mobility of factors of production, the market can be divided into: perfectly competitive market, a model more theoretical and imperfect competitive market where we meet market monopoly, monopolistic competition market and oligopolistic market, the latter manifesting the actual scene of the market economy.

When we refer to a perfectly competitive market, the price can not be influenced, it is resulting from the free play of supply and demand, the manufacturer aiming to maximize the production or cost minimization knowing the identity $R_{mg}=C_{mg}=price$ maximizes profit. If we discuss monopolistic

[1] Assistant professor, PhD, "Danubius" University of Galati, Romania, Address: 3 Galati Boulevard, 800654 Galati, Romania, E-mail: ginaioan@univ-danubius.ro.
[2] Associate Professor, PhD, "Danubius" University of Galati, Romania, Address: 3 Galati Boulevard, 800654 Galati, Romania, Corresponding author: catalin_angelo_ioan@univ-danubius.ro.

competition market, the monopolist is protected by barriers (natural and legal) to the entry of competitors on the market, and he can maximize profits at a price determined by him.

Regarding oligopolistic market (duopoly) uncooperative, the question which is also subject to this scientific approach is how does oligopolistic / duopolistic to maximize profit knowing that its decision-making strategy depends on the behavior of other players, meaning a strategic interaction occurs.
To answer the question above, we report on game theory, Cournot equilibrium and Nash equilibrium.

Elements of game theory provides us the tools required to formulate, analyze, structure and understand the scenarios arising from strategic interaction.

A major contribution to game theory had John Nash, whose research is based on the absence of cooperation assuming that each player acts independently without cooperation with other players.

Nash equilibrium is a holistic strategy and involves two or more players in which it is assumed that each of them predicts the equilibrium strategy of the other players and no player wins nothing by changing their strategy. Games can be with unique and optimal Nash equilibrium and also may be games that allowed several Nash equilibria.

Cournot duopoly is characterized by symmetric role of companies, each agreeing to have the same role in the market. The profit of each firm depends on the amount produced by the other company. The set of options is optimal and it is the Cournot equilibrium occurs when maximizing profits for a given level of production of competitor player. In this reaserch it is studied the delay Cournot duopoly and dynamical behaviors of the game. The decision taken by a player at *t+1* moment depends on the decision taken by the other player at *t* moment, this making decisions more relevant.

2 The Cournot Equilibrium for Oligopoly

Let consider, for the beginning m firms F_i, $i=\overline{1,m}$ with price function: $p(Q)=a-bQ$, $a,b>0$ and the total cost of production being $TC_i=\alpha_i Q$, $i=\overline{1,m}$.

We assume that each firm assumes, successive a leading role. Consider therefore the reaction function of the company F_i to the others at a moment t:

$$Q_{i,t}=f_i\left(Q_{1,t-1},\ldots,\hat{Q}_{i,t-1},\ldots,Q_{m,t-1}\right)\ \forall t\geq 1,\ i=\overline{1,m}$$

where ^ means that the term missing.

If $\exists \lim\limits_{t\to\infty} Q_{i,t}=Q_i^*$ $\forall i=\overline{1,m}$ we shall say that the vector in $\mathbf{R}^m$: $\left(Q_1^*,\ldots,Q_m^*\right)$ is a Cournot equilibrium.

We ask ourselves whether this equilibrium exists, and if so, which yields the equilibrium productions of the m firms.

Considering a fixed time t+1, the selling price of the products of a company F_i, which assumes a leadership role is determined both by its production at this moment, as well as other production companies at the previous time t when the company F_i has informations about the competitors.

Therefore, the selling price will be:

$$p\left(\sum_{\substack{k=1\\k\neq i}}^{m} Q_{k,t} + Q_{i,t+1}\right) = a - b\sum_{\substack{k=1\\k\neq i}}^{m} Q_{k,t} - bQ_{i,t+1}$$

At time t+1, the F_i firm's profit is, for a quantity $Q_{i,t+1}$:

$$\Pi_{i,t+1} = p\left(\sum_{\substack{k=1\\k\neq i}}^{m} Q_{k,t} + Q_{i,t+1}\right)Q_{i,t+1} - TC_{i,t+1} = \left(a - b\sum_{\substack{k=1\\k\neq i}}^{m} Q_{k,t} - bQ_{i,t+1}\right)Q_{i,t+1} - \alpha_i Q_{i,t+1} \text{ from where:}$$

$$\Pi_{i,t+1} = -bQ_{i,t+1}^2 + \left(a - b\sum_{\substack{k=1\\k\neq i}}^{m} Q_{k,t} - \alpha_i\right)Q_{i,t+1}$$

The maximization of the F_i's profit at time t+1 returns to the cancellation of partial derivative of profit with respect to its production at that time, so: $\frac{\partial \Pi_{i,t+1}}{\partial Q_{i,t+1}} = -2bQ_{i,t+1} + \left(a - b\sum_{\substack{k=1\\k\neq i}}^{m} Q_{k,t} - \alpha_i\right) = 0$ from where:

$$Q_{i,t+1} = \frac{a-\alpha_i}{2b} - \frac{1}{2}\sum_{\substack{k=1\\k\neq i}}^{m} Q_{k,t},\ i=\overline{1,m}$$

In a matricial expression the above relations can be written as:

$$\begin{pmatrix} Q_{1,t+1} \\ \dots \\ Q_{i,t+1} \\ \dots \\ Q_{m,t+1} \end{pmatrix} = \begin{pmatrix} 0 & \dots & -\frac{1}{2} & \dots & -\frac{1}{2} \\ \dots & \dots & \dots & \dots & \dots \\ -\frac{1}{2} & \dots & 0 & \dots & -\frac{1}{2} \\ \dots & \dots & \dots & \dots & \dots \\ -\frac{1}{2} & \dots & -\frac{1}{2} & \dots & 0 \end{pmatrix} \begin{pmatrix} Q_{1,t} \\ \dots \\ Q_{i,t} \\ \dots \\ Q_{m,t} \end{pmatrix} + \begin{pmatrix} \frac{a-\alpha_1}{2b} \\ \dots \\ \frac{a-\alpha_i}{2b} \\ \dots \\ \frac{a-\alpha_m}{2b} \end{pmatrix}$$

Noting now for simplicity:

$$A = \begin{pmatrix} 0 & \dots & -\frac{1}{2} & \dots & -\frac{1}{2} \\ \dots & \dots & \dots & \dots & \dots \\ -\frac{1}{2} & \dots & 0 & \dots & -\frac{1}{2} \\ \dots & \dots & \dots & \dots & \dots \\ -\frac{1}{2} & \dots & -\frac{1}{2} & \dots & 0 \end{pmatrix} = -\frac{1}{2}D + \frac{1}{2}I_m \text{ where } D = \begin{pmatrix} 1 & \dots & 1 & \dots & 1 \\ \dots & \dots & \dots & \dots & \dots \\ 1 & \dots & 1 & \dots & 1 \\ \dots & \dots & \dots & \dots & \dots \\ 1 & \dots & 1 & \dots & 1 \end{pmatrix},$$

$$Q_t = \left(Q_{1,t} \ \dots \ Q_{i,t} \ \dots \ Q_{m,t}\right)^t,\ C = \begin{pmatrix} \frac{a-\alpha_1}{2b} & \dots & \frac{a-\alpha_i}{2b} & \dots & \frac{a-\alpha_m}{2b} \end{pmatrix}^t$$

we find that:

$$Q_{t+1} = AQ_t + C,\ t \geq 0$$

Let now P(n): $Q_{t+n}=A^nQ_t+(A^{n-1}+...+A+I_m)C$, $n\geq 1$ (*where I_m is the unit matrix of order m*) – the vector of the production of the m firms at a point t+n with n units of time offset to a reference time t.

How P(1): $Q_{t+1}=AQ_t+C$ is true, suppose that P(n) is true. We have: P(n+1): $Q_{t+n+1}=AQ_{t+n}+C=A(A^nQ_t+(A^{n-1}+...+A+I_m)C)+C=A^{n+1}Q_t+(A^n+...+A+I_m)C$ – true, therefore, we have proved by mathematical induction that:

$$Q_{t+n}=A^nQ_t+(A^{n-1}+...+A+I_m)C,\ \forall n\geq 0\ \forall t\geq 0$$

In particular, for t=0 (reference to the beginning of the m firms), we obtain:

$$Q_n=A^nQ_0+(A^{n-1}+...+A+I_m)C$$

We ask ourselves, naturally the problem of determining the vector Q_n.

Let us note first that the matrix $A-I_m$ is invertible and:

$$(A-I_m)^{-1}=\frac{1}{m+1}\begin{pmatrix} -2m & \dots & 2 & \dots & 2 \\ \dots & \dots & \dots & \dots & \dots \\ 2 & \dots & -2m & \dots & 2 \\ \dots & \dots & \dots & \dots & \dots \\ 2 & \dots & 2 & \dots & -2m \end{pmatrix}=\frac{2}{m+1}D-2I_m$$

For the sum: $A^{n-1}+...+A+I_m$ we will take into account that: $(A-I_m)(A^{n-1}+...+A+I_m)=A^n+...+A^2+A-A^{n-1}-...-A-I_m=A^n-I_m$ therefore:

$$A^{n-1}+...+A+I_m=(A-I_m)^{-1}(A^n-I_m)$$

But we have: $A^n=\left(-\frac{1}{2}\right)^n(D-I_m)^n=\left(-\frac{1}{2}\right)^n\sum_{s=0}^{n}(-1)^s\binom{n}{s}D^{n-s}$ where $\binom{n}{s}$ is the number of combinations of n items taken by s. How $D^{n-s}=m^{n-s-1}D$ for $n-s\geq 1$ follows:

$$A^n=\frac{1}{2^n}\left(I_m+\frac{(1-m)^n-1}{m}D\right)$$

We therefore have:

$$A^{n-1}+...+A+I_m=(A-I_m)^{-1}(A^n-I_m)=\left(\frac{m+1-2^nm-(1-m)^n}{2^{n-1}m(m+1)}\right)D-2\left(\frac{1}{2^n}-1\right)I_m$$

from where:

$$Q_n=A^nQ_0+(A^{n-1}+...+A+I_m)C=\frac{1}{2^n}Q_0+\frac{(1-m)^n-1}{2^nm}DQ_0+\frac{m+1-2^nm-(1-m)^n}{2^{n-1}m(m+1)}DC-2\left(\frac{1}{2^n}-1\right)C$$

or, in other terms:

$$\begin{pmatrix}Q_{1,n} & \dots & Q_{i,n} & \dots & Q_{m,n}\end{pmatrix}^t=$$

$$\frac{1}{2^n}\begin{pmatrix}Q_{1,0} & \cdots & Q_{i,0} & \cdots & Q_{m,0}\end{pmatrix}^t + \frac{(1-m)^n-1}{2^n m}\begin{pmatrix}\sum_{k=1}^{m} Q_{k,0} & \cdots & \sum_{k=1}^{m} Q_{k,0} & \cdots & \sum_{k=1}^{m} Q_{k,0}\end{pmatrix}^t +$$

$$\frac{m+1-2^n m-(1-m)^n}{2^{n-1}m(m+1)}\begin{pmatrix}\frac{ma-\sum_{k=1}^{m}\alpha_k}{2b} & \cdots & \frac{ma-\sum_{k=1}^{m}\alpha_k}{2b} & \cdots & \frac{ma-\sum_{k=1}^{m}\alpha_k}{2b}\end{pmatrix}^t -$$

$$2\left(\frac{1}{2^n}-1\right)\begin{pmatrix}\frac{a-\alpha_1}{2b} & \cdots & \frac{a-\alpha_i}{2b} & \cdots & \frac{a-\alpha_m}{2b}\end{pmatrix}^t$$

from where:

$$Q_{i,n} = \frac{1}{2^n}Q_{i,0} + \frac{(1-m)^n-1}{2^n m}\sum_{k=1}^{m} Q_{k,0} + \frac{\left(m+1-2^n m-(1-m)^n\right)\left(ma-\sum_{k=1}^{m}\alpha_k\right)}{2^n bm(m+1)} - 2\left(\frac{1}{2^n}-1\right)\frac{a-\alpha_i}{2b}$$

Because: $\lim_{n\to\infty}\frac{1}{2^n}=0$, $\lim_{n\to\infty}\frac{(1-m)^n-1}{2^n m}=\frac{1}{m}\lim_{n\to\infty}\left(\frac{1-m}{2}\right)^n=\begin{cases}0 \text{ if } m=2\\ \text{not exists if } m>2\end{cases}$,

$\lim_{n\to\infty}\frac{m+1-2^n m-(1-m)^n}{2^{n-1}m(m+1)}=-\frac{2}{m+1}-\frac{2}{m(m+1)}\lim_{n\to\infty}\left(\frac{1-m}{2}\right)^n=\begin{cases}-\frac{2}{3} \text{ if } m=2\\ \text{not exists if } m>2\end{cases}$, $\lim_{n\to\infty}2\left(\frac{1}{2^n}-1\right)$=-2

we finally have that:

$$\lim_{n\to\infty}Q_n=\begin{cases}-\frac{2}{3}DC+2C=\begin{pmatrix}\frac{a-2\alpha_1+\alpha_2}{3b}\\ \frac{a+\alpha_1-2\alpha_2}{3b}\end{pmatrix} \text{ if } m=2\\ \text{not exists if } m>2\end{cases}$$

We determined so that the process has limit if and only if m=2 so there is a duopoly, in which case we have:

$$Q_1^*=\frac{a-2\alpha_1+\alpha_2}{3b},\ Q_2^*=\frac{a+\alpha_1-2\alpha_2}{3b}$$

$$p^*=a-b(Q_A^*+Q_B^*)=\frac{a+\alpha_1+\alpha_2}{3}.$$

$$\Pi_1^*=\frac{(a-2\alpha_1+\alpha_2)^2}{9b},\ \Pi_2^*=\frac{(a+\alpha_1-2\alpha_2)^2}{9b}$$

Computing the difference: $\Pi_1^*-\Pi_2^*=\frac{(a-2\alpha_1+\alpha_2)^2}{9b}-\frac{(a+\alpha_1-2\alpha_2)^2}{9b}$ we get:

$$\Pi_1^*-\Pi_2^*=\frac{(a-2\alpha_1+\alpha_2)^2}{9b}\left(1-\left(\frac{a+\alpha_1-2\alpha_2}{a-2\alpha_1+\alpha_2}\right)^2\right)$$

The requirement to $\Pi_1^*>\Pi_2^*$ returns to: $\frac{a+\alpha_1-2\alpha_2}{a-2\alpha_1+\alpha_2}\in(-1,1)$ which is equivalent to:

$$\begin{cases} \dfrac{2a-\alpha_1-\alpha_2}{a-2\alpha_1+\alpha_2} > 0 \\ \dfrac{3(\alpha_1-\alpha_2)}{a-2\alpha_1+\alpha_2} < 0 \end{cases}$$

If $a > 2\alpha_1 - \alpha_2$ the conditions become: $\begin{cases} \alpha_1+\alpha_2 < 2a \\ \alpha_1 < \alpha_2 \end{cases}$ and if $a < 2\alpha_1 - \alpha_2$ to $\begin{cases} \alpha_1+\alpha_2 > 2a \\ \alpha_1 > \alpha_2 \end{cases}$.

In order to $\Pi_2^* > \Pi_1^*$ from the same set of conditions, we have: $\dfrac{a+\alpha_1-2\alpha_2}{a-2\alpha_1+\alpha_2} \in (-\infty,-1)\cup(1,\infty)$ that is:

$$\begin{cases} \dfrac{2a-\alpha_1-\alpha_2}{a-2\alpha_1+\alpha_2} < 0 \\ \text{or} \\ \dfrac{3(\alpha_1-\alpha_2)}{a-2\alpha_1+\alpha_2} > 0 \end{cases}$$

If $a > 2\alpha_1 - \alpha_2$ the conditions become: $\begin{cases} \alpha_1+\alpha_2 > 2a \\ \text{or} \\ \alpha_1 > \alpha_2 \end{cases}$, and if $a < 2\alpha_1 - \alpha_2$ to $\begin{cases} \alpha_1+\alpha_2 < 2a \\ \text{or} \\ \alpha_1 < \alpha_2 \end{cases}$.

Considering a system of axes $O\alpha_1\alpha_2$ it follows that in the areas 1 and 2, the first company profit will be strictly greater than that of the second company, and in the third region, the second company profit will be strictly higher than that of the first company (figure 1).

If $a = 2\alpha_1 - \alpha_2$ then: $\Pi_1^*=0$ and how $\Pi_2^*>0$ follows, obviously that $\Pi_1^* < \Pi_2^*$. Similarly, if: $a = 2\alpha_2 - \alpha_1$ then: $\Pi_2^*=0$ and how $\Pi_1^*>0$ follows that $\Pi_1^* > \Pi_2^*$.

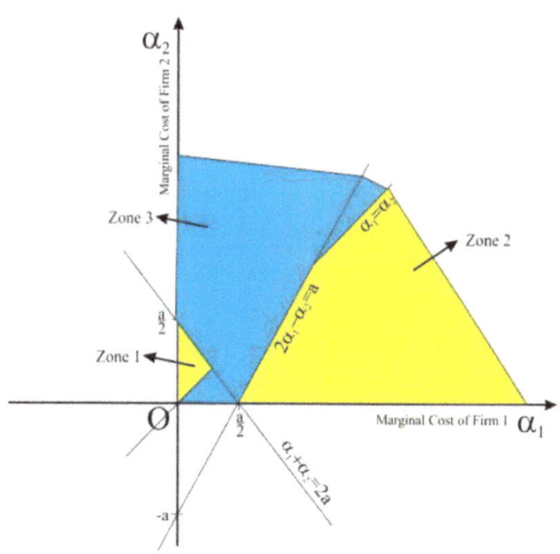

Figure 1

3 The Cournot-Nash Equilibrium

Considering again the m firms above, we assume now that the firms act independently, the selling price being the same for all firms, depending only on the total production.

The profit function for the company F_k is therefore:

$$\Pi_k(Q_1,\ldots,Q_n)=p\left(\sum_{i=1}^{m}Q_i\right)Q_k-\alpha_kQ_k,\ k=\overline{1,m}$$

The condition of profit maximization implies:

$$\frac{\partial\Pi_k}{\partial Q_k}=p'\left(\sum_{i=1}^{m}Q_i\right)Q_k+p\left(\sum_{i=1}^{m}Q_i\right)-\alpha_k=0$$

which is equivalent to:

$$Q_k+\sum_{i=1}^{m}Q_i=\frac{a-\alpha_k}{b},\ k=\overline{1,m}$$

Adding the m relations follows: $\sum_{i=1}^{m}Q_i=\frac{ma-\sum_{i=1}^{m}\alpha_i}{(m+1)b}$ from where, finally:

$$Q_k^*=\frac{a-(m+1)\alpha_k+\sum_{i=1}^{m}\alpha_i}{(m+1)b},\ k=\overline{1,m}$$

The total price is:

$$p^*=p\left(\sum_{k=1}^{m}Q_k^*\right)=\frac{a+\sum_{i=1}^{m}\alpha_i}{m+1}$$

and the profits of companies:

$$\Pi_k(Q_1^*,\ldots,Q_m^*)=\left(\frac{a+\sum_{i=1}^{m}\alpha_i}{m+1}-\alpha_k\right)Q_k^*=\frac{\left(a-(m+1)\alpha_k+\sum_{i=1}^{m}\alpha_i\right)^2}{(m+1)^2b}$$

For m=2 we have:

$$Q_1^*=\frac{a-2\alpha_1+\alpha_2}{3b},\ Q_2^*=\frac{a-2\alpha_2+\alpha_1}{3b}$$

total price: $p^*=\frac{a+\alpha_1+\alpha_2}{3}$ and firms profits:

$$\Pi_1(Q_1^*,Q_2^*)=\frac{(a-2\alpha_1+\alpha_2)^2}{9b},\ \Pi_2(Q_1^*,Q_2^*)=\frac{(a-2\alpha_2+\alpha_1)^2}{9b}$$

It is noted that at equilibrium the two companies will have the same optimal amounts and record the same profits as if taking in the leadership analysis.

Comparing with the first case, when at the time n for two companies (m=2), we have:

$$Q_{1,n}=\frac{1+(-1)^n}{2^{n+1}}Q_{1,0}+\frac{(-1)^n-1}{2^{n+1}}Q_{2,0}+\frac{2\left(2^n+(-1)^{n+1}\right)a+\left(3-2^{n+2}+(-1)^n\right)\alpha_1-\left(3-2^{n+1}+(-1)^{n+1}\right)\alpha_2}{3\cdot2^{n+1}b}$$

$$Q_{2,n}=\frac{(-1)^n-1}{2^{n+1}}Q_{1,0}+\frac{1+(-1)^n}{2^{n+1}}Q_{2,0}+\frac{2\left(2^n+(-1)^{n+1}\right)a-\left(3-2^{n+1}+(-1)^{n+1}\right)\alpha_1+\left(3-2^{n+2}+(-1)^n\right)\alpha_2}{3\cdot 2^{n+1}b}$$

we obtain:

$$Q_{1,n}-Q_1^*=\frac{1+(-1)^n}{2^{n+1}}Q_{1,0}+\frac{(-1)^n-1}{2^{n+1}}Q_{2,0}+\frac{2(-1)^{n+1}a+\left(3+(-1)^n\right)\alpha_1-\left(3+(-1)^{n+1}\right)\alpha_2}{3\cdot 2^{n+1}b}$$

$$Q_{2,n}-Q_2^*=\frac{(-1)^n-1}{2^{n+1}}Q_{1,0}+\frac{1+(-1)^n}{2^{n+1}}Q_{2,0}+\frac{2(-1)^{n+1}a-\left(3+(-1)^{n+1}\right)\alpha_1+\left(3+(-1)^n\right)\alpha_2}{3\cdot 2^{n+1}b}$$

As a result, for n=odd, we have:

$$Q_{1,n}-Q_1^*=\frac{a+\alpha_1-2\alpha_2-3bQ_{2,0}}{3\cdot 2^n b},\quad Q_{2,n}-Q_2^*=\frac{a-2\alpha_1+\alpha_2-3bQ_{1,0}}{3\cdot 2^n b}$$

and for n=even:

$$Q_{1,n}-Q_1^*=-\frac{a-2\alpha_1+\alpha_2-3bQ_{1,0}}{3\cdot 2^n b},\quad Q_{2,n}-Q_2^*=-\frac{a+\alpha_1-2\alpha_2-3bQ_{2,0}}{3\cdot 2^n b}$$

From the above, the following conditions are observed:

Case 1: If $Q_{1,0}<\frac{a-2\alpha_1+\alpha_2}{3b}$, $Q_{2,0}<\frac{a+\alpha_1-2\alpha_2}{3b}$ then at odd moments $Q_{1,n}>Q_1^*$, $Q_{2,n}>Q_2^*$, and then at even moments: $Q_{1,n}<Q_1^*$, $Q_{2,n}<Q_2^*$;

Case 2: If $Q_{1,0}<\frac{a-2\alpha_1+\alpha_2}{3b}$, $Q_{2,0}>\frac{a+\alpha_1-2\alpha_2}{3b}$ then at odd moments $Q_{1,n}<Q_1^*$, $Q_{2,n}>Q_2^*$, and then at even moments: $Q_{1,n}<Q_1^*$, $Q_{2,n}>Q_2^*$;

Case 3: If $Q_{1,0}>\frac{a-2\alpha_1+\alpha_2}{3b}$, $Q_{2,0}<\frac{a+\alpha_1-2\alpha_2}{3b}$ then at odd moments $Q_{1,n}>Q_1^*$, $Q_{2,n}<Q_2^*$, and then at even moments: $Q_{1,n}>Q_1^*$, $Q_{2,n}<Q_2^*$;

Case 4: If $Q_{1,0}>\frac{a-2\alpha_1+\alpha_2}{3b}$, $Q_{2,0}>\frac{a+\alpha_1-2\alpha_2}{3b}$ then at odd moments $Q_{1,n}<Q_1^*$, $Q_{2,n}<Q_2^*$, and then at even moments: $Q_{1,n}>Q_1^*$, $Q_{2,n}>Q_2^*$

Following these considerations, we see that if all firms assume successively the leadership role their outputs can switch on both sides of the equilibrium (if in the case of the existence of the limit or in the contrary case).

More specifically, however, if the initial yields are sufficiently small (large) compared with $\frac{a-2\alpha_1+\alpha_2}{3b}$ and $\frac{a+\alpha_1-2\alpha_2}{3b}$ respectively, the the production alternates at odd or even moments.

If, however, the initial production of a firm is sufficiently small and the other's large enough, then those with low initial production will be directed upward (at any time) to the equilibrium production, whereas those with higher initial production will down to the equilibriu.

The consequence of this is that the company with a higher initial production will not give leadership to the other, preferring to ignore the actions of others and maintaining a constant production.

Now consider a situation in which a new company F_{m+1} enters on market and having marginal cost $MC=\alpha_{m+1}$. The new equilibriums are:

$$Q^*_{new,k} = \frac{a-(m+2)\alpha_k + \sum_{i=1}^{m}\alpha_i + \alpha_{m+1}}{(m+2)b}, \ k=\overline{1,m}$$

$$Q^*_{new,m+1} = \frac{a-(m+1)\alpha_{m+1} + \sum_{i=1}^{m}\alpha_i}{(m+2)b}$$

If before the entry of the new firm the total ammount was: $Q_{old} = \sum_{k=1}^{m} Q^*_k = \frac{ma - \sum_{i=1}^{m}\alpha_i}{(m+1)b}$ now we have:

$Q_{new} = \sum_{k=1}^{m} Q^*_{new,k} + Q^*_{new,m+1} = \frac{(m+1)a - \sum_{i=1}^{m}\alpha_i - \alpha_{m+1}}{(m+2)b}$. The difference between the new and the old ammount is:

$$Q_{new} - Q_{old} = \frac{a + \sum_{i=1}^{m}\alpha_i - (m+1)\alpha_{m+1}}{(m+1)(m+2)b}$$

the total price being: $p^*_{new} = p\left(\sum_{k=1}^{m+1} Q^*_k\right) = \frac{a + \sum_{i=1}^{m}\alpha_i + \alpha_{m+1}}{m+2}$ with the difference:

$$p^*_{new} - p^*_{old} = \frac{a + \sum_{i=1}^{m}\alpha_i + \alpha_{m+1}}{m+2} - \frac{a + \sum_{i=1}^{m}\alpha_i}{m+1} = -b(Q_{new} - Q_{old})$$

Also for the profits:

$$\Pi_{new,k}\left(Q^*_{new,1},\ldots,Q^*_{new,m+1}\right) = \frac{\left(a-(m+2)\alpha_k + \sum_{i=1}^{m}\alpha_i + \alpha_{m+1}\right)^2}{(m+2)^2 b}, \ k=\overline{1,m}$$

$$\Pi_{new,m+1}\left(Q^*_{new,1},\ldots,Q^*_{new,m+1}\right) = \frac{\left(a-(m+1)\alpha_{m+1} + \sum_{i=1}^{m}\alpha_i\right)^2}{(m+2)^2 b}$$

and:

$$\Pi_{new,k}-\Pi_{old,k}=\frac{1}{(m+1)^2(m+2)^2 b}\cdot$$
$$\left[(m+1)^2\alpha_{m+1}^2+2(m+1)^2\left(\left(a+\sum_{i=1}^{m}\alpha_i\right)-(m+2)\alpha_k\right)\alpha_{m+1}-\left(a+\sum_{i=1}^{m}\alpha_i\right)\left((2m+3)\left(a+\sum_{i=1}^{m}\alpha_i\right)-2(m+1)(m+2)\alpha_k\right)\right]$$

Considering the equation of degree II in α_{m+1} we have its roots:

$$\alpha'_{m+1}=\frac{a+\sum_{i=1}^{m}\alpha_i}{m+1},\ \alpha''_{m+1}=\frac{(2m^2+4m+1)\alpha_k-(2m+3)\left(a+\sum_{\substack{i=1\\ i\neq k}}^{m}\alpha_i\right)}{(m+1)},\ \alpha'_{m+1}<\alpha''_{m+1}.$$

In order that: $\Pi_{new,k}>\Pi_{old,k}$ we must have that:

$$\alpha_{m+1}\in(-\infty,\alpha'_{m+1})\cup(\alpha''_{m+1},\infty)=\left(-\infty,\frac{a+\sum_{i=1}^{m}\alpha_i}{m+1}\right)\cup\left(\frac{2(m+1)(m+2)\alpha_k-(2m+3)\left(a+\sum_{i=1}^{m}\alpha_i\right)}{(m+1)},\infty\right)$$

<u>Case 1</u>

$$\alpha_{m+1}<\frac{a+\sum_{i=1}^{m}\alpha_i}{m+1}\Rightarrow Q_{new}>Q_{old},\ p^*_{new}<p^*_{old},\ \Pi_{new,k}>\Pi_{old,k}\ \ \forall k=\overline{1,m}$$

so if the new company will have a marginal cost small enough, then the total output and profits of the old firms will grow, the selling price dropping.

<u>Case 2</u>

$$\alpha_{m+1}>\frac{a+\sum_{i=1}^{m}\alpha_i}{m+1}\Rightarrow Q_{new}<Q_{old},\ p^*_{new}>p^*_{old},\ \text{and}$$

$$\Pi_{new,k}>\Pi_{old,k}\ \text{if}\ \alpha_k<\frac{(2m+3)\left(a+\sum_{\substack{i=1\\ i\neq k}}^{m}\alpha_i\right)+(m+1)\alpha_{m+1}}{2m^2+4m+1}\ \text{and}$$

$$\Pi_{new,k}<\Pi_{old,k}\ \text{if}\ \alpha_k>\frac{(2m+3)\left(a+\sum_{\substack{i=1\\ i\neq k}}^{m}\alpha_i\right)+(m+1)\alpha_{m+1}}{2m^2+4m+1}$$

If the new company will have a sufficiently high marginal cost, then the total production will decline, the selling price will increase and firms with sufficiently low marginal costs will increase their profits, while those with higher marginal costs declines in returns.

Case 3

$$\alpha_{m+1} = \frac{a + \sum_{i=1}^{m} \alpha_i}{m+1} \Rightarrow Q_{new} = Q_{old},\ p^*_{new} = p^*_{old},\ \Pi_{new,k} = \Pi_{old,k}\ \ \forall k = \overline{1,m}$$

When entering a new firm with marginal cost exactly determined by the cost of other companies, according to the formula above, both total production and the selling price and profits old companies will remain constant.

4 References

Azhar S., McLennan A. & Reif H.J. (2005). Computation of Equilibria in Noncooperative Games. Elsevier. *Computers and Mathematics with Applications 50*

Başar T. & Geert J.O. (1995). Lecture Notes on Non-Cooperative Game Theory. *Society for Industrial and Applied Mathematics.* New York: Philadelphia, Academic Press.

Bernhard, v.S. & Theodore L.T. (2001). *Game Theory.* CDAM Research Report, October 8.

Bressan, A. (2013). *Noncooperative Games and Applications*. Pensilvanya: Penn State University.

Ioan, C.A. & Ioan, G. (2012). General Considerations on the Oligopoly. *Acta Universitatis Danubius. Oeconomica*, Vol. 8, No.3, pp. 115-137.

Ioan, C.A. & Ioan, G. (2012). *Matheconomics*. Galati: Zigotto Publishing.

Ledvina, A.F. and Sircar, R. (2011). *Bertrand and Cournot Competition Under Asymmetric Costs: Number of Active Firms in Equilibrium* (February 18)

Nash J. (1951). Non-Cooperative Games. *The Annals of Mathematics, Second Series*, Vol.54, Issue 2, Sept.

Wang J. (1988). *The Theory of Games*. Oxford: Oxford University Press.

15

Linking Government to Academic Research: Lessons from the American Progressive Era

Valentin Filip[1]

Abstract: This paper intends to explore why and how the U.S. government involved academic scholars in the policy-making process during the Progressive Era, with a focus on President Woodrow Wilson's formation and use of the Inquiry. It further attempts to draw upon the lessons learned from this case study in history in order to stimulate new thinking with regard to the interest of the governmental decision-makers in exploiting academic potential. The paper rests mainly on the research dedicated to Progressivism and Wilsonianism and it consists of an analysis based on the literature review and the case study of The Inquiry. The conclusions highlight the impact that the intellectual potential from within universities and research centres might have in informing policies, revealing alternative tracks and finally supporting the process as a whole. Thus, the paper aims to offer "food for thought" for further debates, raise the awareness on the issue of benefiting from a stronger and deeper government-academia relationship and nurture the mutual interest for partnership and even possible integration.

Keywords: government and academia; Progressivism; Wilsonianism

1 Introduction: Progressives and Progressivism in America

At the turn of the 19th and 20th centuries, Progressivism appeared as a reform movement in the United States and evolved for almost four decades to transform the American government and society as a whole. It came in many shapes, as Progressives were equally scholars (John Dewey and Lester Ward) or artists (Woody Guthrie and Upton Sinclair), politicians (Woodrow Wilson and Theodore Roosevelt) or trade unionists (Samuel Gompers and John Lewis), activists (Jane Addams and W.E.B Du Bois) or journalists (Herbert Croly and Ida Tarbell). They all had in common the belief in the idea of Progress and placed a premium on the role of the Government as the main driver of reform.

Born from an era of political turmoil and social unrest, suggestively entitled "The Gilded Age", when America, under the guise of demographic and economic growth, was being predated by corrupted political machines and rapacious corporate trusts, the Progressives took on the mission of "purifying" both politics and the societal dimension. They shared the idea that the changes brought by the Industrial Revolution and modern capitalism needed to be matched with thorough reforms targeting political, administrative, social, and economic issues. The pursuit of Progress called for a new thinking and revision of the intellectual and cultural principles upon which the American state and society were built. Otherwise, graft and waste would have continued to plague a system lagging behind the

[1] PhD, National Intelligence Academy, Romania, Address: 20-22 Odăi str., sector 1, Bucharest, Romania, Corresponding author: valentin_filip@yahoo.com.

technological advances and entrepreneurial tradecraft brought in with the development of a capitalist system that engendered the risk of running unchecked.

Education was considered a key catalyst of the envisaged changes, since the "living", rational government that the Progressives were attempting to set up was heavily based on the input of educated and skilled civil servants, on the one hand, and intellectuals, on the other. Thus, the whole system, from schools to universities, was redesigned so that their product – education – would constitute the much needed ingredient for reform. Moreover, researchers and professors from the academia were given a bigger part to play in the societal and governmental transformation process.

This paper attempts to examine the Progressive perspectives on education and review how the American administration and government harnessed the energies emerging from the academia in order to project them in the policy- and decision-making realm. It is thus trying to set an example to be further elaborated on. Understanding the making of the American societal and political system and its successful evolution as a democratic regime with a functional market and acknowledging the vital part played by the government-university "partnership" may provide a useful map for the decision-makers and researchers in Romania and elsewhere. They would be able to apprehend the challenges of the American Progressive Era, to reciprocate the positive lessons and avoid the negative ones, by adapting the model to the specificities of their own countries. The more so as the Progressive ideology continues to be an inspiration for contemporary academic debates and political thinking in the United States, In this respect, the case of the Inquiry is indicative of this governmental practice of filling its knowledge gaps and informing its decisions by taking advantage of academic thought.

2 Literature Review

Progressivism

The Progressive movement constitutes an appealing topic for the political scientists and philosophers in the United States due to its long-lasting impact on the American society and politics. Explaining who the Progressives were, what were their central ideas and how their thoughts were put into practice involved the use of secondary sources, primarily, as they have the advantage of hindsight in assessing the main traits and implications of Progressivism. In this respect, the use of such works that document the era provide a valuable contribution and supports process tracing as a tool of qualitative analysis. Hence, Tim McNeese examines the context that led to the emergence of the Progressives in the American society and politics, elaborates on their central tenets and sets forth the effect their perceptions, thoughts and actions had with regard to the system of government and the state-society relationship (McNeese, 2010). Likewise, Karen Pastorello approaches the roots of the movement, its development and lasting impact, but with a focus on Progressive recognition of the social, political, and economic demands of a society and system in the midst of sudden changes brought by the rapidly developing capitalism (Pastorello, 2014). Walter Nugent provides a brief but detailed description and explanation of the American Progressivism, starting with the critical exploration of its origins, then chronologically tackling its representative figures and the endeared principles they shared, and finally assessing their accomplishments (Nugent, 2009). Faith Jaycox elaborates on a step-by-step development of the Progressive movement, chronologically arranged, and distils the main issues situated at the heart of the reformers' thought and action by using eyewitness accounts (Jaycox, 2005).

Primary sources are additionally employed when addressing the Progressive debate in the field of education, either from original texts or from tertiary sources that compile excerpts from major works of the main Progressive thinkers and actors. John Dewey, as the "father of Progressive education", is a must in this respect. His selected volume is both a landmark exposition of Progressive educational theory and a philosophical study on the role of education in a democratic regime, aiming to discuss the public education reforms and trigger their implementation (Dewey, 1930). Dewey's advocacy of the democracy was a special and interesting endeavour, as in his views democracy was built upon and centred on schools and civil society, two main ingredients that, fused together, would produce an educated citizen able to actively and constructively engage in public affairs, in the very making of the society, the political system and the economical conditions that would ensure his own security and prosperity. Moreover, education would also impact on the citizen's advancement of the self which gives another argument for reflecting on the topic and reconstructing the concrete reality. To complement the understanding of this seminal contribution to Progressivism, Jay Martin's biographical research captures the birth of Dewey's ideas and work in the context of his own life experience, his family and entourage, based on the published papers in the Center for Dewey Studies (Martin, 2002). William and Susannah Link, in their documentary work that collected and interpreted major readings from the Gilded Age and the Progressive Era, expand the horizon with regard to Dewey's thinking, by presenting his views on the integration of schools into a democratic society, on the fusion of civics and politics through education, as a necessary step in order to fulfil the needs of a modernizing America (Dewey, The School and Society, 2012). Widening the context to the whole Progressive movement, David Labaree's article is vital for understanding the differences Progressive views on education, explaining their divergences and similarities, and assessing their reification in the policy-making process (Labaree, 2005).

Wilsonianism

Due to his huge impact upon world politics, in both theory and practice, Woodrow Wilson is a very popular figure among researchers and authors in the field of political science and international relations. In fact, his valuable contribution to both academic research and concrete politics was so highly appreciated that it gained him the addition of the suffix "-ism" to his name. Wilsonianism was thus born and although it is generally associated with the formulation of foreign policies in the international realm, this paper proposes a wider interpretation of the concept, placing Wilson's thought and action in the Progressive and Liberal environment from which Wilson emerged as a man, intellectual and politician. Therefore, Wilsonianism is considered from a dual perspective encompassing both the internal and external dimension of Wilson's influence on American politics and policies. Ronald Pestritto offers a precise account of Wilson's role in rethinking and reshaping American domestic society and international behaviour (Pestritto, 2005). Moreover, Pestritto's work added value consists in determining the connection between the ideas that Wilson nurtured during his academic career, as student and professor, and the actions he undertook as a public leader in office, first Governor of New Jersey and then President of the United States. From a different angle, Paul Gottfried examines the Wilsonian legacy and defines Wilson's policies as revolutionary, aiming to transfer the democratic reforms at home to the world stage: he was thus attempting to bridge what in international relations terms was dubbed as "the Great Divide" between the domestic and foreign political realms (Gottfried, 1990).

Biographical writings bring also depth and scope to the attempt of examining the genesis of Wilson's ideology and its actual implementation. Scott Berg laboriously defines Wilson as a true architect, one that offered a model for higher education when he was leading Princeton, a model for a different type of government, still liberal but more interventionist, when he took his mandates at the White House, and a model for a new international system, based on a democratic world order, when he rose on the world stage at the Paris Peace Conference in 1919 (Berg, 2013). Charles Zorgbibe vividly portraits Wilson as a crusader, always campaigning in the name of democracy for the weak and the poor, be it students at Princeton, ordinary American people, or nations around the world (Zorgbibe, 2003). Less objectively documented but equally important are the half-biographical half-testimonial writings authored by witnesses to Wilson's life and evolution since they are more endowed to make the readers feel and have a grasp of the era. William Allen White, himself a prominent Progressive leader, attempts to uncover the man behind the facade of the political leader, unveiling Wilson's temper and feelings, his ideals and troubles, and placing him as a part of the higher forces which were moulding America at the time (White, 1925). Joseph Tumulty, Wilson's former private secretary, provides a biography, based on his own personal observations, that sketches a decision-maker willing to be counselled, to accept third views, and to inform himself or be informed by different perspectives (Tumulty, 1921).

The Inquiry and the Peace Conference

A great deal of research was dedicated to the Paris Peace Conference of 1919, as one of the most intense, long-lasting, all-encompassing and high-impact diplomatic events in world history. The U.S. delegation to the peace talks presented an interesting feat: prior to the departure to Europe, it was informed by the research of a group of scholars from the academia set up by Wilson – the Inquiry, and their work continued during the conference itself. The aim is to study the role of this group, virtually a think-tank, in the decision-making process that produced the American official position papers and projects. Lawrence Gelfand offers one of the most in-depth studies with regard to the Inquiry, a masterpiece of documentary research, displaying how the group was formed, how it worked and how it was connected to the policy-making process, as well as a critical analysis, anatomizing the lack of expertise and/or professionalism revealed throughout the Inquiry's evolution, from its structural inception to the final delivery of its products (Gelfand, 1963). Peter Grose briefly pictures the context which led to the creation of the group but, more importantly, presents the Peace Conference from a different angle, the backstage of the experts and scholars that were preparing the meetings of the high officials (Grose, 1996). Focusing on this unofficial perspective, on the peace-making rather than the formal texts of the treaties is the main reason for choosing personal accounts from participants to the Conference in 1919 as references. Ray Stannard Baker offers both selective glimpses of the American delegation in action, with the aim of clarifying the understanding of Wilson's work in Paris, together with his experts and scholars (Baker, 1919), and a documentary record of the activity of U.S. representatives, consisting of original letters and minutes, that expose the informative process that led to decisions and actions (Baker, Woodrow Wilson and World Settlement (volume III), 1922). David Hunter Miller collected an impressive number of documents, a great deal of them elaborated by members of the Inquiry, circulated at the Peace Conference among the members of the American delegation, allowing for a potential correlation of what has been proposed by scholars and adopted by decision-makers (Miller, 1924). Edward House, a proponent of the group that actually established its composition, and Charles Seymour, a senior member of the Inquiry that took part in the American Commission to Negotiate Peace in Paris, tell the inside story of the American delegation in Paris by compiling a series of essays from the participants, most of them previously members of the Inquiry, and reveal how their recommendations constituted the foundation upon which the political decisions rested (House & Seymour, 1921).

3 New Views on Education: Government and Academia during the American Progressive Era

Progressivism: a brief outlook

By the end of the 19th century, the United States were in the midst of complex changes. In the decades that followed the Civil War, an urban and multicultural society had emerged, fueled by the industrial growth and immigration. But the phenomenon of technological and economic modernization was also accompanied by less desirable evolutions, in that a handful of politicians and businessmen sought to control most dimensions of the Americans' life and thus enormously prosper. It was at this time when voices from different backgrounds and in different circles started to be heard, asking to reclaim "a decent society from the forces of economic rapaciousness by expanding the role of collective social action" and "a decent politics – and even democracy – from the forces of corruption that had seized it" (Jaycox, 2005, p. iv). They were warning of the dangers presented by the unlimited power wielded by economic trusts and corrupted politicians and felt that, although America was still "a great nation, but one that still had flaws, gaps in opportunity, and where many people lived in poverty" (McNeese, 2010, p. 90). Their perception was that "the individual and even democracy itself appeared to have been swallowed whole by a huge new economy and a new way of life" (Jaycox, 2005, p. viii) and they simply felt "it was unfair and unjust" that "the rich were getting richer – far richer – than most people" (Nugent, 2009, p. 6). And "most people" was the focus of choice for many of these critical voices; obviously, "this emphasis on ordinary Americans meant that previously unrecognized or marginalized groups attracted" (Pastorello, 2014, p. 9) the attention: debates on women, Native and African Americans, immigrants from around the world, even the workers, added to the already discussed WASP (White-Anglo-Saxon-Protestant) community.

Given their natural propensity to foster hope and to seek progress through changes, these reformers were later labeled Progressives, although they did not constitute a monolithic community but rather a very diverse one. "Progressivism manifested itself in everything from railroad regulation to woman suffrage to immigration control to realist art and literature to the first real mass media and paved roads" (Nugent, 2009, p. 3) and as such included sympathizers and activists from a wide spectrum: "religious leaders, businessmen, professionals, civic leaders, settlement women, suffragists, African Americans, civil right advocates, union members, nativists, immigrants, workers, farmers, and politicians" (Pastorello, 2014, p. 12). In politics they were both from the Republican and Democratic parties and ran as wide as Socialists and Radicals, not to mention that they have even established a short-lived Progressive Party. The bottom line is that "there were many varieties of Progressivism and Progressives" (Nugent, 2009, p. 3) which made it difficult to provide a general, valid definition of the whole ideology. In fact, "the fundamental question of how to define progressivism continues to perplex scholars to this day", realizing that "Progressivism is not a cohesive, unified movement but, instead, the sum of a variety of reform efforts" (Pastorello, 2014, p. 10). In this respect, some may even find adequate the simplistic approach put forth by Justice Potter Stewart: "I know it when I see it" (Murphy, 2013, p. 7).

However, there are some common traits generally tying Progressives together, in terms of motivation or belief. The belief of virtually all Progressives was that there really existed a common good and a public interest (Nugent, 2009, p. 3), specifically that "a society should be fair to its members" (Nugent, 2009, p. 5). They "embraced a religious and secular faith in individual self-determination that infused every area of human behavior" (Murphy, 2013, p. 11), a feature that would become a central theme of Wilsonian action abroad, and strove "to first identify and then to remedy the problems" (Pastorello, 2014, p. 7) emanated from a society that was industrializing, urbanizing and receiving a growing number of immigrants. The pitfalls of these economic and social changes consisted in the emergence of "unwelcome, un-American imbalances in their society": "a new class of ostentatious millionaires, monopolistic and out-of-control corporations, conflict (often violent) between workers and capitalists and supine responses from governments" (Nugent, 2009, p. 2). Governmental languor to these ills was caused both by the lack of institutional and legal instruments, specific to the de-regulated environment of the late 19th century, and, to a greater extent, to a corrupted system that paralyzed all levels of government: local, state and federal. One source of corruption consisted in "the spoils system of job distribution: few publicly funded jobs were funded competitively on the basis of qualifications, abilities, or merit" (Jaycox, 2005, p. 78). The jobs were instead distributed by political machines, the major urban political organizations, and their bosses on the basis of political loyalty or financial support. Then was graft, an ordinary practice at the time, even normal: "men who were otherwise honorable saw no conflict in accepting financial rewards, gifts, commissions, or retainers from businesses and individuals whom they assisted" (Jaycox, 2005, p. 78). Hush money was the virtual currency from both organized crime and legit businessmen and it was given for "inside knowledge of future business or public projects" or "for petty offices and for utility franchises", be it "transit, paving, street cleaning, police protection and in some places even public schools" (Jaycox, 2005, p. 78). This black, invisible administration controlled the existence of entire communities and even the whole nation and its architecture was resistant to change: the bosses were not elected, but instead they were supporting the actual candidates, sometimes nominated by them, and as a result the election process. Bettering the society, politics and economics through reform was then the key dimension of the Progressive spirit, "the very openness to change, that conviction that something needs to be done" (Nugent, 2009, p. 3).

"Good governance" and scientific administration

Government was not only a part of the problem – it was also a part of the solution and most Progressives shared the belief that it was the tool of choice "to regulate economic problems, ameliorate social ills, and reconcile change with tradition" (Nugent, 2009, p. 3). But a different government was needed, since the older one was ill-qualified and corrupted, a new kind of government that "would rely on experts – well educated, highly trained, social and political scientists" (McNeese, 2010, p. 90) to bring knowledge and expertise in the public affairs. On the other hand, the moral dimension would be preached and overseen by "social gospellers", teachers/priests that "merged the sacred and the secular" to address social problems and promote social change "by following Christian doctrine" (Pastorello, 2014, p. 66), "muckrakers", pioneers of investigative journalism that were revealing social problems to the public opinion, and other philosophers or sociologists.

Governmental regulation was thus considered a vital condition for the quality of life of individuals, communities, and the nation. Progressives demanded "a more streamlined and efficient activist government that involved itself in American life": the state was practically required "to step in to play a more active role in solving social, economic, and political problems" (Pastorello, 2014, p. 8), since it was imagined as the most effective means of "social action on behalf of the people" (Jaycox, 2005, p. viii) that could counterbalance selfish private interests. In this respect, "an active and enlarged government" (Jaycox, 2005, p. viii), an interventionist one in modern terminology, was the best instrument to protect ordinary citizens and democracy itself from "the behavior of trusts and the powerful businessmen who had manipulated the traditional language of individual rights to assume unprecedented control over the economy and even the government itself [...] and the political malfeasance" of the corrupted and potent political bosses (Jaycox, 2005, p. viii). Disinterested activism, private charity and pure research were not enough by themselves; they needed to be supplemented by new legislation and public services in order to provide better standards of living. The main functions of the government were to bring social justice, "through redistribution of resources, anti-trust laws, government control over details of commerce and production", and to ensure the development of its citizens, "through protection of the environment, education, and spiritual uplift" by promoting arts and culture (West & Schambra, 2007).

Government started to appeal to Progressive intellectuals as a topic of research and sometimes even as a profession. Reform activism had a particularly strong intellectual inspiration. James' and Mead's "theory of pragmatism emphasized applied knowledge rather than abstract concepts [...] and stressed the importance of using practical action to press for societal reform" (Pastorello, 2014, p. 67). Reforms were assessed in measurable terms of success and the job of the reformers was to push for positive changes "with the assistance of the government to right the wrongs of American life" (Pastorello, 2014, p. 68), and to inform the policy- and law-making processes. In time, these intellectuals, as well as activists from civic groups, turned into "quasi-official and later even official arms of government" (Jaycox, 2005, p. viii), as "investigative bodies and expert advisers", or "brain trusts", intended to help public authorities to alleviate corruption and implement reform (McNeese, 2010, p. 91).

The entire political and administrative system, as a "dynamic, evolving instrument of social change", was built upon "scientific knowledge and the development of bureaucracy" (West & Schambra, 2007). In this context, education was indispensable to government and to the whole reform process of both state and society. It was not just a recruitment pool for professional, competent bureaucrats, but a source of knowledge and expertise for policy. Moreover, it was crucial for the creation of an educated, informed and thus empowered citizen as the actively engaged resource in democratic politics. As such, education as a domain became the focus of Progressive debates and proposed reforms.

Progressive education in a democratic society

The heterogeneous character of Progressivism was also present in the education field. Some historians point at administrative and pedagogical progressives, others divide them into conservative and liberal, while a last category define three schools of thought focusing on social efficiency, child development and social reconstruction (Labaree, 2005, p. 279). Despite similarities such as the dissatisfaction with traditional education or the belief in developmentalism, which meant adapting education to "the capacities of students at particular stages of intellectual and social growth" (Labaree, 2005, p. 283), these strands were fundamentally divergent. While contemporary debates revolve around progressive pedagogy, centered on the nature of learning, needs of the students, and class methodology, the debate in the Progressive Era was won by administrative progressives and their utilitarian vision grounded in scientific curriculum-making and efficient management practices (Labaree, 2005, pp. 281-282). Their success was determined by their better appeal to "people in power, because business and political leaders were attracted to a mode of educational reform that promised to eliminate waste, to organize and manage schools more efficiently, to tailor instruction to the needs of employers, to Americanize the children of immigrants and to provide students with the skills and attitudes they would need to perform and to accept their future roles in society" (Labaree, 2005, pp. 284-285). Utility also had the upper hand over the romantic vision that held in high regard the will and needs of the child (Labaree, 2005, p. 285). Another powerful argument was the authority of science preached by the administrative progressives, eager "to prove the value of their reforms" as well as their "focus on the management of schools and the structure of the curriculum" (Labaree, 2005, p. 285). Last but not least, the fact that

Dewey, a major figure in the camp of the pedagogical progressives, moved early to the higher education system (Labaree, 2005, p. 285), was a decisive blow. However, his ideas on learning and schooling were to become a legacy of the era and in the same time penetrated in the upper spheres of the education realm: universities.

Impelled by the state and societal support, American institutions of higher education encouraged "a scientific approach to agriculture, science and engineering", while in the liberal arts "concentrated on research and developing new disciplines" (Pastorello, 2014, p. 89). In their quest for recognition and capital, universities "professionalized" the social sciences field, providing graduates with skills and ideas for policy-making and public affairs. In the same time, "professors sought public recognition and influence as policy experts in their chosen fields of government and public administration" (Pastorello, 2014, p. 90). The result was that in the Progressive Era, more children and students attended schools and universities than ever in the educational history of the United States (Pastorello, 2014, p. 135) in order to satisfy the rapidly growing needs for "better-educated and trained public, as the society became more urbanized and, at least in certain sectors, more technological" (Nugent, 2009, p. 56). The new research establishments held a different view on societies, economies and policies, in that they were treated as a whole organism. Previously adherent to a rationalist dogma, they now considered that reforms and policies "should be based on empirical evidence, evaluated and sifted by experts in sociology, political economy and allied sciences, who would then devise programs and policies that governments would effectuate for the benefit of the social organism" (Nugent, 2009, p. 59).

John Dewey stood tall among the Progressives. He emphasized the role of schools as social settlements and the need to discuss educational reforms "in a broader, social view" (Dewey, The School and Society, 2012, p. 244). Viewing "public schools as potential agents for social change" (Pastorello, 2014, p. 68), he proposed "radical reforms in public schools curricula" (Pastorello, 2014, p. 133). He had a wider vision than most, projecting schools as "a vital tool to encourage students to become active, responsible citizens who could and would engage as members of a social group in their neighborhood and wider communities" (Pastorello, 2014, p. 134). Thus, educational institutions were a vibrant part of the democratic society, and constituted in themselves "a miniature community, an embryonic society" that needed to be "freed from all economic stress" in order to "open all the possibilities of the human spirit" (Dewey, The School and Society, 2012, p. 244). Education was imagined in its multidimensionality, as "a necessity of life", "a social function" securing "direction and growth in the immature" individual or nation, but in order to fulfill its true purpose it needed to democratize itself in terms of both management and pedagogy (Dewey, Democracy and Education. An Introduction to the Philosophy of Education, 1930). His principles never became dominant in educational philosophy in terms of class practice oriented toward the student, but they have contributed to the proliferation of the view that schools and universities are the means for the development of critical, applied, socially engaged intelligence that increases the awareness of the citizens with regard to public affairs, their understanding of the matter and the competences to effectively participate in decision-making.

4 Wilson and the Inquiry at the Paris Peace Conference (1919)

True to the Progressive spirit, Woodrow Wilson, himself a highly reputable scholar, infused the politics and policies he pursued with the beliefs and ideas of the time. "Exposed to the historical, progressive thinking" of the age, Wilson's most eloquent stance as a Progressive was visible in his opposition to the more libertarian conception of the constitutional system, as proposed by the

Founding Fathers (Pestritto, 2005, p. 10). He wanted a stronger interventionist state, capable of fighting private interests, surging from politics or economics, as the only representative of the common will. In the foreign realm, two capital legacies of Wilsonianism – self-determination and the League of Nations – were based on the historicist and humanist view of the Progressives that believed democracy was the next logical step in the evolution of humanity towards greater civilization and progress.

A case in point is the work a group of scholars and experts – the Inquiry – that Wilson accepted, greeted and used as a basis for policy and action. Moreover, he encouraged their participation to the Paris Conference as members of the American Commission to Negotiate Peace. "It all started as an inquiry, indeed, […] of a working fellowship of distinguished scholars tasked to brief Woodrow Wilson about options for the postwar world" (Grose, 1996, p. 1). Although there is some debate with regard to the actual proponent of creating this "academic band", Colonel House, Wilson's "proto-national security advisor", is credited with this idea aimed at arranging "the U.S. presence at the Peace Conference" and establishing "reliable sources of information about conditions in Europe" (Grose, 1996, p. 3). It is also worth mentioning that the Department of State, led by Bryan, also had the intention to create such a group but (Gelfand, 1963, pp. 14-15), due to "turf-battles", the move was patronized by the White House. In other words, the administration lacked the knowledge and expertise on a number of issues it was expecting and anticipating to discuss in Paris. In fact, even Wilson "had received little formal training in international affairs, nor had he previously manifested any serious involvement in questions of foreign policy" (Gelfand, 1963, p. 1). Anyhow, the President clearly welcomed their recommendations. In fact, six of his famous "Fourteen Points" are based on a report produced by the Inquiry in January 1918 (Baker, Woodrow Wilson and World Settlement (volume III), 1922, pp. 23-41). Since the pursuit of American war and peace aims "might have easily hinged on the very preparations placed by President Wilson in the charge of Colonel House" (Gelfand, 1963, p. 32), the composition of the group was critical. The decision was then to recruit and select mainly professors, since the work of preparing the Conference was intended "to fall within the province of academic scholarship" (Gelfand, 1963, p. 33). Indeed, this "doctrine of government planning making use of expert counselors had emerged as a salient feature of progressive thought" (Gelfand, 1963, p. 33). The result is obvious from the anatomy of the Inquiry (Gelfand, 1963, pp. 53-68): 65% of the members studied in four top universities – Harvard, Yale, Columbia, Chicago – and approximately half of them were researchers and professors in five academic centers of excellence: Harvard, Yale, Columbia, Chicago, Stanford and the American Geographic Society. The human resources "recruiters", most of them renowned intellectuals (Sidney Mezes, Walter Lippmann, Newton Baker, Archibald Coolidge, James Shotwell), who also played the role of leaders and moderators in the group, complained about the difficulty of identifying "qualified talent", "genius" on specific issues. Even though some of the enrolled experts might have been the result of compromise, it may still be concluded that the Inquiry was trying to select "the cream of the crop" from the American academia. It is also worth mentioning that openness and interest were not displayed only by the government, the same response came from the academia: academic societies and universities offered donations and provided logistics, while political scientists, law and economics professors, sociologists, historians and philosophers rushed to provide their CVs in order to "serve the country" (Gelfand, 1963).

In Paris, the former members of the Inquiry left their study groups and libraries in order to work on multinational committees not for research but for pragmatic solutions: "they found themselves down from the ivory tower, testing something with their feet that might be either rock or quicksand" (Grose, 1996, p. 5). Although the story of the Peace Conference is generally told from the political and diplomatic perspective, different talks were held in parallel, "in congenial and civilized encounters" where ideas were shared and expertise was forged. These scholars redrew frontiers, arranged for economic treaties, formulated principles and designed institutions (Grose, 1996, p. 5). Although their work was eventually altered due to national interests and political action, their contribution was nevertheless valuable. "The final decisions rested with others, but these decisions were largely based upon facts and opinions" provided by scholars and it may be said that "the voice of the United States during the memorable Conference at Paris [...] found its first comprehensive and authoritative expression" (House & Seymour, 1921, pp. vii-viii) in the collaborative work and reflection of the "academic band". In fact, House's and Seymour's volume stands proof for the input of the academic laboratory into the political decision-making process.

Learning the lessons from the American Progressive Era leads to an obvious conclusion: good governance is depending on an increasing flow of talented scholars and knowledgeable expertise from the academia. Leaving common interest and openness aside, public authorities simply do not possess a better alternative to academic study as a guide and framework for statecraft.

5. Acknowledgement

This research paper is completed under aegis of the Research Institute for Quality of Life, Romanian Academy, as part of a project co-financed by the European Social Fund through the Sectoral Operational Programme Human Resources Development 2007-2013: "Pluri and interdisciplinarity in doctoral and postdoctoral programmes", POSDRU/159/1.5/141086.

6. References

Baker, R. S. (1919). *What Wilson Dit at Paris.* New York: Doubleday Page.

Baker, R. S. (1922). *Woodrow Wilson and World Settlement (volume III).* New York: Doubleday Page.

Berg, S. (2013). *Wilson.* New York: G.B. Putnam's Sons.

Dewey, J. (1930). *Democracy and Education. An Introduction to the Philosophy of Education.* New York: MacMillan.

Dewey, J. (2012). The School and Society. In W. Link, & S. (. Link, *The Gilded Age and Progressive Era: A Documentary Reader* (pp. 243-247). Chichester, UK: Wiley Blackwell.

Gelfand, L. (1963). *The Inquiry. American Preparations for Peace, 1917-1919.* New Haven, CT: Yale University Press.

Gottfried, P. (1990). Wilsonianism: The Legacy that Won't Die. *Journal of Libertarian Studies, vol. IX, no. 2* , 117-126.

Grose, P. (1996). *Continuing the Inquiry. The Council on Foreign Relations from 1921 to 1996.* New York: Council on Foreign Relations.

House, E. M., & Seymour, C. (1921). *What Really Happened at Paris. The Story of the Peace Conference, 1918-1919, by American Delegates.* New York: Charles Scribner's Sons.

Jaycox, F. (2005). *The Progressive Era (Eyewitness History).* New York: Facts on File.

Labaree, D. (2005). Progressivism, Schools and Schools of Education: An American Romance. *Paedagogica Historica, vol. 41, no. 1-2* , 275-288.

Martin, J. (2002). *The Education of John Dewey.* New York: Columbia University Press.

McNeese, T. (2010). *The Gilded Age and Progressivism: 1891-1913 (Discovering U.S. History).* New York: Chelsea House Publications.

Miller, D. H. (1924). *My Diary at the Conference of Paris. With Documents (volume IV).* New York: Appeal.

Murphy, K. (2013). *Uphill All the Way: The Fortunes of Progressivism, 1919-1929 (Ph.D. thesis).* Retrieved March 20, 2015, from Columbia University - Academic Commons: http://academiccommons.columbia.edu/download/fedora_content/download/ac:156123/CONTENT/Murphy_columbia_0054D_11138.pdf

Nugent, W. (2009). *Progressivism: A Very Short Introduction.* New York: Oxford University Press.

Pastorello, K. (2014). *The Progressives. Activism and Reform in American Society, 1893-1917.* Chichester, UK: Wiley Blackwell.

Pestritto, R. (2005). *Woodrow Wilson and the Roots of Modern Liberalism (American Intellectual Culture).* Lanham, MD: Rowman & Littlefield.

Tumulty, J. (1921, New York Doubleday Page). *Woodrow Wilson as I Know Him.* Retrieved March 20, 2015, from Project Gutenberg: http://www.gutenberg.org/cache/epub/8124/pg8124.html

West, T., & Schambra, W. (2007, July 18). *The Progressive Movement and the Transformation of American Politics.* Retrieved March 20, 2015, from The Heritage Foundation: http://www.heritage.org/research/reports/2007/07/the-progressive-movement-and-the-transformation-of-american-politics

White, W. A. (1925). *Woodrow Wilson: The Man, His Times, and His Task (third edition).* Boston: Houghton Mifflin.

Zorgbibe, C. (2003). *Wilson, un cruciat la Casa Albă / Wilson, a Crusader at the White House.* Bucharest: Fundaţia Europeană Titulescu / Titulescu European Foundation.

16

The Potential Sources of Change in Romania Regional Policy

Gabriela Marchis[1]

Abstract: There have been numerous debates on a new territorial organization of Romania during 2013 and 2014. The miracle of Romania regionalization was deemed to have contradictory effects from *territorial construction* to *dissolution*. Due to the presidential elections from the end of 2014, the process of regionalization was postponed, but some questions are still very alive: It is necessary to *regroup counties into regions*? The low development of Romania regions is caused by the lack of *administrative decentralization*? In Romania, *territorial reform* is synonym with *institutional reform*? Therefore, I consider that it is important to identify the potential *sources of change* in Romanian regional policy. The political debates on Romanian regionalization were mainly focus on *political interests*, without taking into account an important serious of *factors* that can spur growth and socio-economic development across our regions. Through this paper I try to investigate the specialised literature in order to identify some useful policy suggestions from regional scientists, which would be proper for Romania regional development, in the current context of Europe 2020 strategy.

Keywords: Europe 2020 strategy; government role; creative regions; innovation

1 Introduction

Regional integration is an old *desideratum* of Romania, that come into life by law 151/1998, when, in the context of adhering to European Union, 8 regions were outlined in accordance with European NUTS II level. The lack of *expertise* in defining and implementing regional development policies, together with the lack of *a long-run strategic vision* of policy-makers, determine that these 8 regions to be reconfirmed by law 315/2004. Even if, according to Romanian legislation, these regions are not territorial administrative units, the entire regional institution framework was constructed on the bases of these 8 regions and Romania succeeded to attract European financial assistance both in pre-accession and post-adhering periods. Without any scientific justification or practical demonstration, during 2013 and 2014, Romanian politicians advanced the idea that there is a strong need of change in Romanian territorial configuration and a series of debates took place on this issue and different models of how to *regroup counties into regions* arise. These political debates were focus mainly on *institutional reform* and on the *election/nomination procedures of representatives* in different

[1]Associate Professor, PhD, "Danubius" University of Galati, Romania, Address: 3 Galati Boulevard, 800654 Galati, Romania, Corresponding author: gabrielamarchis@univ-danubius.ro.

institutions, without taking into account the real need of harmonious development across the country in accordance with European standards. Romanian regional integration assume to reach certain standards of socio-economic and territorial development that will allow people who live in this community to enjoy in their daily routine that there are European citizens and not to feel the need to emigrate in order to have better living standards. In this context, I consider opportune to review the regional development of Romania from the perspective of the regional science and then to try to reshape (if it is the case) the regions.

2 What is the Regional Policy and Why It Is Important?

A brief incursion in the history of EU regional development policy, reveal that European regional policy is like a *panacea* for overcoming different crisis. Over time, through its technical and financial instruments, European regional policy played a major role in rebuilding regional economies, in order to bring European economies more closely together. Founded 40 years ago, EU regional policy was focused on correcting the imbalances "*resulting notably from agricultural predominance, industrial change and structural underemployment*." (European Commission, 2015)

Throughout history, EU regional policy was the key-drive to restructure and modernizing the European economy. This policy was redesign and improved over the time in order to reach different goals, the funding and the efforts being concentrated on ensuring the widespread of wealth across EU citizens.

Nowadays, the important role of regional policy is fully recognized by all 28 member states, and confirmed by the fact that there were no cuts in budget allocated for 2014-2020, comparatively with many others policy areas. The current European regional policy is focus on investments in line with the objectives of Europe 2020 strategy. Thus, 2014-2020 EU regional policy will finance projects focused on increasing economic development, to the detriment of projects related only on infrastructure. Given that European Union is represented as a kaleidoscope of regions characterized by convergence and also by spatial differentiation, regional policy framework for the next 7 years is designed on the basis of *Partnership Agreements* between European Commission and the EU countries, which outlines the member state's strategy and a list of development programmes. These programmes are implemented by each member state, which means that each country has the major responsibility of selecting, monitoring and evaluating the projects and European Commission is monitoring each programme.

In this context, a good investment agenda in Romania implies a good understanding of regional processes related to existing economic and institutional structures.

3 What are the Factors that Can Spur Growth and Socio-Economic Development across Romanian Regions?

3.1. Romania Portrait in Terms of Innovation and Competition

For 2014-2020 programming period, in line with Europe 2020 strategy, the key-words for a genuine regional policy are: ***innovation*** and ***competition***. In order to measure the territorial competitiveness and the potential for innovation at regional level, European Commission developed the Regional Competitiveness Index, which shows the strengths and the weaknesses of each of EU NUTS 2 region.

(Annoni & Dijkstra, 2013) Accordingly to this RCI-2013, the two southern Romanian regions "Sud-Est" and "Sud-Vest Oltenia" are the worst performers.

Moreover, Romania also is situated on 28th place, the lowest position in the Europe 2020 Competitiveness Index ranking. (World Economic Forum, 2014)

Table 2. Ranks of Romania in accordance with Europe 2020 Index

	Rank (out of 28)	*Score (1-7)*
Smart growth	28	3.5
Enterprise environment	23	3.6
Digital Agenda	28	3.6
Innovative Europe	28	2.9
Education and training	28	4.0
Inclusive growth	26	3.7
Labour market and employment	22	3.7
Social inclusion	27	3.8
Sustainable growth	26	3.9
Environmental sustainability	26	3.9
Europe 2020 Index (2014 edition)	**28**	**3.6**

As it may be observed, Romania has a *very low capacity for innovation* ranking is 28th on the *digital agenda* and the *innovative Europe* pillars. Also, in the *education and training* and *smart growth* pillars, Romania's performance is the worsts. Under these circumstances, translating the European priorities into the real investments decisions at regional and local level becomes a provocative task for our policy-makers.

3.2. Some Guidelines for Romania Long-Run Regional Trajectories

Important efforts are needed in order to develop a *long-term vision* for regional development. First of all, it is important to bring together a variety of representatives from central and local authorities, public and private stakeholders and civil society in order to *set up the priorities for development* for each area, *in accordance with the expectation and the needs of local communities and organisations*.

The real involvement of stakeholders in a decision-making process is necessary, in order to develop a *coherent and efficient agenda for investments*.

Different paths for regional development should be explored, in order to target the intervention towards that sectors that could optimise the regional evolution. Regional scientists [(Gunderson & Holling, 2002); (Folke, 2006)] show that regions, as complex system, are characterized at the same time by *the need for stability and change*. Thus, "*economic growth and human development depend on ecosystems and institutions and how they interact*". Any region has its own capacity for *renewal*, *re-organisation* and *development*. This capacity for *adjustment* and *adaptation* has to be taken into consideration for *redesigning a sustainable future*.

For example, regions should not only preserve and economically enhance their material and immaterial cultural and artistic heritage, but also should transform/adapt themselves in response to external pressures, generating local development and growth. (Lazzeretti, 2013) For instance, local events (such festivals, conferences, etc.) may trigger global effects (attracting people in the region will increase the demand for transportation, accommodation, restaurants, leisure activities, local traditional products, etc. and all of these will determine the raise of funds in the community).

Therefore, innovation as key for regional development, should be understand as well as identifying the key actors and drivers of path renewal and new path creation and seek to find out to which extend such changes are related to existing economic and institutional structures.

Also, reflecting upon innovation, as the creative process by which transformation occurs from interaction between different entities, in the field of regional development, innovation might occur from *knowledge recombination*, which means to take the already existing innovations from one industry and to set and adapt them for wholly different industry solutions. The specialized literature defines this "*exploring the adjacent possibilities*". At this point, the "fertile-soil" of an area is very important. Economies with a higher degree of variety among industries perform better than those without it. Regional scientists demonstrated that "*the more diverse the economic web, the easier is the creation of still further novelty…*[leading to]*…a positive correlation between economic diversity and growth*". (Kauffman, 2008)

In other words, the potential of a region to develop more rapidly is influenced also by its rate of *connectivity*. Moreover, a strongly networked region can have an impact on a larger scale. For instance, a small region but with a high degree of connectivity can respond more rapidly to market demands and can adapt its products to novelty, being an example for the national regime. As in the saying "little strokes fell great oaks", a region may anticipate for example the slow-moving institution from national level regarding eco-innovation, and can act independently, expressing local collective interest for high quality eco-products. In this context, local initiatives are very important to spur economic growth and to transform small awakenings into strategic eco-market niche and further into a dominant design with a high potential for a national adoption. Withal, in regions where *inter-cluster communication* is possible, the knowledge will spill over among clusters and innovation will be disseminated in a more self-organised manner, even trans-national. The success over time of EU cross-border cooperation programs (such as INTERREG or CBS) carried out between different regional entities demonstrates the importance of designing policies in a transnational context, Danube Strategy, being a good example for the current programming period.

But, it is important to notice that applying the same strategy of development in different regions will result in different outcomes. That is way, it is very important to grow *awareness of civil society* and to increase the involvement of local public and private stakeholders in designing their own development strategies/operational plans, in order to better meet their needs. This *collective enlightenment* on indicators that need to change in order to fight stagnation and inertia will lead over time to a better understanding of regional development processes and to a greater involvement in a decisional process. Maybe a new generation of higher-educated policy-makers will rise.

Another aspect that will re-frame regional development concerns to the role of *learning, exploration and exploitation of knowledge*. Human capital endowment is held to be one of the key defining features of a region. Recent work of regional scientists [(Sheppard, 2000); (Porter, 2000); (Martin, 2005); (Bristow, 2005)] reveal that *attracting and retaining innovative firms*, together with *skilled labour* and *knowledge workers*, will guarantee a significant socio-economic change. If the microeconomic environment is ensured at regional level, namely *a top-line working and living conditions*, people will not emigrate and productive firms will operate in these regions, with a long-run consequences related to a strong economic growth, together with new sources of increasing returns and new network connections.

In this attempt to identify the potential sources of change in Romania regional development policy, we cannot neglect the *role of universities in promoting knowledge*. Recent studies [(Youtie & Shapira, 2008); (Power & Malmberg, 2008); (Huggins, 2008); (Benneworth, Charles, & Madanipour, 2010); (Kitagawa, 2013)] illustrates that the regional economic development can be actually achieved through the medium of higher education institutions (HEIs), which play an important role in *connecting knowledge and spanning boundaries to generate innovation*. But, in order to accomplish their mission, universities also need a proper microeconomic environment and a suitable political and socio-cultural space for fostering innovation.

The contribution of universities to the development of their region is not a new phenomenon, but without being integrated in regional growth strategies, recognizing in this way their distinctive role in the formation of the innovation agendas, their input remains unclear. In the development of regional innovation policy networks, local authorities should admit that in a region, the university is the only one that has this unique institutional characteristic of *fostering collaboration* and *building partnerships* with a broader range of sectors involved in innovation processes, such as: other higher education institutions, research centres, organizations, industry players and etc., within and without the region. Therefore, building a regional institutional infrastructure, where universities are embedded as part of the regional innovation architecture may represent the key for promoting economic growth and wellbeing through *workforce development* and *knowledge exchange*. Moreover, through their core activities, such as: professional or vocational training and placements, applied research and consultancy in different areas, universities contribute to their regions also by their *cultural and civic engagement*. According to Kitagawa (2013), "universities collaborate with local organization [...] health sector, education – working with local schools on widening participation initiatives; cultural sector – with local museums, theatres, local cultural amenities or sporting organizations; third sector – including community engagement activities and student volunteering".

4 Concluding Remarks

Reshaping the Romania territory, by regrouping the counties into new regions, is not solving the basic problems of underdevelopment of Romania regions. The current regional portrait of Romania shows that the entire territorial is harmoniously underdeveloped, with the exception of the capital region, which is not very uncommon.

Re-framing regional development in Romania, in my opinion, implies a common effort and public engagement from our decisional policymakers to treat this problem in a more responsible manner, because it has very long-term effects. In the current economic climate, Romanian regional policy-makers should focus their attention in identifying the real challenges in regional development process, which is, accordingly with "The Europe 2020 Competitiveness Report - Building a More Competitive Europe", related with the *lack of basic infrastructure*, which is strictly necessary for the basic functioning of any economy and refer also to *the quality and fairness of governance* and *local public services*, which are important socio-economic determinants.

Another concern for our policymakers should be the *decreasing the bureaucracy for accessing EU financial assistance*, in order to permit the investments which will develop the microeconomic environment at regional level, with spillovers effects over time. The maximum and effective use of EU financial assistance plays a critical role for Romania regional development. Also, finding the way to *target the investments in developing the basic infrastructure* and also to *improve local public services* is a key feature that should take into account. Maybe the institutional reform should be focused mainly in *helping young people to find a job* and make use of their knowledge accumulated in their students years and not only in relation with the selection/nomination procedures of representatives in different institutions.

Moreover given that the role of knowledge and human sensibility in the labour process is essential for further development, public authorities should encourage the *cooperation* between local enterprises and HEIs, because it is essential to focus the entire efforts in developing skills, research, knowledge exchange and innovation. Recognizing the central role of university in local development and involving HEIs in designing strategies for regional development, will produce change and novelty. Furthermore, even if each university has different strengths and mission, their overall role in a region is to provide a *space for dialogue among stakeholders*. Hence, in this highly complex process of regional development, university should be involved, because it may represent not only an important solution to *respond to local skill needs in the community*, but also, through its connectivity and openness can bring partners together, facilitating the *development of ideas and projects*, and *attracting investments* from outside.

5 References

Annoni, P., & Dijkstra, L. (2013). *EU Regional Competitiveness Index RCI 2013*. Luxembourg: Publications Office of the European Union.

Benneworth, P., Charles, D., & Madanipour, A. (2010). Building Localized Interactions between Universities and Cities through University Spatial Development. *European Planning Studies*(18), 1611-1629.

Bristow, G. (2005). Everyone's a winner: problematizing the discourse of regional competitiveness. *Journal of Economic Geography, 5*(3), 285-304.

Dijkstra, L., Annoni, P., & Kozovska, K. (2011). A new regional competitiveness index: Theory, Methods and Findings. *European Union Regional Policy Working Papers*.

European Commission . (2014). *Guidance for Beneficiaries of European Structural and Investment Funds*. Luxembourg: Publications Office of the European Union.

European Commission. (2015). *Regional Policy*. Preluat pe March 19, 2015, de pe InfoRegio: http://ec.europa.eu/regional_policy/index.cfm/en/newsroom/news/2015/03/european-regional-development-fund-turns-40

Folke, C. (2006). Resilience: The Emergence of a Perspective for Social-Ecological Systems Analysis. *Global Environmental Change*, 253-267.

Gunderson, L., & Holling, C. (2002). *Panarchy: Understanding Transformations in Human and Natural Systems*. Washington DC: Island Press.

Huggins, R. (2008). Universities and Knowledge-based Venturing: Finance, Management and Networks in London. *Entrepreneurship and Regional Development*(20), 185-206.

Kauffman, S. (2008). *Reinventig the sacred*. New York: Basic Books.

Kitagawa, F. (2013). City-regions, innovation and universities. În L. (. Lazzeretti, *Re-framing regional development* (pg. 341-358). New York: Routledge Taylor&Francis Group.

Lazzeretti, L. (2013). The remarkable resilience of cities of art: the challenge of a new renaissance in Florence. În P. Cooke, *Re-framing regional development* (pg. 256-274). New York: Routledge Taylor&Francis Group.

Martin, R. (2005). *Thinking about Regional Competitiveness: Some Critical Issues*. East Midlands Regional Development Agency.

Meyer-Stamer, J. (2008). Systematic Competitiveness and Local Economic Development. În B. Shamin, *Large Scale Systemic Change: Theories, Modelling and Practices* (p. 31). Duisburg.

Porter, M. (2000). Location, competition and economic development: local clusters in a global economy. *14*(1), pp. 15-34.

Power, D., & Malmberg, A. (2008). The Contribution of Universities to Innovation and Economic Development: in what Sense a Regional Problem? *Cambridge Journal of Regions, Economy and Society*(1), 233-245.

Schwab, K., & Sala-I-Martin, X. (2012). *The Global Competitiveness Report 2012-2013.* World Economic Forum.

Sheppard, E. (2000). Competition in space between places. În T. J. Barnes, & E. Sheppard, *A Companion to Economic Geography.* Oxford: Blackwell.

Thissen, M., Van Oort, F., Diodato, D., & Ruijs, A. (2014). *Regional Competitiveness and Smart Specialization in Europe: Place-based Development in International Economic Networks.* Edward Elgar Publishing.

World Economic Forum. (2014). *The Europe 2020 Competitiveness Report - Building a More Competitive Europe.* Geneva: World Economic Forum.

Youtie, J., & Shapira, P. (2008). Building an Innovative Hub: A Case Study of the Transformation of University Roles in Regional Technological and Economic Development. *Research Policy*(37), 1188-1204.

17

The Monetary Policy in a Changing World

Mariana Trandafir[1]**, Georgeta Dragomir**[2]

Abstract: In a context where "the economies' evolution is driven by the crisis", the monetary policies are facing, in the post-crisis period, challenges that bring to the forefront of debates the rethinking of objectives, strategies and even implementation tools. This paper presents in a comparative analysis, the relevance of price stability in terms of theoretical fundaments and effectiveness of the concept for the pre and post – crisis periods, in the Eurozone, the US and Japan in an attempt to identify the explicative resorts of the central bank's monetary behavior. At this time when the central banks are obliged to unconventional measures to save the global economy from the danger of deflation, the topic is important and timely addressed. The paper uses statistical data of official documents taken from the International Monetary Fund, European Union and central bank websites.

Keywords: price stability; central bank; the global financial crisis; unconventional measures

1. Introduction

Although in the conception close to the current one, the first central bank was founded in 1694 (Bank of England), the monetary policy occurred during the Great Depression of the years 1929 to 1933, as a government response that aimed at steming the Federal Reserve System US financial panic and bank insolvency and they have over time gained new values. Until the Great Depression, the central banks had to intervene as creditor of last resort to commercial banks and insuring financing of state government spending.

Following the line of Keynesian thought, the expansionary monetary policies implemented after the crash of 1929, designed to stimulate the economic growth by influencing the aggregate demand and which treated inflation as insignificant factor in the development of economy showed prominently its limits.

In the early 70s, the monetary practice, under the sphere of influence of Keynesian theory and theoretical construction of 1958, the Phillips curve, which established an inflation-unemployment compromise, confronted increasingly high levels of inflation, the monetary policy being mainly oriented towards ensuring full employment. It is the time for the emergence of new alternative

[1] Associate Professor, PhD, "Danubius" University of Galati, Romania, Address: 3 Galati Boulevard, 800654 Galati, Romania, E-mail: marianatrandafir@univ-danubius.ro.

[2] Professor, PhD, "Danubius" University of Galati, Romania, Address: 3 Galati Boulevard, 800654 Galati, Romania, Corresponding author: gretadragomir@univ-danubius.ro.

theories, of which it quickly imposed monetarism, as "major pole of opposition to Keynesianism both politically and theoretically" (Beaud & Dostaler, 2000). The basic concepts of monetarism, monetary stability and reliability can be found in the famous "rule of the k percent" of Milton Friedman. Accelerating inflation and rising unemployment in most developed countries, under the impact of the collapse of the Bretton Woods arrangements and oil shocks of the 70s, will require a reassessment of the conventional thinking in monetary policy. The importance of anchoring inflation expectations in the context has represented the catalyst of the institution-building process, aiming at granting a new status to the central bank: independent institutions, with firm mandates for tracking price stability (Isărescu, 2013), which becomes the primary objective of central banks assumed at institutional level, in an intellectual, political and social consensus of the 90s. As a rather pragmatic reply to reality than putting into practice a new academic school of thought (Gill Hammond, 2012), it will be adopted, on a larger scale, a new strategy - targeting inflation, as a solution designed to create the best framework for ensuring price stability. The central banks will say, during the "Great moderation" as "saviors of the global financial system", winners of the "bet with the inflation."

Triggered in an economic context characterized by low levels of inflation, the global financial crisis that began in 2007 as a true "tsunami" has shown that insuring the price stability is necessary, but not sufficient to ensure the financial stability and it was brought into the attention of decision makers (i) the relationship between financial stability and price stability in the context macro-stabilization policies, including the opportunity of assuming a single fundamental objective for monetary policy, (ii) the foremost position of the objective of low inflation or (iii) the most appropriate measure to be expressed in the inflation target. They were brought back to the forefront of debates the attributions of central banks, the opportunity of maintaining the objective of insuring price stability, as the primary objective of central banks and even the institutional existence of the central bank.

2. Literature Review

The primary objective of central banks assumed at the institutional level, the *price stability* ensured by setting a numerical target for inflation, foreseen for a medium time horizon, transmitting clear messages on the task of monetary policy and criteria for assessing the performance of the central bank and it reflects the ability of the central bank ability "to achieve a stable currency based on trust in the interaction between the economic agents, the confidence in property rights, trust in society and, more generally, the confidence in the future." (Issing, 2002)

According to Lucas Papademos (2006) the price stability is that state of the economy in which the general level of aggregates price is stable and the inflation rate is low and stable, so that the considerations on nominal dimension of transactions cease to be a relevant factor for economic decisions.

Emphasizing the dual role of price stability, Ben Bernanke (2006) reveals the qualities of "objective and means for monetary policy": (i) as an objective, the price stability preserves the integrity of the purchasing power of the currency, while affirming as a means by which the policy can achieve other goals; (ii) as a means for monetary policy, the price stability provides a stable monetary and financial framework for the decision on micro and macroeconomic levels, formulated on medium or long time horizons. The effects of these decisions are found in improving the economic growth, increase of employment on long-term and they have a significant impact on the stability of production and occupancy on short and medium term. In a context where the previsions for the medium and long term are well anchored, the low and stable inflation determine the moderation of interest installments on long-term.

In a three-dimensional approach, Otmar Issing (2000) defines price stability as: (i) steady - state deflation experienced by the USA in the last thirty years of the 19th century, during which productivity earnings were found in lower prices and not in the most wages and subsequently laid down by Milton Friedman; (ii) a constant price level or zero inflation (iii) low inflation, accepted definition on reasons regarding both the seigniorage as a source of government revenue, implying the possibility as method of inflation calculation as being inadequate.

In the plan of practical approach, ensuring the price stability, it allows the monetary policy the reduction of uncertainty in the economy, contributing to an efficient allocation of resources (Isărescu, 2013) by:

- facilitating the formulation of long-term business plans / investments;
- improving the functioning of markets, increasing the signaling role of price changes;
- discouraging the speculative activities;
- elimination of undesirable redistribution effects (unanticipated inflation);
- facilitating the formation of resources for investments (savings) and their involvement in productive activities.

Understanding the dynamics of inflationary phenomenon, its causes and its effects on the economy, nationally and globally, and their relevance of the composition of indicators, where it is expressed, represent widely debated topics in the economic literature and practice, identifying the measures that confer quantifiable dimension of the inflationary phenomenon, representing a major concern.

3. Monetary Policy for Crisis or the Crisis of Monetary Policy?

3.1. The Consensus of the Pre-Crisis Period

Many national central banks and the European Central bank define inflation essentially as "a general increase - or generalized - of prices of goods and services for a long time, which leads to lowering the value of money and, therefore, their purchasing power" (ECB, 2011), thus replying to the controversy on the meaning of inflation – the prices increase or increasing the quantity of money in circulation.

The specialized literature (Petursson, 2004; Isărescu, 2013) summarizes, based on international experience, "as what the monetary policy is able to achieve": the central bank can ensure price stability, resulting in long-term the inflation rate level in the economy without affecting the level and growth rate of GDP. Pursuing price stability, the monetary policy contributes to a sustainable economic growth, as on long periods of time, the relatively high economic growth is incompatible with a persistent high inflation. Although it has assumed the price stability as the primary objective, the central banks pursue the impact of monetary policy decisions on aggregate demand in the short and medium term, on the exchange rate and it pays attention to the developments in financial markets. Long-term objective of price stability can be achieved in the context of an effective and free of tension transmission of monetary policy in a stable financial system. (Isărescu, 2008)

In an attempt to restrain the inflationary phenomenon, more and more central banks choose, after 1990, the "road" open by the New Zealand, as a strategy of monetary policy, the direct targeting of inflation, "that frame that attaches the highest importance of a low and fixed inflation or price stability" (Napoleon Pop, 2008). Becoming a "global framework" (Sterne, 2001) the inflation targeting was adopted explicitly or implicitly by the central banks belonging to developed or emerging economies, including Canada (1991), UK (1992), Australia (1993), Sweden (1993), Finland (1993), Spain (1995), Israel (1997), which became, after the financial crises in Asia and Latin America, an attractive alternative for countries with emerging markets: Poland (1998), Brazil (1999), Czech Republic (1997), Hungary (2001), Romania (2005), Turkey (2006), Serbia (2009).

Many central banks, though they do not explicitly target the inflation, they apply elements of this strategy in formulating the monetary policy decisions. The European Central Bank, for example, defines the price stability to be maintained over the medium term, as the annual growth of less than 2% of the harmonized index of consumer prices for the Eurozone and it aims at maintaining the inflation rates at a lower level, but close to 2% on the medium term (the Governing Council, 1998).

Until the global financial crisis, the Federal Reserves of the US were intended as "maximum employment, stable prices, and moderate long-term interest rates." Price stability is defined as "a longer-run goal of 2% inflation", while the Bank of Japan lead the monetary policy based on the principle that the policy aims at achieving the price stability to contribute to the healthy development of national economy. Inflation remains, until 2007, on a path around the proposed target of FED in the Eurozone and ECB in the US, while Japan is experiencing deflation (Figure 1) amid the negative interaction between asset prices, the increase of the financial system malfunction and the deterioration of the real economy.

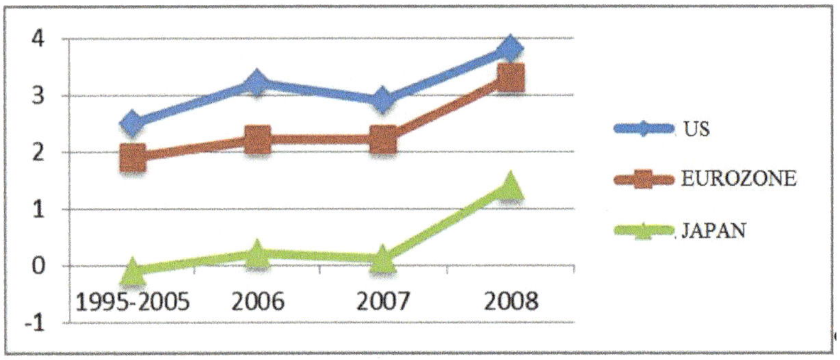

Figure 1. Evolution of Inflation 1995-2008

Source: IMF World Economic Outlook, October 2014

Hazard or best practice in monetary policy during the last two decades of the pre-crisis period, known as the "Great Moderation" was characterized by substantial reductions in inflation, and also on production volatility in almost all developed countries under the impact of structural economic, institutional, technological changes, of perfecting the macroeconomic policies and especially the monetary ones. The "Irrational exuberance" of this period facilitated the emergence of the global crisis, but as evidence of a compelling reality: the monetary theory and the practice of central banks have lagged behind with the development of financial systems in developed market economies and, therefore, many banks plants were unprepared to deal with the financial crisis that erupted in August 2007. (Cerna, 2014)

3.2. Price Stability and the Global Financial Crisis

Occurred amid unprecedented expansion of bank credit and the increase appetite for risk in all financial markets, inducing the adverse selection and moral hazard and creating the impression that only "the sky was the limit," the global financial crisis caused the most severe contraction of economic activity at global level since the Great Depression of the years 1929-1933 and it doubted even the central bank's ability to fulfill its mission amid the inflation rates close to zero in 1990 (US and Eurozone) or 1.3 in Japan (Figure 2)

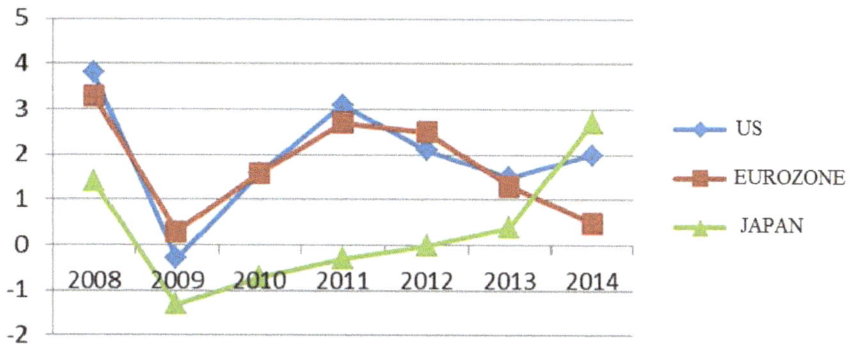

Figure 2. Inflation 2008 - 2014

Facing the shock represented by strong inflationary pressures, each central bank acted, in the post-crisis period, depending on the circumstances and the degree of economic development through measures meant to combat the deep and prolonged recession and financial instability from the Great Depression of the 1930s and to ensure the macroeconomic and financial stability.

The global economic crisis has damaged the transmission channels of monetary policy decisions in the economy and it has forced the central banks to act in the new framework emerged in the developed economies, where (Cerna, 2014):

- the balance sheet of commercial banks has been severely affected by their asset accumulation of a large volume of doubtful debts, generating a massive effort to cut debts (deleveraging), which led banks to restrict the credit supply at a time when the central banks also tried to tighten the monetary policy;
- The interest rate practiced on the interbank markets – as the interest on the private titles market - began to include a risk premium increasingly higher, which countered the effects of lower interest directory rates by the central banks;
- Rapid deterioration of the economic situation required a reduction of interest directories, so that in many countries, the monetary policy rate has reached zero or very close to this level (below which it may not decrease).

In many recent theoretical and empirical works caused especially by the debates on the economic policy pursued in the "lost decade" of Japan, it shows that the central banks may apply a wide range of "unconventional" measures of monetary policy (Cerna, 2014). In practice "the central banks in the United States, United Kingdom, Japan, and euro area adopted a series of unconventional monetary policies with two broad goals (IMF, 2013): to restore the functioning of financial markets and intermediation and to provide further monetary policy accommodation at the zero lower bound, (Bernanke & Reinhart, 2004):

• "The commitment on monetary policy orientation - policy duration commitment", which is to ensure the investors' confidence that short-term rates interest will be maintained in the future at a lower level than expected by the market in the absence of the commitment;

• "Quantitative easing" aimed at increasing the availability of banks' current accounts at the central bank beyond the level necessary to bring the overnight rate to zero;

• "Qualitative easing" (or credit easing), involving usually an expansion of central bank balance sheet, as in the case of quantitative easing, focusing on the structure of assets and not on the monetary base level, aiming at changing the structure of the portfolio of assets held by the private sector and, consequently, changes at the level of relative prices, with consequences on economic activity.

Accordingly, the central banks were forced to abandon the traditional instruments for reducing the real interest in the medium and long term, becoming largely ineffective. The strong return of credit risk and liquidity on financial markets it has put an end to an "age of innocence" in monetary policy (Liikanen, 2012).

4. Challenges of the Global Crisis and even ... Solutions

The crisis has "opened an opportunity" (Issing, 2011) for monetary policy makers and academic research: identifying the explanatory springs of the causes of the crisis, to embed the information in future decisions designed to improve the performance of monetary policies and to avoid repeating the past mistakes.

The importance of low and reduced inflation, as main objective and in many cases the only one, the monetary policy is a concept that the global financial crisis has brought to the forefront of debates: it has shown that maintaining a stable inflation does not necessarily provide a zero level of the GPD deviation compared to the potential. Price stability becomes from the "strong spot" of the pre-crisis to the "weak spot" of the post-crisis period (Table 1).

Table 1. Price stability

Price stability	
pre-crisis period	**post-crisis period**
- main long-term objective of monetary policy, assuming the price stability as the primary long-term objective of monetary policy represent a key element for the whole conceptual framework for policymakers (Bernanke, Laubach, Mishkin & Posen, 2001)	- price stability does not guarantee also the financial stability (Svensson and macroeconomic, 2011); it is necessary redrawing borders or rethinking connections
- maintaining a low and stable inflation is important, perhaps necessary, for achieving other macroeconomic objectives (Bernanke, Laubach, Mishkin & Posen, 2001)	- it is preferably targeting a price level or inflation targeting adapted in the light of the recent financial crisis and recession (Svensson, 2011)
- an explicit mandate for pursuing monetary policy stability and a high degree of operational autonomy (Roger, 2009)	- the ultimate goal should be the output gap and the stable inflation
- insuring price stability is a prerequisite (almost) enough to promote financial stability, being invalidated by the recent global crisis	

The identification of that indicator, while maintaining the set direction, could lead to a greater stability in the economic activity, named by Mankiw and Reis price stability index (2002) representing a debated topic among academics and policy makers in monetary matters.

In the conceptual plan, the crisis requires rethinking flexibility and limits of this flexibility: the liquidity trap into which many central banks fell, it has destroyed the illusion according to which there are no longer shocks that push inflation to zero. A low inflation risk presents the danger of the entry into a negative territory, causing zeroing the monetary policy interest rates, forcing the recourse to quantitative easing measures. (Isărescu, 2012) In order to avoid inflation on negative territory, Blanchard et al. (2010), for example, propose amendments to the inflation target from 2% to 4%, the proposal was not supported by Mishkin (2011) invoking the experience of the 1960s, as a result of accepting the level 4-5%, the inflation has continued to rise over the limit. However, a decision that would meet the consensus is still waiting.

In the field of monetary practice, the ECB has been very active since the beginning of the crisis and its actions helped the financial sector to avoid a complete meltdown and adopted measures that were mainly directed at ensuring the provision of liquidity and repairing the bank-lending channel. The Fed and the Bank of England quickly pursued unconventional monetary policies by implementing quantitative easing programmes that appeared to have a positive impact on financial variables and also on the real economy. (Claeys, 2014) The specialized literature and the international practice shows the effectiveness of the "unconventional" monetary policy measures, but only under certain circumstances, shown in Table 2. (Cerna, 2014)

Table 2. Constraints on non-standard measures

	Communication on future interests	**Targets on *quantitative easing via Credit easing***		***Credit easing in long term***	
		Public	Private	Public	Private
It involves achieving zero level of directories interest	No	Yes	Yes	Yes	Yes
Operational if the financial system is affected by extreme claims	Yes	No	No	Yes	Yes
Credit risk in the central bank's active	No	No	Yes	No	Yes
The risk for central bank independence	No	Yes	No	Yes	No

(*) No – in the first moment, Yes - from a certain level

Source: (Cerna, 2014)

According to official data published by the European Central Bank, for example, (Economic Bulletin no. 2/2015), the Governing Council has decided in January 2015 extending the assets purchasing program so that it includes, from March, titles in euro with low risk (investment grade) issued by governments and government agencies in euro area and EU institutions. The cumulative monthly purchases of securities issued by the public and private sector will rise to 60 billion Euros. It is intended to carry them to the end of September 2016 and, in any case, until the Governing Council shall determine a sustained adjustment of inflation trajectory, which should be consistent with the objective of maintaining the inflation rates below the level, but close to 2% on medium term.

For central banks that have adopted direct targeting of inflation as a monetary policy strategy, the global financial crisis has put into question all the concepts under which they operated, having even its "obituary" by Jeffrey Frankel in the summer of 2012, when announced "with regret, the death of inflation targeting", at only a few months after the FED and the Bank of Japan announced the establishment of medium-term inflation targets, with the stated aim of enhancing the transparency and effectiveness of monetary policy. (Trandafir, 2013)

The intellectual, political and social consensus of the pre-crisis period, crystallized around the belief that inflation is the main source of financial instability and that the ensurance of price stability is a prerequisite (almost) enough to promote financial stability, is invalidated by the recent global crisis. From this perspective, ensuring financial stability returns as an unsolved problem by the central banks. Reconciliation functions of price and financial stability in one institution, supported as possibility by Mugur Isarescu (2012), is considered inappropriate by Lars EO Svensson (2011) as he finds them as being conceptually distinct, each with separate objectives, instruments and control authorities. (Trandafir, 2013) We cannot omit the decision of European authorities which have reached a consensus: the Union Bank, considered an appropriate response in terms of the "impossible trinity", which points out that the financial stability and financial integration are not compatible with the supervision maintenance at national level. (Isărescu, 2012) If the implementation of a unique manual of rules in over 8000 banks, as they are now in Europe, will be able to reach its goal, in the absence of a fiscal union, remains an open subject.

Given the fact that "companies were managed in the past without central banks" Marvyn King (1999), attempts, since the pre-crisis to decipher, based on the realities of the new millennium, the future concept of central bank, imagining "the central bank with no money", as a result of innovations in the technology domain brought by the "new economy" of the 90s: eligible assets could become any financial asset for which there is the possibility of compensating the prices on the market in real time, the system could determine the price of financial assets, in terms of a unit of account, equivalent, probably, with a commodity standard, by confronting the supply with the demand of financial assets and it may perform the deductions. The concern of the central bank to limit the excessive monetary creation would be transferred to the requirement of ensuring the integrity of computer systems. In 2010, Huerta de Soto considers necessary to reform the banking system with the stated goal of "submitting it to its traditional principles of civil and commercial law, according to which every person and company must meet certain requirements (100% reserves), in addition to strict compliance with the terms established in each contract." In this context, the Austrian school followers propose, in in the banking domain, the following three steps (Cerna, 2010):

- Restoring obligatory reserves 100% for banks that receive deposits from the public and all similar institutions;
- Demolition of central banks as financier of last resort (a function which is no longer necessary in terms of applying the previous measures) and as central agency of financial planning;
- Privatization of fiat money issued by the state as monopoly and its replacement by a monetary system that cannot be handled by humans; for now, it can be the classical golden standard system.

5. Conclusion

As a conclusion, we can say that the recent crisis has submitted to the "resistance test" not only the applied strategies, but also the operational framework of central banks, global cooperation and it restored the financial stability in the center of the central bank, changing the very way of thinking of theorists and practitioners on the formulation of monetary policy decisions.

Although the progress registered in the realm of ideas and practice of the economic science, the reality too often does not listen to theory, and the theory claims without grounds from practice (Dinu, 2012) and, regardless of the degree of mastery of the art of distinguishing between cause and effect, it is still affected by the unexpected events, which become points of inflection for economic theory and practice, imposing paradigm shifts of the conventional framework of thinking. As long as it is still valid the consensus of the pre-crisis period and how much it should be rethought the monetarist principles, if the central bank has the right to broaden the objcctives to include, along with price stability also the financial stability are challenges in a world of searches, evaluation, rethinking, where the authorities at the highest level of national and global monetary decision still seek answers. In this world of turmoil, we can say that, unfortunately, crises cannot be anticipated ... so far.

6. References

Blanchard, O., Dell'Ariccia, G. & Mauro, P., 2010. (2010). Rethinking Macroeconomic Policy Rethinking Macroeconomic Policy. *I M F Staff Position Note*. SPN/10/03.

Cerna, S. (2014). Politica monetară neconvențională/Unconventional monetary policy. *Oeconomica*, no. 1, Bucharest.

CernaS (2014). Politica monetară în epoca post-criză/Monetary policy in the post-crisis era. *Economistul/The Economist*, no. 37-38.

Cena, S. (2010). Criza și redefinirea băncilor centrale/The Crisis and the redefinition of central banks. *Oeconomica*.

Hammond, G. (2012). State of the art of inflation targeting. *CCBS Handbook*, Issue 29.

Huerta de Soto, J. (2010). *Moneda, creditul bancar și ciclurile economice/Money, Bank Credit, and Economc Cycles*. Iasi: Ed Universității Al I Cuza.

Isarescu, M. (2008). Probleme ale politicii monetare într-o țară emergentă. Cazul României, Discurs susținut la Academia Regală de Științe Economice și Financiare/Problems of monetary policy in an emerging country. The case of Romania. *A speech held at the Royal Academy of Economics and Finance*, on February 21.

Isarescu, M. (2013). Politica monetară și creșterea economică/Monetary policy and economic growth. Forumul-dezbatere Academica BNR 20/Forum - Academic Debate Romanian National bank 2013. 2nd edition. Constanta. September 2.

Isărescu, M. (2012). Politica monetară în perioada tranziției. Gestionarea modificărilor de paradigm/Monetary policy during the transition period. The management of paradigm changings. *Presentation at the annual Conference of the European Association for Banking History with the theme Public Policies & the Direction of Financial Flows*, Bucharest, June 7 to 9.

Issing, O. (November 2000). Why price stability?. *First ECB Central Banking Conference*.

Issing, O. (2002). *Monetary Policy in a World of Uncertainly*. [Online] Available at http://www.ecb.int/press/key/date/1999/html/sp991203_2.en.html.

King, M. (1999). *Challenges for Monetary Policy: New and Old*. Kansas: Federal Reserve Bank of Kansas City.

Liikanen, E. (May 2012). Monetary policy in unconventional times. *Speech at the workshop Monetary Policy in Unconventional Times*. BCE.

Papademos, L., (2006). Price stability, financial stability and efficiency, and monetary policy. Price stability, financial stability and efficiency, and monetary policy. *Speech at the third conference of the monetary Stability Foundation on Challenges to the financial system – ageing and low growth*.

Petursson, T. G. (2004). Formulation of inflation targeting around the world. *Monetary Bulletin*, Issue 1.

Pop, N. (2008). *Virtuți ale politicii monetare/Virtues of monetary policy*. Bucharest: Expert.

Trandafir, M. (2013). Țintirea inflației – un bilanț provizoriu, Studii post-doctorale în economie, vol 2. – Studii și cercetări financiar-monetare/Inflation Targeting - an interim report, post-doctoral studies in Economics, vol 2 - Monetary Financial Studies and Research. Bucharest: Ed Academiei Române.

*** ECB https://www.ecb.europa.eu.

*** Fed www.federalreserve.gov.

IMF World Outlook Report, October 2014.

18

Energy Efficiency Initiatives on the EU Territory. Comparative Perspective

Crina Radulescu[1], Cristina Elenea Nicolescu[2], Teodora Bitoiu[3]

Abstract: The worldwide population growth and the lower accessibility to the primary energy resources – that have fast diminishing reserves – are reflected in the EU records with the 54 million people affected by the "energy poverty". Therefore, the topic of energy efficiency is gaining a greater weight on the agenda of the governments, especially for countries that mostly depend on the energy resources of other countries. The Directive 2012/27/EU of the European Parliament and of the Council on Energy Efficiency include other requirements concerning the introduction of smart meters and networks to encourage a more efficient power consumption. The paper aims to highlight, from a comparative perspective, a number of provisions adopted by some EU Member States to achieve national targets for energy efficiency in 2020. Some countries have recorded progress, others worrying delays, thus stressing the need for full implementation of the European legislative framework for energy efficiency. The used methodology is mainly qualitative and is based on the analysis of documents and case studies, and the performed analysis aims at providing important information so to strengthen the accountability of the decision makers with regard to policies and measures development to increase energy efficiency, from a concerted perspective aimed at facilitating the Energy Union objectives fulfilment.

Keywords: Energy Union; energy poverty; public policy instruments; smart meter system

1. Introduction

In the context of the natural concern for the energy evolution and global environment, marked by numerous constraints on world energy balance (currently, the oil and gas component is the biggest challenge), many countries have managed to quickly adopt strategies and action programs and alternative energy measures, such as shale gas or renewable energies[4], equally trying to ensure the sustainability maximization of these operations.

---

[1] National University of Political Studies and Public Administration, Romania, Corresponding author: crina.radulescu@administratiepublica.eu.
[2] National University of Political Studies and Public Administration, Romania, Romania, E-mail: cristina.nicolescu@administratiepublica.eu.
[3] National University of Political Studies and Public Administration, Romania, E-mail: teodora.bitoiu@administratiepublica.eu.
[4] See for example the US emphasis on amplifying shale gas, Germany's wishes to reduce its dependence on nuclear power and switch to renewable energy sources by 2022, China's effort for a fleet of vehicles fully electric.

Currently, the energy efficiency is considered as a new "clean" energy resource of the sustainable energy policy[1] understood as that policy that *maximizes the long-term welfare of citizens, while maintaining a reasonable, dynamic balance between food security, competitiveness of energy services and environmental protection, energy system in response to the energy system challenges* (IER, 2003, p. 23).

The challenges facing Europe in the energy field are numerous, such as for example: *increasing dependence on imports, high energy prices and their volatility, globally increased demand for energy, slow progress in energy efficiency* etc.

In view of these uncertainties, the European energy policy benefits from a core of a variety of measures that aim at achieving an integrated energy market and ensuring security of energy supply and sustainable energy sector.

When rising the question on how prepared is the EU to face these new challenges, our attention should be turned first to the current list of priority objectives of the central or local administrations of the EU Member States and found that one of the stringent topics pertains to the *energy efficiency*, its implementing measures at national level being a means of boosting the economic growth and, at EU level, a *means of promoting the competitiveness of European economies*[2].

This bold paradigm shift from traditional policy, centralist and monopolist, *production oriented*, to that oriented towards *energy saving*, was strongly supported by the EU institutions and the concerted action of the EU Member States. The transition has allowed the EU energy market remodelling, and has put under scrutiny the environmental costs and social externalities.

The EU right and competence to act with regard to energy efficiency and energy savings is established in the Treaty on the Functioning of the European Union (TFEU) by art. 194, Para. (1). under this article, some aspects of the energy policy are subject to *shared responsibility*, thus strengthening the effort towards a common energy policy.

Being assessed as the largest energy resource in Europe, the energy efficiency is a central element of the EU's Europe 2020 Strategy for a Smart, Sustainable and Inclusive growth, disconnected from the energy consumption.

For the environmental protection, the current EU policy agenda has set wide-ranging objectives, grouped under the target "20-20-20" (a set of three key-objectives for 2020), for: 20% reduction of greenhouse gas emissions in the EU compared with 1999 levels; 20% increase in the share of energy produced from renewable sources in the EU; 20% improvement in energy efficiency in the EU.

Complementary, on a deeper perspective, the EU has established a set of long term goals within Roadmap 2050[3], the Energy Roadmap 2050 aiming at: reducing the greenhouse gas emissions (emissions GES) 80-95% by 2050 in comparison to the 1990 levels.

A common framework of measures to promote energy efficiency in the European Union is found established by the Directive 2012/27/EU of the European Parliament and of the Council of 25 October 2012 on Energy Efficiency (EED)[4].

---

[1] Energy efficiency needs to be considered as an energy source in its own right, representing the amount in Nw (negawatts) of the energy saved, as demonstrated beyond any doubt by recent world and European history. See more in *European Parliament Resolution* of *23 June 2016* on the *implementation report* on the *Energy Efficiency Directive* (2012/27/UE) (2015/2232(INI)).
[2] See Fact Sheets on the European Union–Energy efficiency.
[3] COM (2011) 112 final, A roadmap for moving to a competitive low carbon economy in 2050. This means the effective reduction of EU emissions internally, and not their compensation through carbon market.
[4] Amending Directives 2009/125/EC and 2010/30/EU and repealing Directives 2004/8/EC and 2006/32/EC.

In trying to remove the existing barriers on the energy market and overcome the market failures the EED rules set down for Member States the national indicative targets for energy efficiency for the 2020 horizon. Thus, art. 3 provides that each Member State shall establish a national indicative energy efficiency objective, based either on the primary energy consumption or on the final energy consumption, either on the primary or final energy savings, or on the energy intensity.

The mix of policy instruments that can be used by national states includes the *regulatory instruments* (e.g. energy taxes or CO2; regulations that allow the application of the energy efficient technology or techniques; standards and rules aimed at improving the energy efficiency of products and services, including buildings and vehicles), *stimulative instruments* (e.g. financing systems and instruments or fiscal incentives that lead to the implementation of the energy efficient technology or techniques), *persuasive instruments* (e.g. energy labelling systems), *instruments for providing administrative goods and services* (e.g. education and training, including programs on energy consultancy).

EED includes, among others, requirements on introducing smart networks and smart meters, as well as providing accurate information on the energy bills for empowering consumers and encouraging a more efficient energy use.

When there is no conditionality of technical, financial and proportionality compliance, the Member States should ensure that final consumers of electricity, gas, heating, cooling and domestic hot water the upgrade of these individual meters at competitive prices, which accurately reflect actual energy consumption and provide information on actual time of use.

If and to the extent that Member States implement smart metering systems and introduce smart meters for gas and/or electricity in accordance with Directives 2009/72/EC and 2009/73/EC they must meet a number of requirements on the reliability and security of smart meters, data protection and privacy, transparency, accuracy in communication with the end users, access to information on energy bills, imposing behavior of market participants to take into account the objectives of energy efficiency and final customer benefits etc.

To ensure transparency and fairness in measuring the individual consumption, should buildings with several apartments be fed either centralized or supersede common systems for heating or cooling such buildings, the Member States may introduce transparent rules for allocating costs for heat or hot water consumption in these buildings.

The conclusions of the European Parliament resolution of June 23, 2016 on the report on the implementation of the Energy Efficiency Directive (2012/27/EU) emphasize that until that time Member States have not properly implemented the EED nor the Directive on buildings of 2010 and recall that the deadline for EED transposition expired on June 5, 2014.

Following these conclusions, on 30 November 2016 the Commission proposed an update to the Energy Efficiency Directive including a new 30% energy efficiency target for 2030, and measures to update the Directive to make sure the new target is met[1].

2. Provisions Enforceable in a Number of Member States of the European Union

Judging by the resolution's conclusions and considering the fact that the deadline for the EED implementation was 2016 and that during its implementation a number of Member States have

[1] See more https://ec.europa.eu/energy/en/topics/energy-efficiency.

encountered difficulties, of which we mention two relevant moments in 2014 when the European Commission has launched infringement procedures for failure to transpose the DEE against the 27 EU Member States (all except Malta) and 2016 when the European Commission has asked Denmark, through a reasoned opinion to ensure translation of the EED in the national legislation, we consider as appropriate for the proposed analysis of this paper to present through a comparative approach the applicable provisions in a number of EU Member States that adopted them so to implement the EED.

For the comparative analysis the paper takes into account 14 EU Member States that have adopted a number of provisions for reaching the national energy efficiency targets in 2020, some countries stood out as they registered a progress, others just worrying delays. The provisions are summarized in Table 1.

Table 1. Provisions enforceable for the energy efficiency improvement in a number of Member States

EU member state	Legal provisions
Czech Republic	2014 – start-up of a vast program of expending the heating network, for implementing new connections with clients in residential, commercial or industrial areas; technology upgrades to improve security of supply and the quality of the network, improving efficiency, and replacing pipes when necessary, with the purpose of updating the heating system to the newest technical standards[1]. The Czech Republic is one of the EU States that have fulfilled the minimum requirements specified by the Directive. Each operator has its own heating rate for its products, which is updated regularly and is currently subject to recent changes in the energy law of this country.
Croatia	It has achieved a partial regulation of the heating domain. Heat cost allocators are subject to individual agreements between service companies and customers (they are able to access their own Internet data, only for splitters), the district heating operators are not involved in this process.
Denmark	There is no special regulation for heat meters, for the district heating system was initiated a broad framework for action: large-scale investment; strong support from central and local authorities; efficient financing; diversification of simple technical solutions; citizens are shareholders of heating companies; detailed planning and monitoring. Heat metering has no impact on actual energy savings, but makes consumers more aware of the amount of their consumption. In Copenhagen, district heating benefit from high technology that allows remote reading, so every consumer is paying as much as he is consuming[2].
Estonia	District heating law adopted in 2003 and amended in 2014[3]provides that the metering process and the installation metering systems allow that quantities of heat entering or leaving a network are counted and data read from the user counters are collected and processed. Network operators have the right to collect justified connection fees, including a fee that may be justified for any changes in the technical conditions of heat consumption at the initiative of the customer. A company which sells heat to customers or to a network operator (which sells heat to customers) or produces heat in the process of generating combined heat and power, must obtain for each network area separately approval of the Competition Council on the maximum sale price of heat.
Finland	The thermal energy consumed in the housing is counted based on the flow sensor, temperature sensor and thermal energy, and the temperature sensor measures the water temperature in a constant way at the entry and exit of the building[4]. The measuring equipment is provided by the heat supplier that is required to provide customers a monitoring report on heat consumption at least

[1] http://ecoheat4.eu/en/Country-by-country-db/Czech-Republic/DHC-Benefits/.
[2] http://dbdh.dk/.
[3] https://www.riigiteataja.ee/en/eli/530102013083/consolide.
[4] http://energia.fi/en/home-and-heating/district-heating/price-district-heating.

	once a year, including adjustments for weather conditions for which are frequently used the S17 system, using an average difference of + 17 ° C between the inside and outside temperature[1]. The price depends on the heat of the thermal energy consumption for each customer, the cost of heating is shared between the inhabitants of buildings, usually on the living space. Charges include energy fee and power fee, in connection with the contractual capacity or the water flow contracted. Control heating regulating activities in Finland is based mainly on competition law and partly on the *Law on the electricity market*. The consumers' position is also protected by the Consumer Protection Act. According to the Competition Authority from Finland, a supplier of heat holds a dominant position on the market in terms of customers connected to the district heating network. Twice a year (on the 1st of January and the 1st of July), Finnish Energy Industries[2] collect information from district heating companies on the heating prices to three residential buildings of different sizes. Approximately 29% of the district heating price is made up of taxes and vary from one region to another. In big cities, district heating is produced in compliance with the energy efficiency in cogeneration with electricity, what is the solution to a favourable price.
France	In 2012 has been regulated by decree the allocation of costs for heating in apartment buildings for a primarily residential use, which has led to stopping the boom in energy prices and reducing the heating bills. The obligation of the cost individualization for heating is imposed after the assessment of the property and shall be made in accordance with the article R131-3 of the *Construction and Housing Code* [3].
Germany	Invoicing the consumption of the hot water and heating was regulated in 2009 by a normative act (ordinance)[4], establishing the distribution of costs for heating and hot water in buildings with at least two apartments, connected to a central network[5]. Buildings/living spaces consisting of only two apartments, one of which is occupied by the owner, are not subject to the provisions of the ordinance. The German federal government has appreciated that in compliance with the obligations of EED Directive implementation is not necessary to develop separate legislation to the ordinance on the costs of heating and has prepared a study on energy saving through the regular gathering of information, over the course of a year, consumption and bills on cooling, heating and the use of domestic hot water. In general, the provisions on cost efficiency are contained in the *Law on energy saving* (of transposition of the European directive provisions on the energy performance of the buildings[6]). In addition, the *National Action Plan* on energy[7] efficiency contains the variants of regulations improvement in the field of the thermal energy costs.
Latvia	The procedures by which the apartments' owners of the residential buildings pay for the services related to the use of real property are regulated by Regulation no.1013/2008. Thus, if an individual property has an autonomous heating system or the hot water from the central heating is not used in the individual property, the owner will pay for the thermal energy consumed for his personal needs, on the basis of the calculation carried out by an authorised specialist, in agreement with the administrator. To facilitate payments, the apartment owners may elect a representative who will monitor the thermal energy, will read the meters and will have other duties, according to the contract.

[1] http://energia.fi/sites/default/files/correct_use_of_districtheat_0.pdf.
[2] Order of 27 August 2012 on the apportionment of heating costs in multi-dwelling buildings for main occupancy.
[3] Order of 27 August 2012 on the apportionment of heating costs in multi-dwelling buildings for main occupancy.
[4] http://www.bbsr-energieeinsparung.de/EnEVPortal/DE/Regelungen/HeizkostenV/Download/HeizkostenV2009.pdf? __blob =publicationFile&v=1.
[5] http://www.bmwi.de/EN/Topics/Energy/Buildings/energy-saving-legislation.html.
[6] http://eur-lex.europa.eu/LexUriServ/LexUriServ.do?uri=OJ:L:2010:153:0013:0035:EN:PDF.
[7] http://www.bmwi.de/EN/Topics/Energy/Energy-Efficiency/nape.html.

Lithuania	The implementation of the energy efficiency principles are faced with some key obstacles: *measuring the amount of heat used* (maximum 10% of the buildings having individual heat meters or heat cost allocators heat installed in the apartments); in the system of heating of a block of apartments built during the soviet period, the radiators are connected in series (not in parallel), and a circuit serves several apartments, which makes it impossible to individual metering, without the consent of all owners of the apartments in a building; the problem of financing; the issue of the population income. For solving the problem of energy efficiency of buildings a standardized system of financing has been released, the period of the loan being determined provisionally between 10 and 20 years.
Holland	For the assurance of equitable conditions and equally comparative prices to consumers a *Law on district heating* was adopted, which entered into force in 2010. Supervision of compliance with legislation in the field is carried out by the Competition Council through its Office of Energy Regulation. The main heat sources for the national networks are cogeneration plants and conventional ones, only a small part deriving from the renewable sources of energy. The main cost factors are the size and age of the heating network of the heat scale.
Romania[1]	In the field of *liberalisation of energy markets*: The law of electricity and natural gas no.123/2012, as amended and supplemented by the Law no. 127/2014 and Law no. 160/2012 for the approval of GEO no. 33/2007 on the organization and functioning of ANRE, transposing the Directive 72/2009/EC concerning common rules for the common market in electricity and Directive 73/2009/EC concerning common rules for the common market of gas. In the field of *energy efficiency*: Law no. 121/2014 on energy efficiency transposes *Directive* 2012/27/EU on *energy efficiency*, amended and completed by Law no. 160/2016. In the field of *renewable sources of energy*: Law no. 220/2008 for establishing the promotion system of energy production from renewable energy sources), with subsequent amendments and additions (Law no. 122/2015). In the field of *high-efficiency cogeneration*: H.G. no. 494/2014 for the modification of H.G. no. 1215/2009 establishing the criteria and necessary conditions for the support scheme implementation for the promotion of high efficiency cogeneration based on useful-effective heat demand in 2011. In the field of *smart metering* [2] In accordance with the provisions of ANRE Order no. 145/2014, on the implementation of smart metering systems of the electrical energy, the concessionaire operators of the distribution have submitted to ANRE proposals for the realization of pilot projects, in 2015, whose results provide the information necessary to establish the conditions and the elements regarding the elaboration of the implementation national calendar of the smart measurement systems, as well as of the *National Plan for the implementation of smart metering systems.* ANRE has approved, in 2015, the 18 pilot projects in the amount of 69.639.770 lei (approx. 15475 euro), on the implementation of smart metering systems of the electrical energy. The support scheme for the promotion of high efficiency cogeneration has been introduced in Romania by HG nr. 219/2007 on the cogeneration promotion based on useful heat (the national transposition of the EC Directive no. 8/2004 on the promotion of cogeneration based on useful heat in the internal energy market that starting June 5th, 2014 has been replaced with the provisions of Directive 27/2012) and implemented by the HG no. 1215/2009 on establishing the criteria and

[1] ANRE Report, Department for Energy Efficiency, Energy Efficiency-Priority for Romania, presented at Romanian Energy Efficiency Forum 2016, Bucharest, 13 October 2016.
[2] ANRE Report on progress towards meeting national energy efficiency targets– 2016.

	necessary conditions for the support scheme implementation for the promotion of high efficiency cogeneration based on useful heat demand. In 2015 the European Commission has adopted a decision on the dismissal of infringement actions brought against Romania, of which the data subjects have been: the Cause 2014/2238 having as their object the infringement of the notification of the National Action Plan for energy efficiency (NEEAPS) according to article 24 paragraph 2 of Directive 2012/27/EU. Directive 2012/27/EU of the European Parliament and of the Council of 25 October 2012 on energy efficiency, amending Directives 2009/125/EC and 2010/30/EU and repeal of Directives 2004/8/EC and 2006/32/EC, has been transposed *in full* into national law by *Law no. 121/2014 on energy efficiency*, with subsequent amendments and additions.
Slovakia	Currently, the district heating system have to cope with the competition between heating based on natural gas, electric heating and the one on coal[1]. District heating accounts for 40% of the market of thermal energy distribution. Over 90% of the apartments in the blocks are heated through the centralized public system. A number of approximately 500 heating companies are serving nearly two million inhabitants. In the pre-accession period to the EU, the Slovak government has transformed all state-owned companies into joint stock companies, in order to start the process of privatization (since 2005). Considering the energy sector as a strategic area, the government has limited the participation of foreign investors in the energy companies to 49% of the shares.
Sweden	Law on district heating (2008) requires that the district heating to ensure the transparency and accessibility of information to the general public on the prices applied for heating or for connection to the district heating network[2]. The government or the regulatory authority may issue decisions on compulsory information related to the prices and principles of working in the field.
Hungary	The development and operation of district heating systems is established by the *Law on district heating* (no. XVIII/2005). The operator shall cover the costs of development of the networks on which they operate, it is obliged to maintain, operate, develop and to bear the necessary costs. Municipalities may require the operator of the district heating extension of heating networks on the basis of local development plans and does not cover the charges made by the operators of district heating, or by their affiliates. The fees provided for the consumption of heat must be in accordance with the actual consumption of the subscriber, data on the amount of heat used being verified by a representative of the local body. Payment obligations and other expenses relating to the condominium shall not be borne jointly. There may be parts of the building for which they charge a user fee for individual taxpayers, as well as other fees for which no owners are responsible, but the local body.

4. Conclusions

The imbalances of the world energy scale, marked by the increasing number of the global population and lower accessibility to primary energy resources whose reserves are quickly diminishing, also affected the citizens of the EU, more than 54 million people affected by energy price increases, low-income and housing with reduced energy performance being identified, as shown by the study of the European Commission in 2015 on energy poverty at the European level. In this context, the issue of energy efficiency, a main pillar of the Energy Union, it becomes more acute, especially for states that are found in a situation of major addiction to the energy resources of other states. The comparative analysis presented by the paper reveals that the Member States, despite the progress made in achieving the objective of 20% increase in energy efficiency by the year 2020, as well as in the implementation of

[1] https://www.kpmg.com/SK/en/IssuesAndInsights/ArticlesPublications/Publicationseries/Documents/Central%20and%20 Eastern % 20European %20District%20Heating%20Outlook.pdf.
[2] http://ei.se/Documents/Publikationer/lagar_pa_engelska/District_Heating_Act.pdf.

the Directive 2012/27/EU on Energy Efficiency, need to step up the efforts on energy efficiency, which requires the full implementation of the European legislative framework for energy efficiency. Measures to increase energy efficiency become the red thread of the Energy Union Strategy, through which the EU wants to ensure European energy consumers, a sustainable, competitive and accessible energy, placing household and non-household consumers' energy in the centre of the Energy Union.

Even if all Member States have implemented a number of energy efficiency measures, in particular in terms of protecting vulnerable consumers or those affected by energy poverty, we consider it necessary to continue their concerted steps, especially in the direction of the development of markets for energy services and increased investment and programmes for energy efficiency.

5. References

***Directive 2012/27/eu of the European Parliament and of the Council of 25 October 2012 on energy efficiency, amending Directives 2009/125/EC and 2010/30/EU and repealing Directives 2004/8/EC and 2006/32/EC.

***Fact Sheets on the European Union–Energy efficiency, Retrieved from http://www.europarl.europa.eu/atyourservice/en/display Ftu.html?ftuld %20=FTU_5.7.3.html, date: 09.03.2017.

***COM(2011) 112 final, Communication from the Commission to the European Parliament, the Council, the European Economic and Social Committee and the Committee of the Regions, *A roadmap for moving to a competitive low carbon economy in 2050* .

***IER - Institutul European din România. (2003). *Despre politica de energie a Uniunii Europene/About the European Union's energy policy*.

***Raport ANRE privind Progresul înregistrat în îndeplinirea obiectivelor naționale de eficiență energetică – 2016/ ANRE Report on Progress in Meeting National Energy Efficiency Goals - 2016.

***Raport ANRE, Departamentul pentru Eficiență energetică, Eficiența energetică-Prioritate pentru România, prezentat la Romanian Energy Efficiency Forum 2016, București, 13 octombrie 2016/ ANRE Report, Department for Energy Efficiency, Energy Efficiency-Priority for Romania, presented at Romanian Energy Efficiency Forum 2016, Bucharest, October 13, 2016.

****Arrêté du 27 août 2012 relatif à la répartition des frais de chauffage dans les immeubles collectifs à usage principal d'habitation/Order of 27 August 2012 on the apportionment of heating costs in multi-dwelling buildings for main occupancy*, Retrieved from http://www.legifrance.gouv.fr/date: 09.03.2017.

19

Evaluating the Quality and Safety of Environmental Factors in Investment Strategies

Stefan Dragomir[1], **Georgeta Dragomir**[2]

Abstract: A participatory risk assessment process engages people through a bottom-up approach that aims to involve stakeholders, the public and specialized agencies in that problem preferred management options and proposing solutions to particular risk problems. In planning a participatory risk assessment, key elements include: -communicating information transparently and using a non-technical or domain – specific language; -defining issues that need to be addressed and the questions that need answered; – scoping the problem and framing the questions;-identifying the data and information needed to deal with the questions;-identifying the sources of data;-deciding how to deal with uncertainty.

Keyword: risk assessment; severity class; probability of consequences

1. Introduction

Risk factors are all factors likely work system to act on the health or integrity of injuries to workers. It's about what the majority of people in the current parlance, they are considered hazards or dangerous situations. In this respect the European norm EN 292-1 defines danger, dangerous situations or events related to hazardous work (risk factors) as being a "reason capable of causing an injury or a sickness attack." This definition is a qualitative risk assessment commonly used in its identification. Between the contractor and the collectivity and within which they operate to create links, dependencies and interference that varies depending on the level of integration in the community and which exerts a decisive influence on his behavior. Concepts and habits within a unit, as well as how that group appreciates the risk, determines in a very large measure behavior in terms of safety at work (Rojanski, Bran, & Grigore, 2000).

1.1. Profession/Job Title, for the Work Place

The most important jobs are represented of technical staff, administrative, financial, budgeting, accounting, human resources, payroll, internal audit, computer science and statistics, administrative, work prevention and protection, mail, medical records, equipment expert. The work consists in the activities of office and outside the unit.

---

[1] Professor, PhD, Dunarea de Jos University of Galati, Romania, Address: 47 Domnească Street, 800008 Galati, Romania, Corresponding author: gretadragomir@univ-danubius.ro.

[2] Professor, PhD, Danubius University of Galati, Romania, Address: 3 Galati Blvd., 800654, Romania, E-mail: gretadragomir@univ-danubius.ro.

The components of work system are:

- The means of production used are: desk, chair; computer and printer; means of transportation belonging to the unit or public transport; outlets, extension cords for power; supplies, office supplies; desktop computers; furniture fixtures;

- The hangman made some wrong operation like: commands; maneuver; positions; establishment; adjustments; misuse of the means of protection; improper work methods or incorrect sequence of operations.

Mechanical risk factors: dangerous movements; functional movements of the machinery: machine parts in motion; fluid flow; movements of the means of transport; automatic self-timer or functional movements against machinery or fluids displacements under gravity: sliding, rolling, rolling on wheels, overturning, falling free, leak free, spill, subsidence, collapse, diving; displacement under the effect propulsion: objects found or particles, deviation from normal trajectory, balance, pushing back, excessive shock, jet, splash.

Risk on action surfaces or contours dangerous (stabbing, slippery, abrasive, adhesive) are:

- Thermal risk factors: - high temperature objects; - low temperature objects or surfaces; flames.

- Electromagnetic: infrared, ultraviolet, microwave, high frequency, medium frequency, low frequency, laser ionizing (alpha, beta, gamma; -electrostatic potential; -lightning, flood, wind, hail, blizzards;

- Chemical risk factor: toxic substances; caustic substances; flammable substances; explosive substances; radioactive substances; excessive vibration of machinery; radiation; gases, vapors, toxic or caustic aerosols; particulate matter in the air, flammable or explosive gases or vapor.

In table no.1 is shown a classification of severity of consequences in function of severity class (Rojanski, Bran, & Grigore, 2000).

Table 1.

Severity class		THE SEVERITY OF THE CONSEQUENCES
Class	Consequences	
1	OMIT	- minor consequences predictable incapacitating reversible up to 3 calendar days (cure without treatment)
2	SMALL	reversible consequences with an incapacity for work predictable 3-45 days that require medical treatment
3	AVERAGE	reversible consequences with an incapacity for work of between 45-180 days that require medical treatment and hospitalization
4	LARGE	irreversible consequences with a reduction of the capacity for work of a maximum of 50% (disability grade III)
5	GRAVE	irreversible loss between 50-100% of capacity, but with the possibility of self service (disability grade II)
6	VERY SERIOUS	irreversible consequences with total loss of capacity for work and self-service capacity (disability grade)
7	MAXIMUM	Out of life

Security is defined as the fact of being sheltered from any danger. Risk and security are closely interrelated and mutually exclusive.

Risk factors acting on the performer by two main components: gravity consequence/event) and probability of occurrence (events/unit time). Combining these components determine the level of risk itself.

Risk factors are all components of the system's own job (executing, the burden of work, means of production, work environment).

2. Research about Own Environmental Risk Factors Work

The environmental risk factors work it is classified as follows:

a. Physical risk factors that include: excessive air temperature (high/low); improper air humidity (high/low); high speed air currents, they define the microclimate and the working environment; Excessive air pressure (high/low); Inadequate lighting; Noise, radiation, vibration, electrostatic potential, natural disasters, aggression to aggression in the workplace.

b. Risk factors of chemical which include: gas, vapours, aerosol dust and toxic pneumoconiogene. Risk factors (potential causes) of system components that form the basis of accidents at work and occupational diseases as well as preventive measures, schematic, are presented in Fig. 1.

Notions of security and risk are opposites being connected by a hyperbolic equation R = (S Security R - risk).

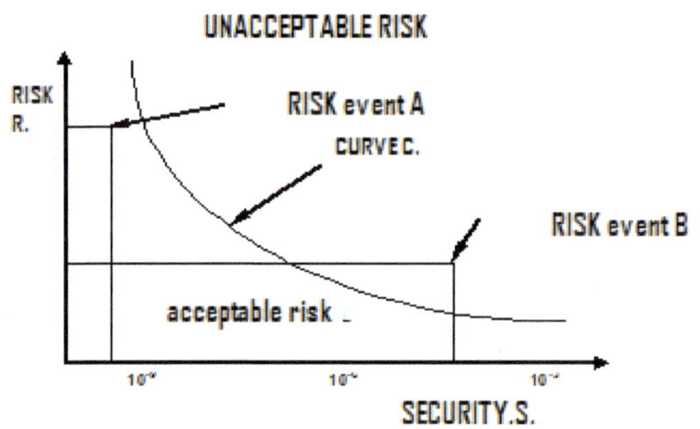

Figure 1. Relationship between Risk – Security

Source: (Negrei, 2002)

y = f(x)

Risk is defined in accordance with the European standard EN 292-1, as "the combination of the probability and severity of an injury or sickness attack that can occur in a dangerous situation." This is a quantitative definition of risk that can be used in prioritizing risks. In other words, the risk is the likelihood of a specific gravity of damage during exposure to the risk factor. Consequently, professional risk associated with a particular situation or a particular technique from combining the following elements:

- foreseeable consequence severity (severity of the most likely consequence);
- the likelihood of such consequences.

Thus defined, the risk can be assessed quantitatively, if severity and probability have been quantified themselves. Quantitative assessment (evaluation) can be used to compare different risks within a system and to determine the priorities of intervention or to compare risk levels before and after the implementation of measures to prevent the manifestation of him.

The absence of a system of review, a small number of accidents or occupational diseases, low severity of consequences of accidents should not be automatically regarded as a presumption of a low risk.

2.1. Risk Severity

Shall be assessed in accordance with MIL-STD-882 C by evaluating the consequences of the most serious accident that could have caused the risk factor.

Consequence severity (severity of the damage possible) can be estimated by considering the following:

- the nature of the protected object (persons, property, environment);
- severity of injuries or damage to health (easy - normally reversible serious - normally irreversible, death);
- the magnitude of manifestation the consequent impact (a person, more than one person).

Categories of severity of consequences allow assigning a qualitative size potential accidents due to human error, environmental conditions, non-compliance project, procedural deficiencies or damage and organ dysfunction product, sub-assemblies or its components.

The product manager, the manager the quality assurance program of safety of the product and the one who carried out the product should be able to lay down exactly what is meant by destroy the product, by major consequences/minor to product/environment and by occupational disease or serious injury. Severity can be defined on the basis of criteria such as:

- temporary incapacity (ITM), permanent work incapacity (disability), death;
- health effects, reversible or not, for risk factors likely to have psychological effects;
- interference with the comfort, satisfaction, worker motivation for social risk factors and organizational (Myrick, Herriges, & Kling, 2014).

2.2. Risk Probability

Probability means in accordance with MIL-STD-882 C frequency of occurrence of the event unwanted and can be described as potential occurrence in the unit time or reported from the population, item or situation.

Probability is conditional on even terms of work processes: reliability of technical equipment, materials, organization of work, time constraints, etc. As with the severity of the consequences for estimating the probability of occurrence of consequences can use multiple grids of appreciation. For a more accurate estimate of the probability of occurrence of consequences is recommended to be taken into consideration:

a) **the frequency and duration of exposure are determined by:**

- need access to the danger zone (normal operation, maintenance or repairs);
- nature of access (e.g. manual feed materials);
- Time spent in the danger zone;

- the number of people who register;
- frequency of access.

b) **probability of occurrence dangerous due to:**

- Technical equipment reliability and other statistical data;
- statistical data related to the frequency of accidents and occupational diseases;
- comparing the risks of system already accepted analyzed risks of systems.

c) **the possibilities to avoid or limit the consequence of a hazardous event by:**

- executing (which can be qualified or unqualified person can perform the task;
- supervised work or not, etc.);
- rate of occurrence of the event estimated dangerous (sharp, fast, slow);
- any form of risk awareness (through general information by direct observation;
- by means of warning and indicating devices;
- possibilities to avoid or limit performer consequence (e.g. reflexes);
- the skill saving opportunities that make the chances contractor to avoid;
- or limit the result to be possible in certain circumstances possible, impossible);
- practical experience and knowledge of the performer (on the job);
- examined, on a similar work process or inexperienced).

2.3. Level of Risks

The level of risk is an indicator quantity absolutely once rated allow knowing to what extent the security of a system, in terms of the possibility of accidents and occupational diseases, it is acceptable or not.

In practice it is considered that a system is secure, if having a non-zero risk, but small enough, known as residual risk or acceptable. Interventions while the residual risk increases as the work degrade and age under the law of increasing entropy. Where as the risk cannot be null (infinite security) must be determined which couples probability of occurrence-consequences can provide an acceptable level of risk.

Graphic representing acceptable risk in the form of rectangles with areas equal to F1 = F2 = F3. gravity/probability, data in Figure 2, the curve variation in the severity of consequences.

Risk severity

Under the curve (A) the risks are acceptable, and above the curve (B) the risks are unacceptable. The curve in Figure 2 called risk acceptability curve and corresponding function p hyperbole. g = const. In Romania currently accepted value of this constant is to be 3.The main objective of the evaluation is to establish acceptable risk and bringing in acceptability.

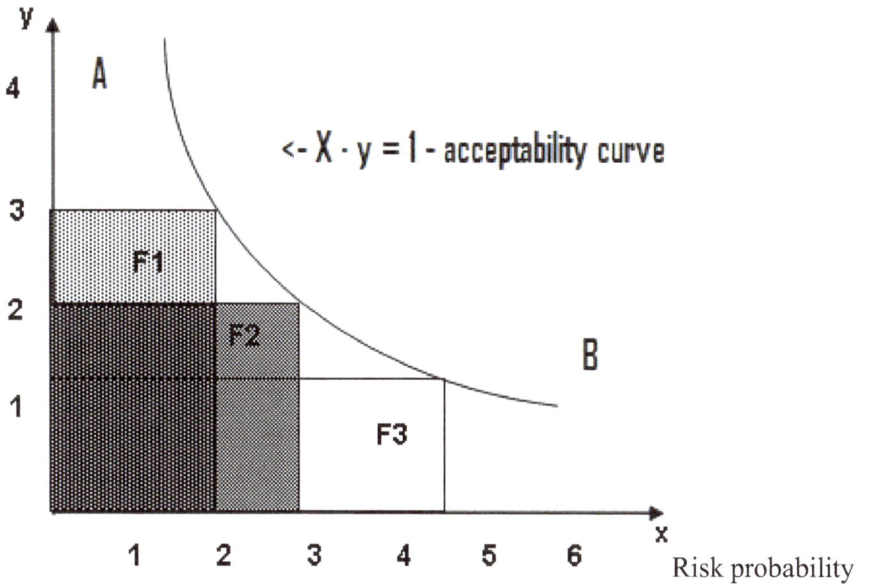

Figure 2. The curve variation curve: severity of consequences/risk probability

A-acceptable risk; B-unacceptable risk (Rojanski, Bran, & Grigore, 2000)

Evaluation of Environment Impact

Assessment of environmental impact shall be carried out using the matrix method (for index of quality) and V. Rojanschi method (calculation of global pollution index).

An assessment of the impact on the environment shall be based on:

- indices of quality on environmental factors (water, air, soil-sub soil, noise, human settlement, biodiversity, landscape)(I_C);
- index of global pollution (I_{PG}).

Quality of a environment factors is falling within the allowed limits of STAS or Normative reglementations.

It is estimate defects "project" on the environment based on "factor size" which are to be analyzed taking into account the level of quality indicators that characterize its effects.

The formulas of environmental quality index is (I_c):

$$\mathbf{I_c = L_{project} / L_{reglementation} = E^{-1}}$$

$L_{proiect}$ – project actions

$L_{reglementat}$ – reglementations of Normative actions;

E – environmental effects

Interplay between actions project ($L_{project}$) and environmental effects (E) can be highlight by marking the appropriate box of its size estimated by a common system to the whole assembly (with +, - , or 0), as follows (Negrei, 2002):

Table 2

I_c = **0** to **+1**	- positive influences. Environmental is influenced in admissible limits.
I_c = **- 1** to **0**	- negative influences. Environmental is influenced over admissible limits.
I_c = **0**	- Environmental is not influenced.

An assessment of the impact on environmental factors by the quality indexes (I c)

Matrix for impact assessment

Table 3

Environmental actions	**Effects on environmental factors**			
	Noise	Air	Water	Soil
Air	0	-	0	0
Wather	0	0	-	0
Soil	0	0	-	-
Landscape	0	0	0	0
Noises	-	0	0	0
Human settelment	0	0	0	0
Effects -E	**-1**	**-1**	**-2**	**-1**

The values of Effects (E) are:

For noise, E =-1

For air, E =-1

For water, E=-2

For soil, E=-1

3. Assessment of Quality Index Values

These assessments are based on: Quality index values (I_c) for each environmental (Negrei, 2002) factors and worthiness note that corresponding of I_C values like in the table 4.

Table 4

Wothiness note	**Ic value**	**Environmental effects**
10	**I_c = 0**	Environmental is not affected by the developed activity.
9	**I_c = 0,0 ÷ 0,25**	Environmental is affected in admissible limits. Level 1. Positive effects.
8	**I_c = 0,25 ÷ 0,50**	Environmental is affected in admissible limits. Level 2. Positive effects.
7	**I_c = 0,50 ÷1,00**	Environmental is affected in admissible limits. Level 3. Positive effects.
6	**I_c = -1,0**	Environmental is affected over admissible limits. Level 1. Negative effects
5	**I_c = -1,0 ÷ -0,5**	Environmental is affected over admissible limits. Level 2. Negative effects
4	**I_c = -0,5 ÷ -0,25**	Environmental is affected over admissible limits. Level 3. Negative effects

3	**I_c = -0,25 ÷ -0,025**	- The medium is degraded, level 1. - The effects are harmful to **long** periods of exposure.
2	**I_c = -0,025 ÷ -0,0025**	The medium is degraded, level 2. - The effects are harmful to **medium** periods of exposure.
1	**I_c = sub –0,0025**	The medium is degraded, level 3. - The effects are harmful to **short** periods of exposure

$I_{PG} = S_i/S_r$

I_{PG} = 1, no polluted existence

I_{PG}> 1 it existing environmental quality modification

Quality scale by Global Polluted Index is shown in table no. 5:

Table 5

I_{PG} = 1	- environmental is not affected by human activity
I_{PG} = 1...2	- Environmental is affected in admissible limits
I_{PG} = 2...3	- Environmental is affected and existing a discomfort for life forms.
I_{PG} = 3...4	- Environmental is affected and existing troubles for life forms.
I_{PG} = 4...6	- Environmental is severe affected and existing a multiple dangers for life forms.
I_{PG}> 6	- The medium is degraded, unsuitable for life forms.

3.1. Calculus of global Polluted Index

It is considered a number of four environmental factors affected by polluted risk like: air, water, soil-subsoil, noises:

- Global Polluted Index (Negrei, 2002) $I_{PG} = S_i/S_r$
- S_i value (ideal state) – resulting by geometrically figure have the surface:
- $Si = 200cm^2$
- S_r value (real state)

It was built by pooling related points values Nb (note worthiness) for each environmental factor taken into account.

N_b value shall be obtained for each environmental factor scale of worthiness as a function of the value of the pollution index

- N_b for Noise:

I_c = -1.0⇨ N_{bnoise} =6

- N_b for Air:

I_c = 0.25 ⇨ N_{bair} = 8

- N_b for Water:

I_c = -1.0⇨ N_{bwater}= 6

- N_b for Soil:

I_c = 0.25 ⇨ N_{bsoil} = 8

Surface Sr: $S_r = 100\ cm^2$

$$I_{PG} = \frac{S_i\ 200\ cm^2}{S_r\ 100\ cm^2} = 2$$

Global Polluted Index =2

Graphically representation for Index of global polluted is shown in figure no. 3:

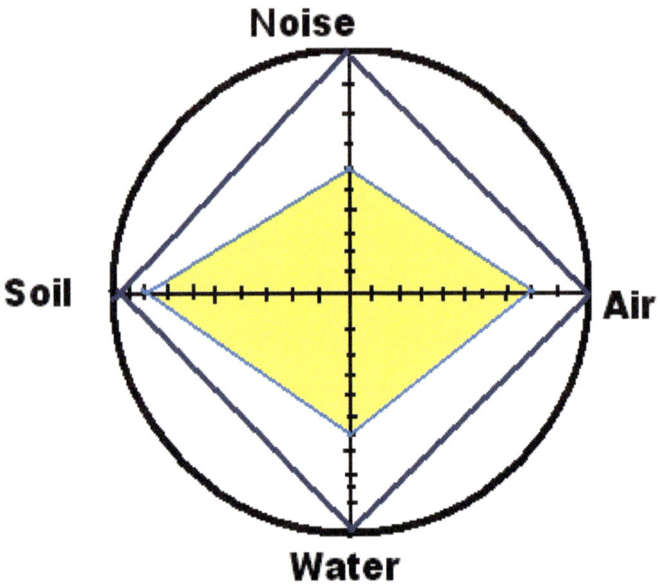

Figure 3. Graphically representation for Index of global polluted

Index of global polluted value is: $I_{PG} = 2$- Environmental is affected in admissible limits

4. Conclusions

An acceptable risk may be characterized by a probability of occurrence (frequency), but the seriousness of the consequences (F1) - nuclear accidents, or vice versa-a high frequency with low severity of consequences (F3) - traffic accidents.

Risk level assessment method and its classification as acceptable or unacceptable risk has the advantage that it can be applied both to existing employment systems and those in construction-design phase. Establish risk acceptability curve (delineating acceptable risks) is a difficult issue. This is done through a strategic decision be based on the cost of human life, whether from the comparison with other risks already accepted.

Exposure to risk factors, represents the duration in the time or frequency in time at which the contractor is exposed to a risk factor and the level to which it is exposed. Assessment of exposure may be carried out, in some cases, in terms of quantitative metrics. Needs analysis can choose diverse exposure assessment rubrics. Exposure is often integrated into the concept of probability, the assessment of risk, taking into account the duration or frequency of exposure. Consideration of exposure, in a separate probability is subtle and it requires a complex approach for assessing occupational risks.

5. Bibliography

Myrick, F. A., Herriges, J. A., & Kling, C. L. (2014). *The Measurement of Environmental and Resource Values: Theory and Methods.* RFF Press.

Negrei, C. C. (2002). *Economia si politica mediului/Economy and environment policy.* Bucharest: EDP.

Rojanski, V., Bran, F., & Grigore, F. (2000). *Elemente de economia si managementul mediului/Elements of economics and environmental management.* Bucharest: Editura Economica.

20

The Competitiveness of Commodity Chains in Albania toward the EU Integration on focus: Farmers of Korca region

Dorjan Marku[1], Eleina Qirici[2], Oriola Theodhori[3]

Abstract: The aim of this paper is to present a clear overview of the competitiveness of the commodity chains of the Albanian agriculture and identify the main difficulties that farmers and smallholders are facing, in order to access local and regional agricultural markets. Addressing weak points along the agro-food chain, and increasing the competitiveness of the agricultural chains by improving support services at producer level, linking them with competitive agricultural markets is very important for the economic growth of rural areas, as Albania aspires to enter EU in the upcoming years. In order to identify the main problems that farmers and small holders are being faced with, when their products access agricultural markets, we conducted a survey that consisted on questionnaires distributed to farmers. Based on the statistical analysis resulted that the main barriers that affect the access of agricultural products on the market were: low selling prices, lack of transportation facilities, lack of contractual trade agreements and lack of modern technology. This study also addresses to a greater extent different steps that should be followed in order to improve agriculture policies, and to achieve a sustainable agriculture model, so that the Albanian agricultural products can compete with those of the region and EU.

Keywords: market access, agriculture policies, commodity chain, Korca,

1. Introduction

Agriculture in Albania faces important challenges aiming to achieve successful structural changes that can increase productivity and restate its competitive advantages. In order to reach at a certain level that can align toward the EU, the sector has to improve its physic capital, and adapt practices at all levels of the agriculture, similar to those of the EU countries.

Many smallholders in developing countries face different risks in their production processes. Constantly they are exposed to different negative influences such as natural disasters, conflicts, price instability and uncertainty about the access of resources and markets.

In Albania, farmers face difficulties accessing local and regional agricultural markets, often without adequate means to manage risks. This issue must be addressed in order to prevent price volatility, reduce poverty in rural areas and enable smallholders to meet the growing demand for food. These negative influences reduce farmer's willingness to invest and considering market liberalization between countries they become more exposed to such market risks. In order to create value chains, it is required an

[1] Lecturer, PhD, Faculty of Agriculture, "Fan S. Noli" University, Albania, Address: "Shetitore Rilindasit", Korçw, Albania, Corresponding author: dorjanmarku@gmail.com.

[2] Associate Professor, PhD, Faculty of Economy, "Fan S. Noli" University, Albania, Address: "Shetitore Rilindasit", Korçw, Albania, E-mail: qirici.elena@yahoo.com.

[3] Associate Professor, PhD, Faculty of Economy, "Fan S. Noli" University, Albania, Address: "Shetitore Rilindasit", Korçw, Albania, E-mail:theodhorioriola@yahoo.com.

interaction between different actors of the sector because the nature of these linkages determines the value of the chain. This may be enriched based on a more developed level of support, through the improved conditions for a sustainable development of the sector, private initiations and responsible institutions for planning, monitoring and implementing policies.
Market access for farmers means the ability to acquire farm inputs and farm services, and the capability to deliver agricultural produce to buyers (IFAD, 2010a). Markets provide the opportunity to generate income, contributing to a reduction in poverty and hunger in developing countries. Markets also drive production to meet consumer demand in terms of quantity and quality (van Schalkwyk et al., 2012). Sustainable access to markets is required to guarantee smallholders an increase in income and to lift them out of poverty.

Switching from traditional to highly competitive products, based on quality, seems to be the most important challenge of the Albanian agriculture in the future toward the EU integration. In order to achieve it, farmers, commodity suppliers, as well as small and medium enterprises needs support in their efforts in order to improve the value chain.

Based on SSBU 2007 – 2013, since the transition period the financial support of the agriculture sector has been focused mainly on indirect financial support, consisting on creating a favorable business environment, support on extension services of farmers, institutional strengthening and rehabilitation of infrastructure. Direct financial support has been applied since 1997, mainly based on payments in the form of grants distributed to farmers through different support schemes, based on the cultivated area. Since 2014, the financial support schemes has undergone through an essential transformation process, focusing on investment schemes aiming to promote storage capacities. These financial schemes support the delivery of agriculture production on wholesale warehouses, storage capacities, conservation, processing and agriculture markets, agriculture technology, safety and quality products based on competitive advantages of Albania. Also, new financial schemes on agriculture support the interest rate until 70%, for a period of seven years, for investments based on bank loans. This form of support it is not limited only for agriculture cooperatives and organizations but include even individuals, legal subjects and new enterprises that are directly related with the investment.

Nowadays, various theoretical analysis in the world focus on agriculture policies, mainly on the role of direct payments which have become part of different evaluations. In fact, support policies of agriculture lead to structural changes, influencing to a large extent the stimulation of production and farm income (OECD, 2011).

Also, Roe et al. (2002), suggests that the application of direct payments compared to the case when payments are not applied at all, may improve the access of farmers on goods and services, increasing their wealth, while may indirectly increase the value of land.

The sustainable growth of the sector depends on the level of technology, knowledge and the efficiency of land inputs that affect the performance of farms. High productivity and competitiveness, market access of products, growth of income and improvements on the living standards of farmers are identified to be the basic factors of production.

Despite the improvements and developments that have occurred during the last years, the agriculture sector in Albania should reach a higher level of productivity and competitiveness in the local and international markets, in order to reduce the gap with other countries across the region and EU. Following this direction, weak points along the agro-food chain should be addressed and a comparative advantage analysis must be considered compared to other regional countries.

In order achieve a more realistic approach and to reach the objectives of this paper, we decided to conduct a survey, contacting directly with farmers (in the form of questionnaires) of Korca region. The aim of the questionnaires was to identify demographic evidence, experience on agriculture, the sector involved and identify difficulties that the Albanian farmers are being faced with. The study was developed based on a detailed review of the available literature aiming to determine clearly the situation of competitiveness between farmers in Korca region.

2. Materials and Methods

The research method used in this study is formulated based on the information and data's that were gathered, the presented issues, data location and their purpose. The form of research used it's a combination between qualitative and quantitative research, benefiting from the advantages of these two research types.

The quantitative approach the study consist on the formulation of a questionnaire, in order to obtain a clear overview of the targeted population and identify the main problems that affect access of products on agricultural markets, as the final destination of the value chain. The qualitative method used in this study focuses mainly on obtaining specific information on farmers and the interpretation of different issues based on their perception.

The nature of the research applied in this paper is to identify and explore over a phenomenon, being more familiar and have a better understanding of it. This study was conducted in Korca region. We chose this region because it is considered to be one of the most developed in Albania in terms of agriculture, and we believe that the indicators that we get from this survey represent similarities with those of the whole country.

In order to achieve the objectives and to expand the interest and contribution of this paper, the information and data gathered were developed in two phases. Initially was gathered information about farmers that operate in Korca region, from the Regional Directorate of Agriculture. The second phase consisted on the fulfillment of questionnaires from the selected sample. After these steps, all the information and data gathered was processed statistically, reaching concrete results on the main influences of the access of products on agriculture markets. The population that was analyzed in this study represents an intentional probability sample. The reason that we chose this form of sample was to include as many as possible diverse characters of the studied population, and obtain diversified perceptions of farmers. The sample population of this study was represented by 168 farmers and diversified based on Korca municipalities. The scale that was used for measuring directly farmer's attitudes is the Likert Scale. Likert – type or frequency scales use fixed choice response formats and are designed to measure attitudes or opinion (Bowling, 1997; Burns, & Grove, 1997). Based on the frequency of the answers of farmers, a simple statistical analysis was raised consisting on the mean and standard deviation.

Another procedure before setting up the final questionnaire and enhance the reliability of the instrument used during this study, was the test of the questionnaire. This step was taken in order to make the questionnaire more valuable and concise. This phase resulted very important because we were able to acquire a preliminary answer from farmers. Furthermore, during this stage farmers were encouraged to identify other problems and add questions that they considered important for the goals of this study.

3. Results and Discussions

Returns on investments in the Albanian agriculture have a strong effect on development, especially if channelled through productive investments that focus on addressing weak points along the agro-food chain. The objective of support in this context is to achieve a better distribution balance of wealth and power. In order to intervene it is important to identify the main difficulties of farmers when selling their products. According to farmers, lack of access on agricultural markets prevents the sale of their products on the market. For this reason we decided to identify the main influences that cause this occurrence. Most of them admitted that there are no trading facilities on their rural areas, forcing them to sale their products alone without any reliable information on the market. Poor communication and long distance from the market increase artificially the cost of their products and time. Figure 1, shows the frequency of their answers about the distance that they follow until the regional markets of Korca in order to sell their products.

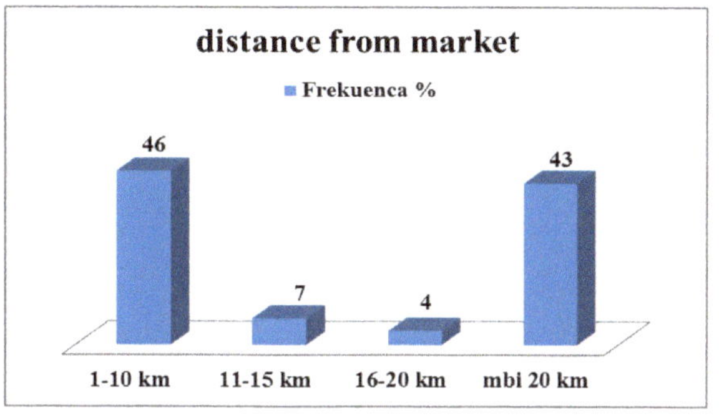

Figure 1. Distance from the agricultural markets

Based on the figure above, 46% of them follow a distance to 10 km away from the market while 43% described a distance that overcomes 20 km. If we consider the conditions of infrastructure on rural areas in Albania and the lack of facilities, these numbers are not so encouraging.

Another important question directed to farmers consisted on the distribution channels that they use for selling their products. Figure 2, shows the frequency of their answers.

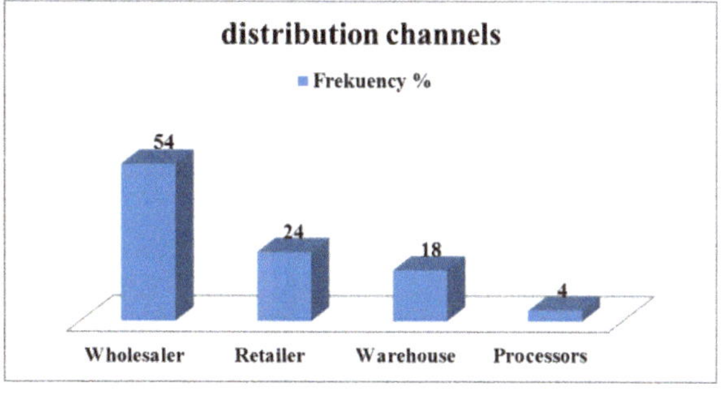

Figure 2 Distribution channels of farmers

As the evidence shows on figure above, 54% of the farmers sell their products on wholesalers, 24% on retailers, only 18% deliver products on warehouses, while 4% delivered them on processors.

Conservation and storage capacities are important processes that affect directly natural values, form, and lifecycle of agricultural products. Figure 3, shows the frequency of the answers of farmers that were interviewed. To be more specific, most of the farmers that answered this question and that are reflected on the graph are mainly involved on the production of fruits.

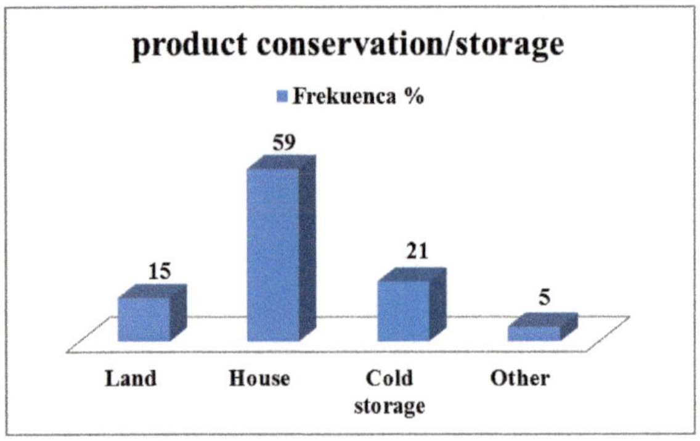

Figure 3 Conservation and storage of agricultural products

The results of figure 3, show that only 21% of farmers were keeping their products on cooling capacities, 59% were keeping them in house conditions, while 15% on the land.

Low level of agriculture technology was identified by farmers of Korca region as one of the most important barriers that affect level of production and quality. Based on the survey as shown on the graph below, resulted that only 28% of farmers were using modern agriculture technologies, while 72% of them were mainly using old production technologies, figure 4.

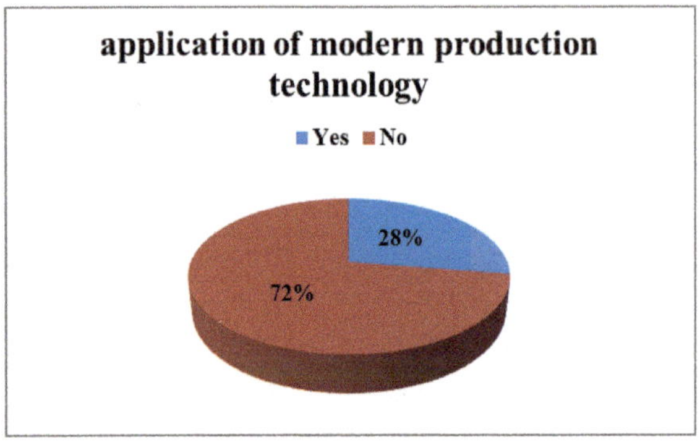

Figure 4 Application of modern technology by farmers

Based on the statistics that are shown above, it is necessary that the financial support from the national schemes to be addressed on improvements on the level of production technology.

Related to the data's processed from the questionnaires and the statistical analysis that was conducted, resulted that the main barriers that affect access of products on agricultural markets on the region, are as shown on table 1.

Table 2 Identified barriers that affect access of products on agricultural markets

Barriers	Mean	Std. Deviation
Low selling prices	4.7250	.72641
Lack of transportation	4.3625	.85772
Lack of contractual trade agreements	4.3125	1.01056
Lack of agriculture technology	4.3125	.99803
Uncertainty	4.2875	.99298
High taxes	4.2250	1.06369
Lack of packing materials	4.0500	1.15361
Distance from market	3.7875	1.24581
Poor information services	3.5750	1.21598

According to data's shown on table 1, resulted that all the identified barriers that affect the access of products on agricultural markets in Korca region are statistically important, because the mean of the identified variables is statistically different from the neutral value 3. Based on the analysis, the most important barriers that affect access of products on the market are as follow:

1. Low selling prices
2. Lack of transportation
3. Lack of contractual trade agreements

The mean of the variables lies on the level *"very important"*, statistically different from level 4 (important level), for $P = 0.000 < 0.05$.

4. Comparative Advantage Analysis

The concept of comparative advantage as a determinant of international trade became popular for the first time from Ricardo (1817), underlying the importance of physic and natural influences of competitiveness, technological and human factors.

The application of agriculture policies may be effective only if we are clear where we should intervene, so that the Albanian agriculture can reach in the future or come closer to EU standards in terms of competitiveness and quality. In this context, we believe that if we develop a comparative advantage analysis compared to other countries in the region, the application of these policies may be very successful. Compared to other regional countries, we possess against them competitive advantages that derive from the following factors:

i. Climatic conditions
ii. Appropriate land conditions
iii. Wealthy and diversified biological resources
iv. Old tradition on agriculture

All these factors are a great basis for developing healthy and productive agriculture activities, and serve as an impulse that shows that agriculture sector will continue to play an important part on the Albanian economy in the future. However, our country has a lot of disadvantages compared to other regional countries that derive from different barriers and structural problems of the rural sector. Some of them are as follow:

i. Small size and fragmented farms
ii. Difficult management of the agriculture sector because of the large number of small farms and rural population.
iii. Large diversification of agriculture products because of high level of uncertainties and difficulties of agriculture marketing.
iv. Difficulties of implementation of modern technologies. Low levels of technology.
v. Small numbers of farm organizations and cooperatives.
vi. Poor regional infrastructure, lack of storage/conservation capacities and transportation facilities.
vii. Low levels of financial support

Based on the factors mentioned above, government financial support should be higher and focused on all stages of the production chain, so that the output could be positive.

5. Conclusion

During this study were identified important conclusions conceived based on the results derived from the questionnaires that were addressed to farmers, resulting as follows:

Despite the improvements of the agriculture sector and the increased level of support during the last decade, reality shows that the support schemes are still away from those applied in the EU.

Based on the applied analysis resulted that the main variables that affect the access of products on agricultural markets are low prices of agricultural products, lack of transportation facilities and lack of contractual trade agreements.

All the variables that were identified by farmers as "very important", have a great impact on the production chain, meaning that improving each one of them will have a positive impact on the final output.

Wholesaler warehouses are the intermediate actor of the agriculture production, specialised and informed on local and foreign trading contracts of agricultural products. Supporting and strengthening this part of the chain, will encourage and secure the market for all farmers products.

Farmer's organizations play a key role on poverty reduction and enhancing food security. The Albanian government should promote equitable distribution of investments, involve and allow them to participate in the decision – making process to overcome their weaknesses.

Assistance to farmers should be increased and help them initiate dialogue and build trust between each other, aiming to develop long agreements.

Financial support schemes should take farmers needs into consideration and support them with more insurance schemes, microcredit and start-up funds, so that they can link contractual agreements between producers and buyers and facilitate contractual arrangements, based on a secure supply of inputs and accomplish each other requirements in the long run.

Considering the small size of farms and the high level of land fragmentation, supporting farmer's cooperatives will encourage the development of intensive production. In this context, responsible institutions that compose and implement agricultural policies, should promote these forms of cooperation, as they serve to increase linkages between small farmers and other actors in the chain.

Considering the difficulties that farmers in Albania are being faced with, it is recommended that support policies should be addressed on enhancing the number of storage and conservation capacities.

Low level of the agriculture technology rank farmers in Albania in a difficult position compared to farmers in other regional countries. In order to reduce this gap, better policies are required in terms of the support of modern technologies.

6. References

Agroweb: www.agroweb.org.

Andy Field, (2009). *Discovering statistics using SPSS.* 3rd Edition, pp. 688-689.

Bowling, A. (1997). *Research Methods in Health.* Buckingham: Open University Press.

Burns, N., & Grove, S. K. (1997). *The Practice of Nursing Research Conduct, Critique, & Utilization.* Philadelphia: W.B. Saunders and Co.

Cochrane W.W. (1979). *The Development of American Agriculture.* Minneapolis, MN. University of Minnesota Press.

International Fund for Agricultural Development. Annual Report 2010.

MBUMK, *Strategjia Ndërsektoriale për Bujqësinë dhe Zhvillimin Rural 2014-2020/ Crosscutting Strategy for Agriculture and Rural Development 2014-2020.*

MBUMK, Strategjia Sektoriale e Bujqësisë dhe Ushqimit 2007-2013/ Sector Strategy of Agriculture and Food 2007-2013.

OECD (2011). Disaggregated Impacts of CAP Reforms: Proceedings from an OECD workshop, Edited by C. Moreddu. OECD Publishing, Paris.

Rikardo (1817). *Principles of Political Economy and Taxation.*

Roe, T., Somwaru, A. & Diao, X. (2002). *Do direct payments have intertemporal effects on U.S. agriculture?* Manuscript. University of Minnesota.

Strategjia Sektoriale e Bujqwsisw dhe Ushqimit/Sector Strategy of Agriculture and Food (SSBU) 2007 – 2013.

Van Schalkwyk, et al. (2012). *Unlocking markets to smallholders.* Lessons from South Africa. Vol. 10, page 13.

21

The Icelandic and Romanian Profile. Different Patterns in a Converging World

Ionel Sergiu Pirju[1]

Abstract. The majority of intercultural studies are preferring a sample with two cultures, even such a study can't provide a complex understanding about the importance of culture in the international context. The most complex Cross Cultural studies (Schwartz, GLOBE, Hofstede, and Trompenaars) include a large number of cultures, but time and costs remain major obstacles for an exhaustive analyses. The aim of this article is to present relevant intercultural values that characterize Iceland and Romania: history, language, power distance and conflict management. This study it is a synchronic one because in its content will be analyzed the contemporary situations in the two countries. The analysis is exploratory and it will be used the Locke`s consensual inductive system which involves mostly the collections of scholars` opinions but with personal reflections.

Keywords: Iceland; Romania; cultural values; performance; power distance

1. Introduction

Along the history, the cross cultural adaptation offers solutions for individuals to become skilled by identifying critical situation in order to avoid severe consequences for their particular situations. Based on former scholar experience, the assumption of this research is that in the international field, if cross-cultural knowledge is mastered, there is an additional opportunity to develop and maintain an excellent relationship with international partners. At the same time, according to the principle of concordance, in case of identifying common values between two countries, it seems natural that there should be a greater intensity of common projects, compared to that achieved with other regions.

This article will try to present first the main strategy of Icelandic and Romanian policy regarding the European integration. Also, by comparing the cultural values betweent the two countries, the study will emphasize how much the Romanian society will try to increase the level of stability and establish credibility on the international arena. To integrate the article into the extention demanded by the cross cultural methodology, it will be also analized the differeces between Power distance and Performance orientation. Both values are presenting the perefect benchmarking model for practical implications in order to benefit the societal culture from the two countries. The approach I propose tries to capture the influence of these two cultural dimensions on the international performance of a state by comparing the values and norms between the two countries. It aims at emphasizing the importance of multiculturalism (Bercovitch & Foulkes, 2012) and is focused on the importance of cultural synergy in interstate relations.

---

[1] Senior Lecturer, PhD, Danubius University of Galati, Faculty of Communications and International Relations, Romania, Address: 3 Galati Blvd., Galati 800654, Romania, Corresponding author: pirjusergiu@univ-danubius.ro.

This article does not claim an exhaustive analysis; it will reflect some aspects of the contemporary cultural values between Iceland and Romania because the most important aspects of the world situation can be passed through cultural lenses. The in depth comparison could be seen as a diagnosis method "whose main content is to identify the strengths and weaknesses of the analysed domain, highlighting them and finalizing into corrective recommendations". (Nicolescu & Verboncu, 2008, p. 135)

In order to achieve the proposed objective, the subject of the study is structured in two parts where it will be presented the intercultural paradigms required for this cross cultural study. In each part the intention is to demonstrate the need for understanding of the cultural values between the two countries, because on the global market the cross cultural knowledge is underlying the innovative skills for international cooperation.

2 Historical Background and the Policy Regarding the European Integration

The main integrators factors from a cultural point of view are: language, religion, ethnicity, social and political values, (Fox, 2002) but the history is the pillar of them. History is highlighting the following feature of national cultures in intercultural research: the country's specificity is identical with the specificity of the dominant national culture. National history identifies with of the values promoted by a group of people transformed it into a national state. It is also favored by a number of factors that must be considered together: geography, religion and so on, each of them acting as a binder for that group of people.

The mismatch between national culture and the intercultural communication inevitably lead to the reduction in the efficiency. The first literary mentions about the history of Iceland were in *Islendigabok* (the Book of Icelanders) written only after 200 years after the arrival of the first settles (Karlsson, 2013). The first parliament in the World, the *Althingi,* who now is second time active starting with 1944, was the perfect manifestation of the Old Commonwealth.

The modern political background of Iceland and the national culture were formed during the 1800s as an important part in creating independent Icelandic political platforms (Duelung, 2003). For many Icelander there is a feeling that their old society was one of the best possible in those times. In history, the dynamics of adaptation of Icelanders to new situations involves a flexibility of their ego for achieving competitiveness in the international market. Iceland was and still it is now a pure cultural space (as in the beginning of the last century was also the German or Japanese) and in present days its history is characterized by a conjunction which is in harmony with the global system. The Discovery of America started from here.

In Romania the national history is characterized by the struggle of a homogeneous human group which from 2000 years, living only in the same determined space, tried not to be integrated in other former neighboring empires. The Romanians are very proud of their history (especially the victorious fights against the Ottoman Empire) but very unhappy with the present. The history in Romania has a self-centered character and its values should not be judged based on some ethnocentric criteria, instead they should be valued by their contribution to the European heritage. The present national history is seen now like a political problem because the 45 years of Communism were an imposed situation for the people.

The Romanian and Icelandic histories are integrated in the mainstream of European values (even on opposite geographical polls) and represent ones of the most important cultural pillars of the continent. In both countries the stories "help us understand how others negotiated the cultural attitudes of the past that have relevance for the present" (Martin & Nakayama, 2014, p. 77).

After the World War II the price of fish rose and this situation was very stimulating for the Icelandic Economy. For Romania it was the beginning of a new political era, the forced introduction of Communism. In the rising of New Europe, after the 1945, the two countries had an insignificant role, Romania because it was a satellite state of Moscow and Iceland because the new formed European Coal and Steel Industry had few implications on its direct export strategy. For that period Iceland had an unusually high volume of trade with the countries of Eastern Europe: 33% of its exports went to Eastern Bloc Countries (Thorhallson & Vignisson 2004, p. 24).

At January the 1st 1959: Great Britain, Sweden, Norway, Denmark, Austria, Switzerland and Portugal formed European Free Trade Association (EFTA). Due to the fishery dispute with Britain (the Code Wars) Iceland was not invited to join the treaty. The agreement with the European Community was signed in 1972 when was ended the dispute between the Iceland and European Community regarding the fishing boundaries (Iceland extended the maritime line to 200 km).

The interest of Iceland for the European Community (EC) was from the beginning a practical one. In 1986 Spain and Portugal, the most important buyers of the Icelandic Fish, joined to the European Community and if until 1885 Iceland exported to the EC 23% of its salt fish after that date the amount of exports raised over 95%. After the historical discourse of Jacques Delors from the European Parliament in 1986 regarding the necessity of strengthening the collaboration between the EFTA and EC, the Icelandic Political Parties started to became interested on European Integration.

For Iceland the acceptance of European Economic Agreement (EEA) does not require the acceptance of EU's common agricultural and fishery policies. Also, the full membership to the European Union it was never a strong option for the country (both for political elite or common citizens). The only interest it was on strengthening the collaboration with European Economical Agreement which provides access to European Market with limited tariffs.

The Icelandic euro skepticism is based on the population strong beliefs on self-determination and on the intention that in the future the nation should be able to decide on its inner policies in the fishing strategy. "There was a clear consensus that the Icelandic Nation was unique and had to be protected when it came to international cooperation". (Bergmann, 2012)

Like all the other countries of the former communist bloc, Romania has made efforts to substitute the totalitarian system with democracy and free market policies, which has impacted upon political structure and social behaviours (legislation is under construction and the political and business communities are getting more sophisticated). Until 1989 the Romanian state was a factor of restriction for political freedom. Today, after 25 years, new research initiatives are required about the role of Romania in South Eastern Europe (Bibu & Brancu, 2008).

In the same frame of time, between 1960-1970, Romania was the most Western oriented country from the Warsaw Pact. The South Eastern country was the first communist country with opened an Embassy in Western Germany (1967) and also the first communist state with established commercial relations with European Community by signing two agreements. The first one was signed in 1974 named General System of Preferences and the second in 1980 – Agreement of Industrial Products. (Angelescu, 2012)

The ex-communist president Nicolae Ceausescu (who was executed after a very quick simulation of trial on 25 December 1989) was characterized by "The Economist" as "de Gaulle of the Warsaw Pact". After the 1980 the Romanian dictator became paranoiac with an anti-western attitude and Romania started to be an autarchic society.

Romania was the only communist state which not invaded Czechoslovakia after the social riot from 1968 and a lot of western leaders came as political guests in the communist era - French President Charles de Gaulle, the US Presidents Nixon and Ford. Also, Romania was the first country for the communist bloc with join IMF and General Agreement for Tariffs and Trade – GATT (Constantiu, 2011).

Immediately, after the December Revolution from 1989, Romania was perceived like an East Oriented country, being the last ex-communist state which signed a diplomatic path to NATO - 12 October, 1990. Iceland was a founding state of the Alliance in 1949 and also signed a historical agreement with USA in 1951 which allowed the opening of a military base on Keflavik peninsula, closed in 2006. It is important to mention that a part of the logistical and human resources from Keflavik base was moved to a new open NATO base in Romania. The new base located in the proximity of the Black Sea is now an important part of the European Defense Strategy regarding possible Russian or Middle East (Iran) aggressions.

Unlike Iceland, in Romania the idea of European integration was very popular among the population but not among the politicians with left orientation, who in the 1990 had expressed nostalgia about ex communism society. A survey made in 1995 demonstrated that 97% of the Romanians are in favor for EU membership – the highest score in Europe. (Angelescu, 2012)

In the next period Romania failed in achieving the progress in implementing the European "Aquis Communautare" and in consequence (together with Bulgaria) was excluded from the first wave of European Enlargement. On January 2007 Romania was accepted as a new member in the European Family but with some restrictions regarding the Schengen space and monetary policy.

Both Iceland and Romania had to face the economic crises from 2007. In Iceland the phenomenon had a very strong impact on the civil society because 90% of the financial system collapsed and the currency lost half of its value. Mostly because of fishery industry the economy was able to recover but it is important to mention the assistance program provided by the IMF, Nordic States and Poland (Polish are the first minority in Iceland).

In Romania, the politicians` strategy was not centered on the welfare of common citizens; even the IMF recommended the taxation of large fortunes, the Government "in its wisdom" chose to reduce the common wages with 25%. It is important to notice that in Iceland the Parliament took measures in favor of the borrowers by creating the "Debtors Ombudsman" with enough power to reduce the value of the debts. If the credits in foreign currency are considered in Iceland a violation of the national law, in Romania there is not a similar mentality and a large number of common people are still having serious problems due to the exchange fluctuations.

As a positive aspect the economic growth was positive in the both countries and Romania is the leader of the European Union with an economic increment of 3,6 % in 2015. It is important to mention the non-conventional response of the Icelandic society regarding the "classical" way to make policy. In 2010 the Best Party promoted by the show-man Jon Gnarr obtained 35% of Reykjavik`s votes and the actor become the mayor of the Capital.

In Iceland and Romania we can find a constant struggle against acculturation and assimilation by powering neighbors. Acculturation refers to the changes that took place in a human community, caused by constant interaction with a dominant social group. (Schmidt et all, 2007, pp. 21-22) Assimilation of cultures implies also the existence of an asymmetry against the methods of distribution of power, or the degree to which a minor culture is active in the community in which it is integrated. (Vlăsceanu et all, 1998, p. 45) In both situations there was no assimilation and acculturation and the icons of the past are still present in the daily life situations. The resistance to foreign oppression is the most important historical value in Iceland and Romania

3. The Cross Cultural Values of Iceland and Romania

The approach for this section tries to capture the influence of the cultural dimensions on the international performance of a state by comparing the values and norms between the two countries. It aims at emphasizing the importance of multiculturalism for public collaboration (Popa, 2015) and is focused on the importance of cultural synergy in interstate relations. Intercultural communication occurs in every day relations and power relations are very present in these encounters. "Communication across power divides can be very difficult, particularly when there is a cultural difference in how power is viewed or how power distance is expressed". (Martin & Nakayama, 2014, p. 316)

Without no doubt Iceland and Romania are cultunits nations with very strong linguistic identities. By cultunit we understand a group of persons who speaks the same language and belonging to the same territory or social group. (Lun & Firkola, 2000, p. 142) The Icelandic language is the purest manifestation of the Viking spirit and Romanians are the only people from South Eastern Europe who are preserving their Latin language amidst the Slavic nations. The conservation of linguistic legacy is the most valuated issue in these two countries regarding their past. Even so, where people are speaking the same language can be differences in communication style and language use. (Martin & Nakayama, 2014)

The jewellery of Icelandic language it have been transmitted across the World through the Saga. From the beginning the Icelandic literature was an open one to the World because "the poets and storytellers of Iceland followed events in the rest of Scandinavia with keen interest composing new works about contemporary matters" (Olason, 2006, p. 5).

In both languages the linguistic metaphors teach how should behave with paradoxes and the complexity of the international realities. The metaphors are used in daily life situations and using them makes us aware about the complexity of our way of thinking.

The practical importance of the metaphor with the acquisition of the ability of using it refers to the fact that Icelanders and Romanians are using it as a basis for explaining and discovering new perspectives. The metaphor requires a fine spirit of analysis, it focuses on the more subtle manifestation of national behaviour, and these are reported to the meanings given by the members of a country regardless of the place they occupy in the society. Working with metaphors, as integrative parts of intercultural diagnosis in Iceland and Romania implies "the ability to follow simultaneously both literal and symbolic communication the symbolic and metaphoric communication, forms a self-expression and a presentation of all the situations where the subject cannot be aware or able to express itself analytically" ((Grant & Oswick, 1996) cited by (Huţu, 2007, p. 124)).

The cultural metaphor offers a new way for understanding the life and behind each structure it is a universe of meanings which determines the human relations. The linguistic metaphor presents the important role of the system of believes, values, ideology etc. in the national reality in both countries. In Iceland as in Romania very important is the establishment and acceptance of a linguistic common code of behaviour etiquette (abstaining from religious and ethnic comments, establishing clear the individual responsibilities, the private delimitations) which can develop the solving of the fundamental dilemma of communication (Teodorascu & Arsith, 2014). In both countries there is a diachronic vision of national language which it is the catalyst bridge to different time periods of the history – the living link with the ancestors.

For cultural values, the Geert Hofstede model presents the dynamics of the common values in a country. For the majority of the people their native values are a very important lens through which the World it is accepted or not. Hofstede identifies six cultural dimensions: power distance, uncertainty avoidance, individualism, masculinity, long term orientation and indulgence. Those represent independent preferences for the citizens of a state which differentiate them from the people belonging to other countries.

In the next figure there are presented the cross cultural values between Iceland and Romania.

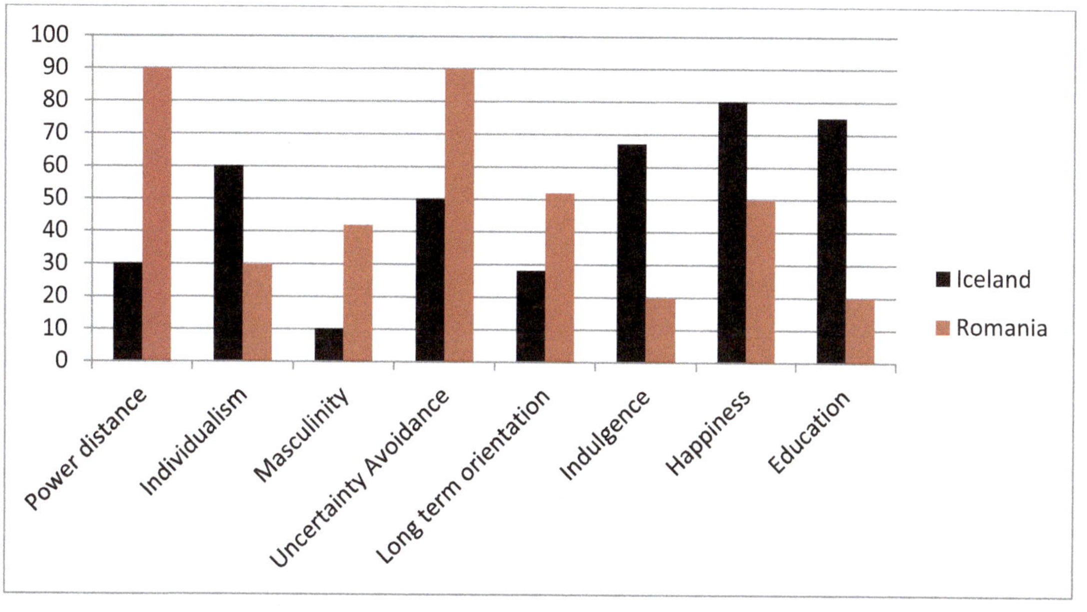

Figure 1. Cross cultural values of Icelandic and Romanian society. Adaptation of the author for Geert Hofstede values, http://geert-hofstede.com/iceland.html

Power Distance (PD) is the degree to which members of an orgnization and society encourage and reward unequal distribution of power with greater power at higher levels or expect power to be shared equally in that society (Chokkar et alli, 2008, p. 4).

Hofstede Center (2017) reported a PD score of 90 for Romania and 30 Iceland (ranking Romania as an unequal society where the people feel that they should not have aspirations beyond their rank). The Romanian score of this dimention is significantly higher than the World average, comparable vith Guatemala (95), Panama (95), Philippines (94) and Russia (93). The essence of this dimention demostrate a huge gap between the elites and the mases, a strong segmentation and an acute inequality in incomes. It is important to observe how it it possible in Romania to make the transition from "the status from ascription" to "the status by acievement" (Trompenaars, 1993).This means demonstrating how much, in present days, a person's performances accounts for a high status rather than his alliegence to a political group, or sex (Sorcaru, 2016).

Icelandic culture could be presented like USA culture and be described as a: "very egalitarian society whose Constitution not only guarantees the existential equality of every man and woman, of whatever ethnic or national background, but in which people have come to expect that differences in status and power are minimized and hierarchical structures primarily express inequalities in roles established for convenience or efficiency's sake". (Chhokar et alli, 2008, p. 508)

Performance Orientations (PO) reffers to the extent to which an organization or society encourages and rewars group members for performance improvevent or excelence (Chhokar et alli, p. 45). As a country of the former European communist block, Romania is characterized by a transitional economy wich has to face to the substatial changes in political structure, economy and cultural configuration. No discussion of leadership and performance in Iceland or in Romania can be fully understood without, even if ever so briefly, paying attention to the historical, political, economic and social context from which it emerged (Hofstede, 2002). In particular, Romania has been influenced in the last 90 years by succesive waves of political ideologies (from Monarchy through Communism to Parliamentary Republic) which shaped a pardox society with oscilate between a non-combative mentality and European Union values.

Even if it is higly evaluated and encouraged in management, the perfomance is jeopardized in Romania due to the clientelist relations, but there exists a stong expectation of the society to emerge the country as a performance and future oriented nation. Therefore, it is very useful in Romania to present how much the competence counts in obtaining top levels on political or business hierarchy and not the social connetions or any other such criteria. And becouse Icelandic culture is perceived all over the world as a future oriented society, which invests in rationality and pragmatism and guarantees a great egalitarism among its citizens, its model is an realistic benchmark for improving the Romanian *status quo*.

The hapiness index and the importance of education for the Icelandic people is strictly conected with the role of performance orientation in the community. The Icelandic Performance orientation it is related to the country`s openness to change, its willingness to take risks and try new things, its pragmatic mentality and its desire to excel in order to achieve tangible results. The democratic ideas, support of others and sense of fair play may help in real life situations in Iceland. Icelandic management style can offer for a recent South-Eastern European democracy the models for the wealth of recognition to encourage competition and to accept the legitimacy of the victorious party in the competitions.

The conflict situations appears in everyday situations and "the way in which people respond to conflict may be influenced by their cultural background…most specifically, most people deal with conflict in the way they learned with growing up – their default style" (Martin & Nakayama, 2014, p. 235).

The intention of conflict management strategies is to generate performance using a free communication style. An increase with 1% of level of economic freedom will generate an increase of economic, political, and social effectiveness with 3,8%. Also an increase with 1% of the quality of rule of law will contribute with 7,5% at the effectiveness area (Pohoata et alli, 2013, p. 31).

As a country from South Eastern Europe, Romania is characterized by a conflict management strategy wich has to face to the substatial changes in political structure, in economy and in cultural configuration.

The solving of conflicts is jeopardized in Romania due to the clientelist relations (if you are better political connected you have the chance to solve all the problems) but there are stong expectations from the people to emerge the country as a performance oriented nation.

The Icelandic conflict management strategy it is related to the country`s openness to change, its willingness to take risks and try new things, its pragmatic mentality and its desire to excel in order to achieve tangible results. Conflict management situations can be solved through trough a "theta reddast/it will sort itself out" attitude because no matter how complex the situation is, in the end things will all work out and even the rules exist can be stretched and expanded as needed (Kristjansdottir et alli, 2015).

In general, for a conflict management audit Vanderlinden et alli (2010) identify four key stages: observing, analyzing, evaluation and formulation recommendation. Also is recommended to place the cultural values in the general context of the cooperation, taking into account the main objectives, but also the particularities of the external environment.

Drennan D. (1992) proposes, for example, the approach of the conflict as an internal approach, as a factor that shapes the internal culture, the main objectives of the managers, having the role to create a team spirit between the employees[1]. Is important taking into consideration the objective pursued by the all (staff or employees) and the ways in which they can turn it into performance.

The strategy of conflict management should be based on dialogue, where those interested could be able to ask questions, because in such complex matters always can appear useful new directions. A competent person trained in the research field, is able through its interventions to correct any errors or deficiencies who escaped to those who have served the project, and conversation inevitably is helping to discover new truths.

The Icelandic tradition in conflict management and in political science (the oldest Parliament in the World) can provide for the Romanian elite the civic obligation to seek wealth not only for personal use, but equally to the well-being of the community – a high human orientation.

4. Conclusions

The dynamics of Globalization encourages the study of cross cultural differences between countries and their impact on effectiveness in the proximity. Making progress is quintessential for Icelandic and Romanian societies in the recent European context. The best way for selecting foreign partners involves a complex process in which each partner (with his unique cultural background) it is evaluated.

Icelandic society is a second chance culture and, according to Harold Bloom theory (1997), an *anxiety of influence* is necessary for the Romanian people, because after 45 years of communism and 25 years of hard transition, the Romanians needs to struggle in the global market since the entire South Eastern Europe is still embedded in the historical, political economic, social and cultural frame of the past.

In Romania there is also a need for Innovative Leadership (the Icelandic style) to be seen as a process of influence in which the individual leader exercises considerable impact on others by inducing them to think and behave in an effective way. The Leadership has to be seen as an expression of the democratic will and a process oriented to global collaboration through cultural sensibility and adaptability.

We can note that for the Icelandic culture the country right to self-determination is stronger in the economical agreements with the European Union. In the first part of the study it is noticed that for Iceland the first steps for a European Integration had a strong economical and national importance. In Iceland more than in Romania, it is possible to identify the importance of ethno political identity because the groups are "organized around their shared identity and seek gains for members of their groups" and the "material and political demands as claims arising from their cultural concerns" (Gurr, 1996, p. 53). The welfare of the nation and the security of the fishing boundaries are directly connected with the rejection of EU integration.

In Romania the group leaders have not a common identity with a political doctrine, the loyalty is strictly to the restricted clan (family, business associates etc.) end it is very common to change often the political party (There are Members in Parliament who in 3 mandates changed 3 or even more political Parties etc.). Even Romania is better linked with European Union (from the institutional point of view) this

---

[1] Cited by (Huțu, 2007, pp. 120-122).

country it is much more limited than Iceland in achieving performance, in part due to the huge phenomenon of corruption. In Romania, future-oriented behaviours, planning, investing in the future are not highly ranked. In Iceland, an expression of Performance orientation is represented by investments in education and personnel development (postgraduate education, competence development, etc.).

The approach which I proposed here, the comparison of several values between Iceland and Romania will help in the future to analyze the contemporary educational and business environment between the two nations. This study helps to understand the importance of the cultural mediator who could be able to provide suggestion which may have a strategic role in any research area.

Similar studies emphasize the conditions through which a project could be operative by involving the collaboration and concentration of all the interested parties. The synergic participation it is achieved only when people identifies themselves with a common project and take collective responsibilities. It is recommended to place the cultural values in the general context of the cooperation, taking into account the main objectives, but also the particularities of the external environment.

We can infer that understating the cultural values of each person is the key factor in the evolution of international collaboration. In conclusion, this limited research could be the basis for an extensive study focused on deeper understanding of the Icelandic political culture and can improve the Romanian cultural adaptability with cross-cultural effectiveness in the South East Europe.

5. References

Angelescu, I. (2012). *European Integration studies in Romania from Analyzing European Union Policy*. Edited by Bundi Federig; Eliassen A. & Kyell, Bologna, Societa editrice il Mulino.

Bercovitch, J. & Foulkes, J. (2012*).* Cross cultural effects in conflict management: Examining the nature and relationship between culture and international mediation. *International Journal of Cross Cultural Management*, pp. 25-47.

Bibu, N. & Brancu, L. (2008). *Convergences of the Romanian societal culture with European culture clusters in the process of European integration. The role of intercultural teams management in increasing European cohesion*. Munich Personal RePEc.

Bergmann, E. (2012). How National Sentiments have influenced Iceland`s European Policy. *PhD dissertation*, Reykjavik, Department of Political science, University of Iceland.

Bloom, H. (1997). *The Anxiety of Influence. A Theory of Poetry.* New York, Oxford: University Press.

Chhokar, J. & House, R. (2008). *Culture and Leadership across the World, the GLOBE Book of in – Depth Studies of 25 Societies.* London: Taylor & Francis Group.

Constantiniu, F. (2011). *Honest history of the Romanian People*/O istorie sincera a poporului roman. Bucharest: Publisher Univers Enciclopedic Gold.

Duelung, P. (2003). *The Nordic Cultural Model.* Copenhagen Nordic Cultural Institute.

Fox, R.G. (2002). *Anthropology, by comparison.* London: Routledge.

Gurr, T.R. (1996). *Minorities, Nationalists, and Ethnopolitcal Conflict, Managing Global Chaos: Sources of and Responses to International Conflict*. Ed: Crocker, Hampson & Aall, Washington DC: United States Institute of Peace Press.

Hutu, C.A. (2007). *Organizational culture and leadership/*Cultură organizaţională şi leadership. Bucharest: Publisher Economică.

Hofstede, G. (2002). *Culture's consequences: Comparing values, behaviours, institutions and organizations across nations.* Thousand oaks, C.A.: Sage.

Hofstede, Geert (2017). The Hofstede center. http://geert-hofstede.com/iceland.html.

Karlsson, G. (2013). *A Brief History of Iceland.* Reykjavik, Printing: Isafoldarprentsmiodja.

Kristjansdottir, S.; Bjanadottir, T. & Saphiere, D.H. (2015). *Cultural detective. Iceland*, www. culturaldetective.com.

Lun, L. & Firkola, P. (2000). Methodological issues in cross cultural management research: Problems, solutions and proposal. *Asia Pacific Journal of Management*, vol. 17, pp. 133 – 154.

Martin, J.M. & Nakayama T.K. (2014). *Experiencing Intercultural Communication.* Mc Graw Hill Education.

Nicolescu, O. & Verboncu. I. (2008). *Managerial Methodologies/*Metodologii Manageriale. Bucharest: Publisher: Universitara.

Olason, V. (2006). *Old Icelandic Poetry*. In a History of Icelandic Literature. Vol. 5 of Histories of Scandinavian Literature. Edited by: Daisy Neijmann.

Popa, D.A. (2015). *Introduction in Public Relations/*Introducere in Relatii Publice. Galati: Editura Universitara Danubius.

Pohoata, I.; Socoliuc, O.R. & Diaconasu, D.E. (2013). *Institutional Quality – Determinants of Transitional Performances in Eastern European Nations.* Review of Economics and Business Studies, Iasi.

Schmidth, W.V. (2007). *Communicating Globally – Intercultural Communication and International Bussines.* London, Sage Publications.

Şorcaru, S.L. (2016). *Sexism – Topical Issues – Case studies.* Personal article: The Female Leaders in a Society with Many Prejudices. Saarbrucken, Lambert.

Teodorascu, F. & Arsith, M. (2014). *Communications and public relations in political organizations*/Comunicare şi relaţii publice în organizaţii politice. Galaţi: Editura Zigotto.

Thorhallson, B. & Vignisson, H.T. (2004). (A) *Iceland's policy on European Integration from the foundation of the republic to 1972*, from Icelandic and European Integration. Edited by Thorhallson, B., Publisher Routledge, Taylor and Francis Group.

Thorhallson, B. & Vignisson H.T. (2004). (B) *A controversial step membership of the EEA, from Icelandic and European Integration.* Edited by Thorhallson, B., Publisher Routledge, Taylor and Francis Group.

Trompenaars, F. (1993). *Riding the waves of culture: Understanding cultural diversity in business*. London: The Economist Books.

Vanderlinden, B.; Frasila, C. & Dupriez, P. (2010). The multiple perspective in cross cultural audit/Perspectiva multiplă în auditul cultural. *Management Intercultural*, Anul XI, nr. 21. Iaşi: Publisher Alexandru Ioan Cuza.

Vlasceanu, M. (1999).*Organizations and organizational culture*/Organizaţiile şi cultura organizării. Bucharest: Trei.

22

Claw-back Tax - a Fang of Romanian Health or a Moral Duty?

Viorica Puscaciu[1], Florin-Dan Puşcaciu[2], Rose-Marie Puşcaciu[3]

Abstract: This study belongs to the scientific field of economics, more precisely to finance area. The scientific challenges to which this approach tries to find answers are the so controversial claw-back tax. It is a fee that even if is applied to different fields of the economy, it succeeded to set up only the national health system from our country, and that is why, this approach try to clarify it. The obtained results of this work intends to bring more light in this dispute between the manufacturers of drugs and the state authority; in this matter, one part considers this claw-back tax as being a moral one, and the others think that it is something abusing their profits. The aim of this study is to clarify this matter, by objectively analyzing the problem from both sides, with their arguments, and with the scientific instruments. So, these are our objectives, treated with the qualitative scientific methods, trying to reach the results and getting the conclusions of this research.

Keywords: claw-back tax; health system; money; manufacturers of medicines; taxpayer

1. Introduction

The choice of this theme came from its importance and topicality of the subject. The scientific frame of this paper is circumscribed to the most present theme from time to time in our economic life. The scientific work is circumscribed economic area, specifically financial one, whose events and changes never ceases to amaze us, causing us to constantly seek new answers to other questions that always gives this area of research. The theme is both a challenge, and also a desire to add some more clarification to this matter. The research hypothesis is chosen from this multitude of taxes, and the reason is that this claw-back tax which affects the sanitary system in our country, the problem is: if this claw-back tax is a legal in sense of moral one, or not? This theme is important to be clarified, even if for its topicality, in our days, and of course for its implications in our life. As for the research methodology used in our work it is about a qualitative analysis. The paper proposes a theoretical and doctrine clarifying of the areas. The intuitive method used is because of the lack of data and qualitative approach to areas further research which implies a balanced approach and in terms of quantity. It is also used a prospect method of the impact of claw-back tax on the main undertakings involved: producers, consumers and the state.

Our paper begins with the clarifying the theoretical concept of claw-back fee, by iterating both the best respectful sources as international dictionaries, and also continuing with a pleiade of illustrious authors which have researched this area. After this starting presentation of the subject, this paper continues with the explanation of the topic applied from the theory into practice: that is in the medical system, with special mention to our country. It is fully explained the background of this fiscal measure in the

[1] Professor, PhD, University of South-East Europe Lumina, Romania, Address: 64B Sos. Colentina, Bucharest, Romania, E-mail: viorica.puscaciu@lumina.org.

[2] Professor, PhD, Department of Economics, Danubius University of Galati, Romania, Address: 3 Galati Blvd., Galati 800654, Romania, E-mail: fdpuscaciu@univ-danubius.ro.

[3] Senior Lecturer, PhD, Department of Economics, Danubius University of Galati, Romania, Address: 3 Galati Blvd., Galati 800654, Romania, Corresponding author: rosemarie.puscaciu@univ-danubius.ro.

Romanian sanitary system, and also the short "history" of this applying of the claw-back tax. It is also analyzed with details the impact of this fee on the health system, and on the public budget as well. Our study further presents the position both of the supporters of this claw-back fee, and also the criticizers of it. The final part of this paper shows the consequences of applying this tax for all the implied factors. As normally used, this approach ends with the conclusions of our research.

2. General Presentation

Accordingly to the basic definition, type claw-back fee is actually a financial penalty applied to companies that have violated certain provisions. In this case, however, it represents a surcharge revenues obtained from pharmaceutical companies that make sales over the state budget for medicines. First of all, we shall have a look to the different approaches of this topic in literature.

In the British & World English dictionary, the Claw-back tax is defined as two acceptors, as follows: "Money or benefits that are distributed and then taken back as a result of special circumstances, and the second acceptor is: a retraction of stock prices or of the market in general". (British & World English Dictionary, 2015)

Oxford Advanced Learner's Dictionary explains claw-back as: "the act of getting money back from people it has been paid to; the money that is paid back"[1].

Cambridge Dictionary precised: "A claw-back refers to the recovery of money which has been already paid to a person or company, typically because that payment should not have been made for legal (or occasionally moral) reasons. It can also refer to the recovered money itself. Claw-back provisions in a contract may entitle a party (e.g. the company's shareholders or creditors) to claw-back (= recover) excessive salaries or bonuses paid to the company's directors, for example, if it can be shown that those payments damaged the company's ability to fulfill its commitments to that party. As the news headlines below suggest, the expression is usually used in a compound noun (e.g. claw-back provisions, claw-back clause) or as a phrasal verb (to claw something back)"[2].

Investopedia explains "claw-back" both in two ways, like this: the first acceptor is: "purchasing certain investments provides taxable benefits contingent upon holding periods. When you sell these investments before they have reached maturity, the benefits must be returned; and the second acceptor is: in layman's terms, a fall in a stock's price right after an increase is called a claw-back of the price"[3].

Farlex Financial Dictionary defines claw-back as: "a drop in a security's price after a previous rise, and the second acceptor is: "money that must be refunded or given back for some reason or other. The term especially applies to tax advantages extended to a taxpayer subject to certain conditions that the Eurostat taxpayer did not fulfill"[4].

Webster's New World Finance and Investment Dictionary describes claw-back tax as follows: "a word used in the venture capital industry to describe a common term found in partnership agreements. A claw-back requires venture capitalists to refund fees to their investors if it turns out that the venture capitalists received more than their 20% share of a fund's overall profits. Claw-backs became common in 2002, occurring when a venture capitalist took its 20% share of a fund's early investment success, but the fund later lost money. Claw-backs also are used in other financing contexts, such as private equity".[5] This matter was studied and deeply analyzed by some important researchers, among which we remind the followings: the adoption of a claw-back is followed by higher proportions of equity based pay and long-term pay. Firms with a greater proportion of equity based pay are more likely to suffer from managerial actions such as earnings manipulation (Burns and Kedia, 2006). They find that

---

[1] Oxford Advanced Learner's Dictionary, published by Oxford University Press, 2015.

[2] Cambridge Dictionary, printed by Cambridge University Press, 2015.

[3] http://www.investopedia.com.

[4] Farlex Financial Dictionary. © 2012 Farlex, Inc.

[5] Webster's New World Finance and Investment Dictionary

executives are more likely to manage earnings when they receive higher levels of equity-based pay. Efendi, Srivastava, and Swanson (2007) find that firms where the CEO has significant holdings of in-the-money options are more likely to restate earnings.

Levine and Smith (2010) theoretically explore the incentive properties of mechanisms that can retract previously awarded cash bonuses, but provide no empirical analysis. Chen, Greene, and Owers (2012) also develop a model of claw-back incentives.

Brown, Davis-Friday and Guler (2011) examine 252 claw-backs over 2005-2009 (Corporate Library data) and find that adopting firms are larger, have less influential CEOs, and have higher M&A bonuses and goodwill impairments.

Paquita Y. Davis-Friday, Abraham N. Fried and Abraham N. Fried (2011) examine whether the adoption of claw-back provisions in executive compensation contracts improves the informativeness of accounting information. Contrary to conventional wisdom, they find that claw-backs do not lead to improved financial reporting. Specifically, they also document a significant decline in the market's response to earnings surprises after the adoption of both fraud and performance based claw-back provisions. Their results provide a cautionary tale of how some types of claw-backs may produce an unintended consequence in terms of deteriorating the established relation between reported earnings and stock price.

Fried and Shilon (2011) provide information on usage rates for firms in 2010 in the S&P 500.

Some of the contemporaneous research on claw-back adoption often focuses on policies triggered by one specific event, such as accounting restatements (e.g., Chen, Green, and Owers (2012).

This is consistent with the notion that a primary reason for adopting a recovery policy is concern over accounting or stock price manipulation by executives to increase bonus payments or increase the likelihood of clearing the performance hurdles defined in performance-based vesting provisions (Bettis, Bizjak, Coles and Kalpathy, 2012).

Ilona Babenkoa Benjamin Bennettb John M. Bizjakc Jeffrey L. Colesd, in their work named *Claw-back Provisions* (2012), contrary to some prior studies, they do not find that claw-back adoption lowers the incidence of financial restatements (Chan, Chen, Chen, and Yu, 2012) or reduces shareholder litigation or discretionary accruals. Nonetheless, on average the market reaction to report of a clawback policy prior to Dodd-Frank[1] is positive and significant, on the order of 0.5%.

3. From Theory to Practice: Applying Claw-Back Fee

Claw-back is a tax applied in the pharmaceutical industry and assumed that all drug manufacturers to help fund public health system with an amount of money ranging between 5% and 11% of the income made by selling the products. The contribution shall be paid quarterly until the 25th of the month following the quarter in which delivery took place drugs in a special account opened at the Treasury on behalf of the Ministry of Health.

Claw-back tax, paid by drug manufacturers that have products on the list of compensated and free, was first introduced in 2009, but since then until now has suffered a series of changes. Given that GEO 104/2009 contained quite a lot of doubt about the calculation algorithm and the time you have paid this fee additions were made by WHO 928/2010. The new order brings certain clarifications regarding previous interpretations of the provisions relating to the declaration, calculation and payment of "claw-back". The most important changes concern:

- date on which the contribution ("claw-back" tax) becomes chargeable - only after receiving a fully revenues from sales related to a quarter;

- the date on which contributions must be paid - date of payment "claw-back" is set by the House

[1]The Dodd–Frank Act: *Significant Impact on Public Companies*, Skadden, Arps, Slate, Meagher & Flom. Retrieved July 25, 2010.

National Health Insurance by notification addressed to each payer;

- introduction of additional statements containing the details of the consideration medicines collected on a certain quarter;

- replacing "2010" by "year..." in the Annexes 1 to 5 of the Order 928/2010.

The Order of the Health Ministry no. 351/2011 changes the rules for calculation, declaration and payment of the claw-back fee. This becomes due only after receiving entirely by payers of income related to a quarter. Accordingly to the Order no. 928/591/2010, quarterly total revenue is the amount resulting from the sale in Romania by tax payers, as follows: medications included in national health programs that benefit the insured in outpatient treatment, with or without personal contribution, based on prescription, health insurance system, and medicinal insured persons in hospital treatment. Under the rules issued earlier, the persons liable to pay the tax declared National House Health Insurance drug sales by suppliers of drugs used in the outpatient treatment or medical units with beds, using the forms 2a, respectively 2b. The rules introduced by WHO 351/2011 is inserted and the obligation to declare, via new forms 2a1 and 2b1, full collection of these revenues corresponding quarterly sales previously reported. The new statements are submitted in the first 5 days of the month following the month in which they were fully collected revenues of a quarter.

As for the calculation of tax, Order no. 351/2011 clarifies the fact that the established percentage based on the total revenues from sales of medicines for outpatient and hospital use related to each quarter is applied to the proceeds from the sales of drugs for treatment outpatient and hospital use same quarter related (such as GEO 104/2009 also provides that introduced this contribution). Under the new provisions, and succession procedures for determining tax "claw-back" would take place as follows:

- in the first 5 days of the end of each quarter is still mandatory submission to the National Health Insurance House of the Declaration on the list of medicines sold in one quarter, for suppliers of drugs used in outpatient treatment (Form 2) and/or the Declaration on the list of medicines sold in one quarter for health facilities with beds (Form 2b). Maintain the health facilities with beds for compulsory transmission of health insurance houses lists of medicines purchased in that quarter;

- in the first 15 days of the end of each quarter is maintained for the National Health Insurance House mandatory transmission centralizer drugs purchased by the medical bed in the quarter;

- In the first 5 days of the month following the month in which they were entirely related revenues collected in a quarter (where income for that quarter were previously reported by Form 2a and/or 2b). Persons liable to pay tax are obliged to submit to the National House of Health Insurance, if applicable, the Declaration on the list of drugs used in outpatient treatment related to a quarter of the value of the services was collected (Form 2a1), and/or Declaration on drugs list used by health facilities with beds, relating to a quarter of the value of the services was collected (Form 2B1);

- within 15 days of filing Form and Form 2a1 2b1: National House of Health Insurance contribution due notice according to data reported;

- by the date specified in the notification received from the National House of Health Insurance, the persons liable to pay tax must make its remittance to the date specified in the notification (before payment is made until the 25th of the month following each quarter).

GEO 77/2011 was tried improvement and tax regulation "claw-back", amid countless controversies and complaints that sparked a claw-back the old regulation, namely, GEO 104/2009, as amended and supplemented.

According to GEO 77/2011, quarterly contribution is calculated by applying a percentage "p" on the value of consumption of medicines, supported the National Fund for Health Insurance and the Ministry of Health budget, consumption related sales contribution of each payer. This percentage "p" is calculated by CNAS and communicates the marketing authorization holders of medicines following the expiration until the end of the quarter.

In turn, GEO 77/2011 has undergone some significant changes by GEO 110/2011 which again change the formula for calculating the contribution and the Ordinance 17/2012 regulating certain fiscal measures which came into force on August 24, 2012 which focuses on the following aspects:

- cancellation "delay penalties" for people who owe tax claw-back for the period between fourth quarter 2009 and third quarter 2011 are fulfilled cumulatively the following two conditions:

(1) people who owe claw-back declare and fully pay tax within 30 days from the date of entry into force of GO 17/2012

and

(2) pay the legal deadline for payment of interest due for principal obligations;

- the obligation of submission to the National Health Insurance House's updated list of drugs for which the claw-back tax is due until the 15th of the month following the quarter for which the tax is due;

- remove the value added tax (VAT) of the formula for calculating state budget incurred related to drugs, but only since the fourth quarter of 2012.

On 5 February 2013, the Constitutional Court decided that the inclusion of value-added tax (VAT) in the formula for calculating the claw-back (for the period prior to the fourth quarter of 2012) is unconstitutional. Therefore, even if the GO 17/2012 removed VAT from the calculation formula claw-back just starting the fourth quarter of 2012, according to the decision of the Constitutional Court, VAT not to be taken into account even before the appearance of Ordinance 17/2012.

Conclusively, the calculation of "claw-back" is a laborious present case involves a close relationship between the taxpayer and the CNAS, preparing statements provided by the legislation listed above for each period they were in force, the calculation and payment contribution/tax coming as a consequently their data and communicate directly to the taxpayer by CNAS (market authorization holders of medicines).

Not least the calculation of "claw-back" involves taking certain decisions of the entity's legal representative on the interpretation and implementation of the legal framework applicable.

The latest version, which will come into force on October 1st 2011 brings the news eliminating value-added tax (VAT) of the calculation formula and increased the amount reference value of 1.42 billion lei 1,51 billion lei (without VAT). This reference amount is paid quarterly approved budget for medicinal National Unique Fund Health Insurance (FNUASS) and from the Ministry of Health (MOH). Generic Drugs Manufacturers Representatives Association of Romania (APMGR) argue that while the government eliminated the formula for calculating VAT, pharmaceutical companies are still required to pay a fee for the entire chain of distribution revenues, which include the additives applied by distributors and pharmacists. Moreover, the amount of reference, although it was raised, not the actual consumption of drugs in 2011. "Returning to the calculation formula of GEO 77/2011 which was widely criticized including by the IMF because of unfair character - similar charge applied to all producers, regardless of drug sales growth recorded by each company - and unpredictable (percentage "p" is calculated on the basis of erroneous non-transparent manner provided by CNAS and companies can not in any way anticipate the amount thereof)", reads a release of APMGR.

Claw-back was adopted since October 2011 and now has begun to create problems for patients with serious diseases. The amount of an industry amounted to 400 million lei in the first three months of this year, i.e. 33.6% of the entire value of compensated drugs consumed during this period. The claw-back applies Romanian pharmaceutical industry for drug manufacturers to help fund public health system with a variable amount of money depending on the income. Although modified in order to be more friendly for the taxpayers, it remains rather controversial and the new project on claw-back public discussion launched by the authorities does not include requests from industry. But, four years after the introduction of this tax has not solved the health budget deficit, moreover, is, in the opinion of industry representatives, a brake on the development of generic drug companies by reducing local production, delaying investments in development and even reduction personal.

Although, for many seem like a visually impaired claw-back tax can be understood by a single word: claw. The main actors in health care - the state, manufacturers and retailers of medicines - are fighting to seize a larger part of the money those Romanians who contribute to National Health Insurance Fund. And as the stakes consistency, claw-back tax has become one of the most disputed legislative provisions of the last three years.

The underfunding of the health system threatens to impede the access of Romanians to new pharmaceutical treatments to eliminate from the market affordable medicines and the pharmaceutical industry to cancel investments in production and development.

Romanian authorities ask drug makers a review of the method of financing the deficit in the health system. Claw-back tax on producers to cover the difference between the state budget and actual consumption generated by drug treatment needs of patients Romanian, recorded in the last quarter of 2013 a significant increase of 30% compared to other quarters and reached a unsustainable level for the pharmaceutical industry.

Grand drug manufacturers complain that the fee claw-back corresponding first quarter of this year, in Romania represents about 30% of the sales of most drug manufacturers compensated. Curiously, small producers argue that the actual percentage is only 11%. Great producers of medicines, namely multinational companies, seeking annulment of the tax claw-back current form and asked the government to amend the law involved and the need for proper budgeting at national pharmaceutical, real consumption from 2013.

"Claw-back amount of the fee cannot be supported by the industry, it represents more than 400 million euro per year (calculated for 2011), averaging 33.6% of total sales of pharmaceutical manufacturers compensated over any company related taxes trade in this form unique in Europe", reads a release of the Romanian Association member companies of International Medicine Manufacturers (EFPIA) and the Association of Generic Medicines Producers in Romania (APMGR). But what the medicines producers forget to say is that drugs manufacturers claw-back exists in all European Union countries and is designed to curb abusive consumption of drugs. Furthermore, fee has designed to help small producers in their fight with drug multinationals. The truth is that claw-back is good for small fee. It penalizes the major manufacturers offering huge discounts to pharmacies. Basically fee is charged to the final price at which the drug reaches the consumer. How multinationals offering 75% discounts at pharmacies, and they sell to the consumer medicines are now obliged to pay this tax and discounts. And this is not convenient. What they forget to say is that the major manufacturers in the European Union tax discounts offered to pharmacies are of 90%", as declared a Romanian producer of drugs.

Romanian health system is among the most poorly funded in the European Union, as Romania is among the last countries in Europe in terms of percentage of GDP allocated to health, with only 3.9% compared to the European average of 9%. Expenditure on drugs are only about 80€/year/capita, while even in neighbor countries - they start from 150€/year/capita.

The Romanian state has huge debts to suppliers of medicines, debt accumulated in recent years. One of the priority requirements of the International Monetary Fund was paying these debts (arrears) whose size threatens medical system crashes. In August 2010, the government allocated 1.9 billion lei to pay debts to suppliers of medicines, but after making payments, the IMF staff found that the absolute amount of arrears decreased by only 600 million lei. How was that possible? It seems that pharmacies have not submitted all the bills health insurance houses because they knew that the funds allocated were insufficient to compensate drugs. When new money appeared, the bills were reported. And as a story of bottomless pitcher began to rise incessantly new and new arrears. This situation was triggered in the 2008 election year, when the Health Ministry has eliminated the ceilings of pharmacies, which were kept under control with medication expenses compensated. To private reaction it was a natural one: both higher sales to make profits as large. In Romania, the main business partner pharmaceutical industry is the state, which totally or partially compensates for the price of a number of drugs.

As statistics reveal, only in 2012-2013 period, 2 of 10 patients were treated exclusively Romanian contributions from the pharmaceutical industry through claw-back. Manufacturers of drugs and APMGR gathered together in ARPIM associations point out that, under a budget well below the European average, as is currently updating the list in terms of compensated drugs, deficit financing exclusively to producers through claw-back it is impossible. In the last two years they have funded health system 2.8 billion lei, and the situation seems to change in 2014 as the authorities have allocated only 6.6 billion lei, while consumption amounted to 8 billion lei, without taking into account the updating of the list of free and subsidized medication. The amount of the claw-back tax reached 25.23% of the sales of subsidized drugs that manufacturers have had in the fourth quarter of 2014 showed Generic Medicines Industry Association in Romania (APMGR), which states that the National Insurance data health (CNAS) which was calculated based on the rate of duty are wrong.

4. Technical Explanation of Claw-Back Tax

Currently, all pharmaceutical companies pay to the State a claw-back fee amounting to about 14% of turnover (i.e. 14% of total company sales). The tax is paid only by the drug companies, but is calculated including distribution and pharmacy margins that you do not receive the drug companies. According to the Emergency Ordinance no. 77/2011, quarterly contribution (claw-back) is calculated by applying a percentage "p" on the value of drug consumption FNUASS budget support and that of MS, related sales contribution payer in each hand.

$$p = ((CTT - BAT) / CTT) * 100$$

in which CTT is total consumption of medicines paid from fund quarterly national unique health insurance and the Ministry of Health budget.

(CTT means total consumption of medicines paid quarterly budgets FNUASS and MS BAT quarterly approved budget for the drugs covered FNUASS and MS budgets, calculated by dividing the annual budget initially approved in April by state law).

The coefficient "p" shows APMGR in a statement, it rose to 25.23% in Q4 2014 compared to just 20.92% in quarter 3. Increased percentage "p" in calculating the claw-back tax to 26.1% in the 1st quarter of 2015, from 25.23% in Q4 2014 is a direct consequence of increased consumption of innovative medicines whose price was maintained at a very high level in recent years through violation of the laws on drug pricing. APMGR reiterates that the only solution that could make things normal, saving the insolvency generic manufacturers is the immediate implementation of a differentiated calculation of the tax claw-back for generics, based on the introduction of a maximum proportion of 65% in calculating the variable "p" the claw-back formula, thus correlating with the fiscal burden in the drug pricing policy.

In 2014 was published Government Emergency Ordinance no. 69/2014 on the establishment of financial measures in health and amending certain acts. GEO 69/2014 brings a number of changes and, especially, additions to the quarterly contribution regime (claw-back tax) regulated by Government Emergency Ordinance no. 77/2011 on the establishment of contributions to fund health spending, as amended, that have been instituted other financial measures applicable in regional or research and development. Quarterly total consumption value of drugs (CTT) used to determine the percentage "p" will be reported CNAS by health insurance funds on the basis of data recorded in the informatics platform of social health insurance; in turn, the value related to consumption of drugs centralized notified each taxpayer (tax base) will draw all the data recorded in the said platform, as follows:

- taxpayers, that authorization holders for medicines ("MAH"), Romanian legal persons and foreign legal representatives MAH will submit quarterly CNAS updated list of medicines for which the tax due according to a methodology and a format approved by order of the President of CNAS;

- tax payers will determine and calculate VAT excluding tax due from the volume of quarterly consumption of medicines notified by CNAS (in fact, regulation of current practice);

- appeals against consumption values will be notified by CNAS to see only the data for the first quarter for which they were communicated.

GEO no. 69/2014 supplements 77/2011, by establishing a separate tax regime for those drugs, as a result of the health technology assessment procedures, receiving conditional inclusion decisions DCI list. In short, the new rules thus established are:

For mentioned products may conclude price-volume/cost-volume-outcome ("CV Contracts") with the funds obtained from the exclusion and/or compensation percentage change of medications included in the DCI list, as well as the implementation of policies pharmaceuticals (MAH interested potential elements apparently unknown); failure to conclude such contracts will attract unable to include relevant medicines DCI list.

CV contracts are qualifying as mechanisms to ensure the financial sustainability and predictability of costs in the public health system by which local MAH MAH foreign or local representative undertakes to supply medicinal products included conditioning DCI list under the rules of GEO no. 69/2014, for a certain category of patients and for a certain period of time;

Initiate contract negotiations CV is according to prioritization criteria and model contract expressly provided and methodology of the negotiation, conclusion and monitoring of the implementation of such contracts shall be determined by the Minister of Health and CNAS president;

Claw-back tax payable by taxpayers is determined by applying the CV based contracts provided these contracts to the value of consumption in individual quarterly statement of CNAS.

Consumption value is calculated by multiplying the quarterly retail price excluding VAT/wholesale price with the volume of medicines consumed quarterly volume limit set by contracts CV; and the percentage claw-back tax consists of the percentage value "p" for the previous quarter Contract conclusion CV, calculated according to the formula set out in art. 3 paragraph (2) of the Emergency Ordinance no. 77/2011 (the common percentage applicable fee unconditionally compensated medicines), plus between 5 and 30 percentage points in the proportion the number of patients for each therapy to shrink the number of eligible patients (percentage found in the relevant contract CV). If the cumulative excess volumes of drugs consumed volumes determined by contracts CV, taxpayers bear the full amount of the related drug consumption exceeded, excluding VAT; this value is not included in the calculation exceeded quarterly total consumption of drugs (CTT). Within 15 days of the issuance of conditional listing decision DCI list, foreign MAH must appoint a legal representative, Romanian legal person to negotiate and conclude contracts CV or to declare and pay claw-back payable; also, within 30 days from the date of conclusion CV MAH local or foreign legal representatives must register for tax purposes at the National Tax Administration Agency as contributors to claw-back.

Note that the rules on the submission of quarterly by CNAS, challenging them and the applicable payment terms relating to medicinal products included conditioning DCI list, although regulated distinct, are identical/similar to those for subsidized drugs without restrictions in the health insurance system, which is due to determine claw-back according to article 3 of GEO no. 77/2011. It also established the obligation of all foreigners holding MAH drugs included in the list DCI (including new products) that have not yet designated a legal representative, within 30 days of the entry into force of the ordinance, communicate CNAS data Identification of that representative, whilst tax recorded in the same period.

In essence, the new law establishes two tax regimes and determination of tax applicable claw-back drugs that are currently granted state social insurance system, i.e. new drugs conditioning included in the list comprising international common names for medicinal products for insured persons in the system health insurance or national health programs ("DCI List"). The Association states that the already high level of claw-back tax forced drug manufacturers only generics in Romania last year to lay off more than 300 employees and a decrease in production for the domestic market by 10% , and delay major investments in local production facilities. In addition, since 2011, when claw-back tax was introduced, there have disappeared from the market more than 1,300 medications. GEO 69/2014[1] brings a number of changes and, especially, additions to the quarterly contribution regime (claw-back tax) regulated by Government Emergency Ordinance no. 77/2011 on the establishment of contributions to fund health spending, as amended, that have been instituted other financial measures applicable in regional or research and development.

In essence, the new law establishes two tax regimes and determination of claw-back tax applicable to drugs that are currently granted state social insurance system, i.e. new drugs conditioning included in the list comprising international common names for medicinal products for insured persons in the system health insurance or national health programs ("DCI List"). We note the following changes in applicable tax claw-back already compensated medicines in the public: quarterly total consumption value of drugs (CTT) used to determine the percentage "p" will be reported CNAS by health insurance funds on the basis of data recorded in the informatics platform of social health insurance; in turn, the value related to consumption of drugs centralized notified each taxpayer (tax base) will draw all the data recorded in the said platform.

The Association states that the already high level of tax claw-back forced drug manufacturers only generics in Romania last year to lay off more than 300 employees and a decrease in production for the domestic market by 10% and delay major investments in local production facilities. In addition, since 2011, when it was introduced claw-back, they have disappeared from the market more than 1,300 medications.

Generic Drugs Manufacturers Association of Romania (APMGR), the representative body of generic drug companies in Romania, announces that the claw-back tax on the 1st quarter of this year reached a new historic high of over 26% of sales to the public sector which will lead to the disappearance of several drugs and cheapest on the market and the collapse of the local pharmaceutical industry.

The tax is paid only by the drug companies, but is calculated including distribution and pharmacy margins that you do not receive the drug companies. And the producers of drugs accused that: Claw-back tax level in the fourth quarter of 2013 reached a level of 20% of the sales of medicines, it means that we pay, in addition to the flat 16%-20% of turnover. We are talking about higher taxation, somewhere at 40%. We have to stop all investments in 2014 until a solution is found for this claw-back tax.

Manufacturers, distributors and pharmacies selling drugs offset the debt: the state debt promptly honoring promises and citizen expect to receive subsidized drugs in payments that you make monthly to the National Health Insurance Fund, under the quiet approval of the State. If a manufacturer/importer of drugs cannot pay the quarterly fee (calculated based on a formula that takes into account the market share and sales growth), when products are withdrawn from the list of compensated and free of charge ones.

In this dispute, in Romania there are two different parties: one sustaining the claw-back tax, and another one rejecting and criticizing it, as follows: the Proponents of the tax say that, in Romania, the consumption of drugs crazy. They are right; CNAS spends a quarter of its funds with medicines, one of the highest percentages in Europe. 20 most prescribed medicines in Romania are new and expensive pharmaceuticals, which is unusual in Europe. Most often, they are part of national health programs - which recorded the largest increase in funding in recent years - and are usually prescribed total cleared and especially in poor districts and universities (according to World Bank experts). Manufacturers of generic drugs are required to pay for additions distributors and pharmacists as claw-back is calculated at retail price of drugs, which includes over producer prices and trade margins.

Maintaining reporting errors reported by member companies APMGR the National Health Insurance Fund (NHIF) and the total lack of transparency regarding the calculation of tax claw-back. Keeping the basis for calculating the tax claw-back of drugs purchased in hospitals are reimbursed twice by CNAS hospitals are funded under the DRG system. The existence of proven fraud and counterfeit

[1] GEO – Government's Emergency Ordinance.

medicines into the system, resulting in artificially raising the claw-back tax. Keeping prices above those of the rest of the EU for most settled 50 drugs, resulting in increased tax claw-back.

In the National Health Programs are recorded fact and the largest state debts to the pharmaceutical industry. Sometimes, even certain segments of state encourage such reckless spending. Process the lists of compensated drugs - entering the prerogative of the Ministry of Health committees - is "nontransparent, inconsistent and too little based on practical data" (IMF staff report). Thus, it follows that, in Romania, to compensate for treatment with extracts of ginkgo biloba, for example. In addition, sales of drugs on large international manufacturers which no longer have patent (so called generics) are not encouraged, their volume decreasing in recent years. When you asked last time the pharmacy "aspirin cheapest, not the most expensive"? As the opponents say that tax, in Romania, the consumption of drugs is much lower than in the rest of Europe. And they are right. Romania's per capita expenditure on drugs are the smallest, only 172 euro compared with the European average of EUR 376 maximum or registered in Greece (584 euro). As a percentage of GDP, expenditure on medicines Romania is 1.4%, below 1.7%, as is the European average (Eurostat)[1].

Then the drugs trade is already overburdened in Romania, offset VAT on medicines being 9% compared to zero in the UK or Sweden.

Romania is one of the European countries and origin of parallel trade, given the low price imposed by the Romanian producers. Parallel, trade occurs when a dealer buys drugs from manufacturers in countries with cheap medicines (Romania being one of the European countries with the cheapest drugs when put on the market) and exports them to countries with higher prices where they are sold directly pharmacies. This practice legal but immoral lowers the Romans access to certain drugs. The full truth is that the Romanian state invests far too little money in medication use compared with other European countries (Romania allocate health under 5% of GDP last place in the EU), and this consumption is not modeled in favor of the patient, but rather in favor the interests of the pharmaceutical industry.

It is a good measure taken by the government but whose application would be unfair for some players in the system that it encompasses manufacturers, distributors and pharmacies. Of these, only producers will bear the burden, because the difference will be charged (50 million in the example above) contains the profit margins of pharmacies and distributors. Romania is a special case here: the producer price of the drug enter the market, add distributor and the pharmacy margin, which grow (with VAT) acquisition final price to the patient. This price is settled by CNAS and taken as reference in calculating the claw-back, and distributors and pharmacies in Romania have among the highest margins in the European Union (Scrip Report).

Manufacturers of drugs warn that this claw-back tax increase is not supported by market developments. In addition, they fear that the growth trend will continue and even accelerate in coming quarters while the indicative budget for the calculation of the claw-back is as low medicine consumption in 2011.

The underfunding of the health system threatens to impede the access of Romanians to new pharmaceutical treatments to eliminate from the market affordable medicines and the pharmaceutical industry to cancel investments in production and development.

Romanian authorities ask drug makers a review of the method of financing the deficit in the health system. Claw-back tax on producers to cover the difference between the state budget and actual consumption generated by drug treatment needs of patients Romanian, recorded in the last quarter of 2013 – as example - a significant increase of 30% compared to other quarters and reached a unsustainable level for the pharmaceutical industry.

Every year, drug manufacturers cover the claw-back, the entire difference between the state budget and actual consumption generated by drug treatment needs of patients Romanian. In other words, the claw-back was transformed from a budget control measure in a tax burden which resulted in the creation of a business environment lacking transparency and predictability. The burden is even greater

---

[1] www.eurostat.

as the list of compensated and free drugs has not been updated for six years, which means a negative economically and socially strong impact. As a consequence, they say that about a thousand of drugs will disappear from the market. Manufacturers of drugs warn that this claw-back tax increase is not supported by market developments. In addition, they fear that the growth trend will continue and even accelerate in coming quarters while the indicative budget for the calculation of the claw-back is as low medicine consumption in 2011. Keeping that tax in its present form, it can have serious economic and social consequences, primarily for population by the total disappearance from the market of medicines and inability to introduce new drugs and for drug companies, which will have to postpone or cancel investments in local production capacities.

In recent years, they say that the market disappeared almost 1.000 types of medicines in all therapeutic areas, both because of the claw-back, but also to the calculation. Head APMGR says that currently, there are 120 active trials of pharmaceutical companies on the claw-back, won at first instance, and if they will be won definitively, National Health Insurance must return differences and budgetary effort will be a huge one.

5. Conclusions

The truth is that claw-back tax is good for small producers. It penalizes the major manufacturers offering huge discounts to pharmacies. Basically fee is charged to the final price at which the drug reaches the consumer. How multinationals offering 75% discounts at pharmacies, and they sell to the consumer medicines are now obliged to pay this tax and discounts. And this is not convenient. What they forget to say is that the major manufacturers in the European Union tax discounts offered to pharmacies is 90%. Note that if a manufacturer/importer of drugs cannot pay this quarterly fee (calculated based on a formula that takes into account the market share and sales growth), when products are withdrawn from the list of compensated and free.

But this claw-back tax is not a panacea for the Romanian medical system. If it is not matched by few essential measures such as rebuilding a new list of compensated drugs and the introduction of clear criteria for their therapeutic efficiency and economical, the claw-back will only be placed in a claw-back producers, that will improve the Balance Sheet State but not human health. That is why there are some problems that were pointed out by the Association of the manufacturers of the drugs in relation to claw-back: manufacturers of generic drugs are required to pay for additions distributors and pharmacists as claw-back is calculated at retail price of drugs, which includes over producer prices and trade margins; maintaining reporting errors reported by member companies APMGR the National Health Insurance Fund (NHIF) and the total lack of transparency regarding the calculation of tax claw-back; keeping the basis for calculating the tax claw-back of drugs purchased in hospitals are reimbursed twice by CNAS hospitals are funded under the DRG system; the existence of proven fraud and counterfeit medicines into the system, resulting in artificially raising the claw-back tax; keeping prices above those of the rest of the EU for most settled 50 drugs, resulting in an increased claw-back tax.

6. References

Babenkoa, I., Bennettb, B., Bizjakc, J. M., Coles, J. L. (2015). Clawback Provisions. *SSRN (Social Science Research Network), Tomorrow's Research Today*, issue of 24th April.

Bergman Brown A., P.Y. Davis-Friday P.Y. & Guler L. (2011). Economic Determinants of the Voluntary Adoption of Clawback Provisions in Executive Compensation Contracts. *SSRN (Social Science Research Network),* Social Science Electronic Publishing, Inc.

Bettis, J.C., Bizjak, J.M., Coles, J.L. & S.L. Kalpathy, S.L. (2013). Performance-Vesting Provisions in Executive Compensation, published in *Social Science Research Network, Tomorrow's Research Today,* December 18, 2013 and also Paris December 2014 Finance Meeting EUROFIDAI - AFFI Paper.

Burns, N. & Kedia, S. (2006). The impact of performance-based compensation on misreporting. *Journal of financial economics,* 79 (1), 35-67.

Chan, L., Chen, K. & Y. Yu. (2012). The effects of firm-initiated claw-back provisions on earnings quality and auditor's behavior. *Journal of Accounting and Economics*, Vol. 54, Issues 2-3, pp. 180-196, Presented at 2011 JAE Conference at the Wharton School, Univ. of Pennsylvania.

Chen, M.A., Green, D. & Owers, J.E. (2014). The Costs and Benefits of Clawback Provisions in CEO Compensation. *Social Science Research Network, Tomorrow's Research Today, Review of Corporate Finance Studies.* Forthcoming, November.

Skadden, Arps, Slate, Meagher & Flom, *The Dodd–Frank Act: Significant Impact on Public Companies*. Retrieved on July 25, 2010.

Davis-Friday, P.Y., Fried, A. N. & Jenkins, N.T. (2011). The Value of Clawbacks. *Social Science Research Network, Tomorrow's Research Today*, June 17.

Efendi, J., Srivastava, A. & Swanson, E. P. (2007). Why Do Corporate Managers Misstate Financial Statements? the Role of Option Compensation and Other Factors. *Social Science Research Network, Tomorrow's Research Today,* April 2.

Fried, J. & Shilon, N. (2011). Excess-Pay Clawbacks, published in Social Science Research Network, Tomorrow's Research Today. *Journal of Corporation Law, Vol. 36, pp. 722-751,* March 28.

Levine, D.I. & Smith, C. (2010). *The Global Challenges in Responsible Business.* Cambridge: Cambridge University Press.

Webster's New World Finance and Investment Dictionary Copyright © 2010 by Wiley Publishing, Inc., Indianapolis, Indiana. Used by arrangement with John Wiley & Sons, Inc.

***(2015). *British & World English Dictionary.* Oxford: Oxford University Press.

***(2015). *Cambridge Dictionary.* Cambridge: Cambridge University Press.

Permissions

All chapters in this book were first published in EIRP PROCEEDINGS, by Danubius University Press; hereby published with permission under the Creative Commons Attribution License or equivalent. Every chapter published in this book has been scrutinized by our experts. Their significance has been extensively debated. The topics covered herein carry significant findings which will fuel the growth of the discipline. They may even be implemented as practical applications or may be referred to as a beginning point for another development.

The contributors of this book come from diverse backgrounds, making this book a truly international effort. This book will bring forth new frontiers with its revolutionizing research information and detailed analysis of the nascent developments around the world.

We would like to thank all the contributing authors for lending their expertise to make the book truly unique. They have played a crucial role in the development of this book. Without their invaluable contributions this book wouldn't have been possible. They have made vital efforts to compile up to date information on the varied aspects of this subject to make this book a valuable addition to the collection of many professionals and students.

This book was conceptualized with the vision of imparting up-to-date information and advanced data in this field. To ensure the same, a matchless editorial board was set up. Every individual on the board went through rigorous rounds of assessment to prove their worth. After which they invested a large part of their time researching and compiling the most relevant data for our readers.

The editorial board has been involved in producing this book since its inception. They have spent rigorous hours researching and exploring the diverse topics which have resulted in the successful publishing of this book. They have passed on their knowledge of decades through this book. To expedite this challenging task, the publisher supported the team at every step. A small team of assistant editors was also appointed to further simplify the editing procedure and attain best results for the readers.

Apart from the editorial board, the designing team has also invested a significant amount of their time in understanding the subject and creating the most relevant covers. They scrutinized every image to scout for the most suitable representation of the subject and create an appropriate cover for the book.

The publishing team has been an ardent support to the editorial, designing and production team. Their endless efforts to recruit the best for this project, has resulted in the accomplishment of this book. They are a veteran in the field of academics and their pool of knowledge is as vast as their experience in printing. Their expertise and guidance has proved useful at every step. Their uncompromising quality standards have made this book an exceptional effort. Their encouragement from time to time has been an inspiration for everyone.

The publisher and the editorial board hope that this book will prove to be a valuable piece of knowledge for researchers, students, practitioners and scholars across the globe.

List of Contributors

Romeo Bosneagu
Naval Academy" Mircea cel Batrân", Romania, Strada Fulgerului 1, Constanța 900218

Florin Sorescu
Tomis University, Constanta, Romania, 100 Vulcan Petru Str., Constanta, 900628, Romania

Rodica Elena Faida
Master Student, Spiru Haret University, Bucharest, Romania. 13, Doamnei Str., Bucharest, Romania

Ana Alexandru
Student, Faculty of Economic Sciences, "Danubius" University of Galati, Romania,3 Galati Boulevard, 800654 Galati, Romania

Ana-Maria Teodora Andronic
Assistant at the International Cooperation Center and Master Student at Danubius University of Galati, Romania, 3 Galati Blvd., Galati 800654, Romania

Andy Puşcă
Rector of Danubius University of Galati, Romania, 3 Galati Blvd., Galati 800654, Romania

Anişoara Popa
Department of Comunications International and Relation, Danubius University of Galati, Romania, 3 Galati Blvd., Galati 800654, Romania

Daniela Aurelia Popa
Danubius University of Galati, Faculty of Comunication and International Relations, Romania, 3 Galati Blvd, Galati, Romania

Ionuț Ştefan and Sergiu Pîrju
"Danubius" University of Galati, Faculty of Communication and International Relations, Galati, 3 Galati Boulevard, 800654 Galati, Romania

Florin Iftode
Danubius University of Galati, Faculty of Communication and International Relations, Romania 3 Galati Blvd, Galati, Romania

Jeta Goxha
Faculty of Law and Political Sciences SHPAL Pavaresia Vlore, Albania, Bulevardi Vlorë-Skele Posta Vlorë AL-9401 Vlorë Albania

Mirela Arsith
Dean of Faculty of Communication and International Relations, "Danubius" University of Galati, Romania, 3 Galati Boulevard, 800654 Galati, Romania

Iulian Georgel Savenco
Senior Lecturer, PhD, Faculty of Law, "Danubius" University of Galati, 3 Galati Boulevard, 800654 Galati, Romania

Tache Bocanială
Faculty of Law, "Danubius" University of Galati, Romania, 3 Galati Boulevard, 800654 Galati, Romania

Paul Zai
University Babes-Bolyai, Romania, Address: 1 Mihail Kogălniceanu Str., Cluj-Napoca 400084, Romania

Cristina Nicoleta Caranica
Department of Management Information Systems, The University of Economic Studies, Romania, Piața Romană 6, Bucharest 010374, Romania

Ermira Sela
Student, University of Tirana, Albania, Bulevardi Zogu I, Tiranë, Albania

Fanel Teodorascu
Faculty of Communication and International Relations, Danubius University of Galati, Romania, 3 Galati Blvd., Galati 800654, Romania

Gina Ioan and Catalin Angelo Ioan
"Danubius" University of Galati, Romania, 3 Galati Boulevard, 800654 Galati, Romania

Valentin Filip
National Intelligence Academy, Romania, 20-22 Odăi str., sector 1, Bucharest, Romania

Gabriela Marchis Georgeta Dragomir and Mariana Trandafir
"Danubius" University of Galati, Romania, 3 Galati Boulevard, 800654 Galati, Romania

Crina Radulescu, Cristina Elenea Nicolescu and Teodora Bitoiu
National University of Political Studies and Public Administration, Romania

Stefan Dragomir
Dunarea de Jos University of Galati, Romania, 47 Domnească Street, 800008 Galati, Romania

Dorjan Marku
Faculty of Agriculture, "Fan S. Noli" University, Albania, "Shetitore Rilindasit", Korçw, Albania

Eleina Qirici and Oriola Theodhori
Faculty of Economy, "Fan S. Noli" University, Albania, "Shetitore Rilindasit", Korçw, Albania

Ionel Sergiu Pirju
Danubius University of Galati, Faculty of Communications and International Relations, Romania, 3 Galati Blvd., Galati 800654, Romania

Viorica Puscaciu
University of South-East Europe Lumina, Romania, 64B Sos. Colentina, Bucharest, Romania

Florin-Dan Puşcaciu and Rose-Marie Puşcaciu
Department of Economics, Danubius University of Galati, Romania, 3 Galati Blvd., Galati 800654, Romania

Index

S

T

U

V